CONCORDE INTERNATIONAL

ARNETT HOUSE
HAWKS LANE
CANTERBURY CT1 2NU
ENGLAND
01227 451035
FAX: 01227 762760

Total English

Pearson Education Limited
Edinburgh Gate
Harlow
Essex CM20 2JE
England
and Associated Companies throughout the world.

www.pearsonelt.com

© Pearson Education Limited 2011

First published 2011
Ninth impression 2014

ISBN: 978-1-4082-6716-5
Book with Active Book Pack

Set in MetaPlusBook-Roman
Printed in China
CTPSC/09

Acknowledgements

The publishers and authors would like to thank the following people and institutions for their feedback and comments during the development of the material:
Serpil Acar, M.E.V. Özel Basınköy High School, Turkey; Brasshouse Language Centre, Birmingham, UK; Angel F. Briones-Barco, EOI Alcala de Henares, Spain; Manuel Bueno, Brazil; Isabel Abellán Clemente, Escuela Oficial de Idiomas de Villarrobledo Albacete, Spain; EC School, Brighton, UK; EOI Getxo Heo, Spain; EOI Bilbao, Spain; EOI No 1 Zaragoza, Spain; Eliana González Giraldo, Universidad EAFIT, Colombia; English Language Centre, Lodz, Poland; Eva De Andres Gomez, EOI de San Fernando de Henares, Spain; Ryszard Kalamarz, Katowitz University, Poland; Margarita Gutierrez Navaro, EOI de Coslada (Extension of the EOI de San Fernando de Henares), Spain; Ramon Lapena Prieto, EOI Sant Feliu de Guixols, Spain; Aldo Antonio Roque, The Learning Center, Brazil; Margareth Vitoria Pacheco dos Santos, Sociedade Brasileira de Cultura Inglesa, Brazil; Adrián Luis Schiavelli, Centro Universitario de Idiomas, Argentina; Justyna Smigiel, Poland; Szkola Wyzsza Psychologii Spolecznej, Poland; University of Warsaw, Poland; Katarzyna Wasylkowska, Academy of Physical Education, Warsaw, Poland

We are grateful to the following for permission to reproduce copyright material:
Logos
Logo 11.3 from The Open University, www.open.ac.uk, copyright © The Open University.
Text
Extract 11.3 about 3UA Company, www.u3a.org.uk, reproduced wit permission of 3UA.

In some instances we have been unable to trace the owners of copyright material, and we would appreciate any information that would enable us to do so.

Photo acknowledgements

The publisher would like to thank the following for their kind permission to reproduce their photographs:

Alamy Images: D. Hurst 25, David Lyons 102br (D), Jeff Greenberg 20br (D), John Glover 25bl, Jon Arnold Images Ltd 60br, 136tl, 140cl, Jon Arnold Images Ltd 60br, 136tl, 140cl, Juniors Bildarchiv 25tl, Mike Booth 25br, PeerPoint 126tr, shinypix 25b; Corbis: Mark Edward Atkinson / Blend Images 20cl (A), Pierre-Auguste Renoir / The Gallery Collection 94bc (E); **Getty Images:** John Powell 122tr (A), Stephen Frink 29t, Taylor S. Kennedy 119bl; **Ronald Grant Archive:** Hammer Film Productions 92cr (D); **iStockphoto:** 12br, Atlantagreg 25tr, jsemeniuk 137, miloslutz 35b, stuartbur 25cl, travellinglight 102tr (B); **Kobal Collection Ltd:** Paramount 92tl (A); **Lonely Planet Images:** Richard I'Anson 62cr; **Panos Pictures:** Mark Henley 99bl; **Pearson Education Ltd:** Luis Espana 65bl, 65br, Luis Espana 65bl, 65br; **Photolibrary.com:** 54cl (2), 60l, 69cl, 99tl, Chad Ehlers 102tl (A), 119t, Kristian Cabanis 99cl, Michael Siluk 123tl (B); **Press Association Images:** Ng Han Guan / AP 124b; **Reuters:** Herwig Pramm 15cr (L); **Rex Features:** 20thC.Fox / Everett 122tl, 60cl, 70tl, 88br, 90cr, Tony Kyriacou 104cr; **Richard Waite Photography:** 22tr, 22br, 23tl; **Robert Harding World Imagery:** Richard Cummins 81cr; **Thinkstock:** Goodshoot 14tl (A)

Cover images: *Front*: Alamy Images: GYRO photography/ amana images

All other images © Pearson Education

Illustrated by Ian Mitchell, Jode Thompson, Kveta, Steven Hall (All from *Three in a Box*) and Roarr Design.

NEW

Total English

ELEMENTARY

English

Students' Book

A1-A2

Diane Hall and Mark Foley

Contents

Contents

Contents

Contents

Do you know...?

1

a 🔘 1.01 Do you know the alphabet? Listen and repeat.

a b c d e f g h i
j k l m n o p q r
s t u v w x y z

b Listen to the alphabet again. Write the letters in the correct place.

sounds	letters
/eɪ/	a h _j_ _ _
/iː/	b c d _ _ _ _ _ _
/e/	f l m _ _ _ _ _
/aɪ/	i _
/əʊ/	o
/uː/	q _ _ _
/ɑː/	r

c 🔘 1.02 Listen and check your answers.

d Write six consonants and three vowels. Read them to your partner. Write your partner's list.

Consonants: _____

Vowels: _____

2

a 🔘 1.03 Do you know numbers? Match the numbers with the words. Then listen, check and repeat.

0 1 2 3 4 5 6 7 8 9 10

eight five four nine oh/zero one
seven six ten three two

b 🔘 1.04 Complete the list with numbers from the box. Then listen, check and repeat.

> eighty   fifty   ~~fourteen~~   nineteen   ninety
> seventeen   seventy   sixteen   thirty
> twenty-two

11	eleven	21	twenty-one
12	twelve	22	_____
13	thirteen	30	_____
14	_fourteen_	40	forty
15	fifteen	50	_____
16	_____	60	sixty
17	_____	70	_____
18	eighteen	80	_____
19	_____	90	_____
20	twenty	100	a hundred

3

a Do you know classroom instructions? Match the instructions with the pictures.

> Ask and answer.   Check your answers.
> Complete.   Correct.   ~~Listen.~~   Look at page ...
> Match.   Read.   Read the tip.   Repeat.   Write.

b 🔘 1.05 Listen and check your answers.

4

a 🔘 1.06 Do you know classroom questions? Complete the questions. Then listen and check.

How to... ask questions in class

How do you _say coche_ in English?
How do you (1) _____ that?
What does _grandmother_ (2) _____ ?
I don't understand. Can you (3) _____ that?

b Practise with a partner. Ask and answer questions about the photos.

A: _How do you say_ kahve _in English?_
B: _Coffee._
A: _How do you spell that?_

1

Lead-in

A

B

C

1 **a** 🌐 1.07 Choose the correct words in *italics*. Then listen and check.

1 Woman: (*Hi*)/*Goodbye*, I'm Silvia. What's *the*/*your* name?

   Man: Hi, Silvia. *My name's*/*Name's* Pedro.

2 Man: *What's*/*Who's* your name, please?

   Woman: *Is*/*It's* Caroline Stacey.

   Man: *Who*/*How* do you spell that?

   Woman: It's C–A–R–O–L–I–N–E S–T–A–C–E–Y.

3 Man: Hello. *My name*/*My name's* John Logan.

   Woman: Hello. *I'm*/*I called* Maria Burton. Nice to meet *you*/*it*.

b Match the three dialogues with photos A–C.

c Practise the dialogues with your classmates.

2 **a** 🌐 1.08 Listen and repeat this phone number.

020 651 3472

b 🌐 1.09 Now listen and write the phone numbers.

01452 946 713

c Practise with your classmates. Find out their names and phone numbers.

1.1 People and places

Vocabulary | countries and nationalities

1 Find the countries on the map.

United States of America ☑C☐   Argentina ☐
Australia ☐   Brazil ☐   China ☐   Czech Republic ☐
England ☐   France ☐   Germany ☐   Greece ☐
Italy ☐   Iran ☐   Japan ☐   Poland ☐
Russia ☐   Spain ☐   Turkey ☐

2   **a**   Look at the photos and the box. Ask and answer questions.

> Daniel Craig   Donatella Versace   an iPod   Jet Li
> Marat Safin and Dinara Safina   a Mercedes car
> Michelle, Malia and Sasha Obama
> Nicole Kidman   a Panasonic Blu-ray Disc player
> Penelope Cruz   ~~Ronaldo~~

1   A: *Who is he?*   B: *He's Ronaldo.*

2   A: *Who is she?*   B: *She's …*

3   A: *What is it?*   B: *It's …*

4   A: *Who are they?*   B: *They're …*

b   Match the photos with the countries in exercise 1.
Ronaldo – Brazil

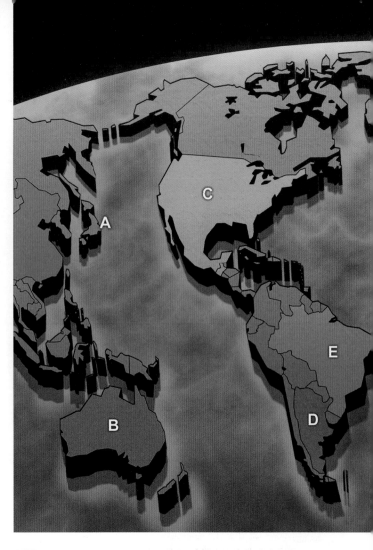

3   **a**   Complete the table.

Country	Nationality	Ending
Australia	1 *Australian*	(i)an
Argentina	2 _____	
United States of America	American	
Brazil	3 _____	
Italy	4 _____	
5 _____	German	
Iran	6 _____	
Russia	Russian	
7 _____	Spanish	ish
Poland	8 _____	
England	9 _____	
Turkey	Turkish	
China	10 _____	ese
Japan	Japanese	
11 _____	French	
Czech Republic	Czech	
12 _____	Greek	

b 🔊 1.10 Listen and check your answers.

Pronunciation | word stress

4 🔊 1.11 Listen and repeat the countries and nationality words.

5 Look at the Lifelong learning box. Read the tip and complete the exercise.

Recording stress

! <u>Underline</u> the syllable with the stress.

Austr<u>a</u>lian

Listen to the countries and nationality words again. <u>Underline</u> the stress.

Austr<u>a</u>lia   Austr<u>a</u>lian

Lifelong learning

see Pronunciation bank page 148

Grammar | *to be*: positive

6 **a** Complete the Active grammar box with *is* or *are*.

Active grammar

I am (I'm)   *We are (we're)*
You are (you're)   *You are (you're)*
He _____ (he's)   *They _____ (they're)*
She _____ (she's)
It _____ (it's)

see Reference page 17

b 🔵 **1.12** Complete the sentences. Then listen and check your answers.

I'*m* Brazilian. *I*'m from São Paulo.

1 Jennifer Lopez _____ American. _____'s from New York.
2 We'_____ Polish. _____'re from Warsaw.
3 A: Excuse me, where are you from?
   B: I'_____ from Colombia.
4 A: What is _____ ?
   B: I think it'_____ a Japanese car.
5 A: Who are _____ ?
   B: They'_____ students in my class.
   They'_____ from Brazil.

7 Talk about the people and objects in the photos on page 10.

A: *Ronaldo?*
B: *He's from Brazil. He's Brazilian.*
A: *iPods?*
B: *They're from the United States. They're American.*

8 Where are the things from? Work in pairs.

A: *I think A is from China.*
B: *No, I think it's from Italy.*

Listening

1 Look at the photo above. What is the occasion? Who are the people?

2 a 🔊 1.13 Listen to Amber and choose the correct words in *italics*.

1 Amber talks about her *job/family*.
2 Rafael is Amber's *husband/brother*.
3 Rafael's family is from *England/Brazil*.

b Listen again and complete the family tree with names from the box.

> Connor   Eileen   Nathalia   Nilza   Steve

3 What are their relationships?

Nilza and Nathalia *mother and daughter*

1 Connor and Amber
2 Steve and Connor
3 Rafael and Amber
4 Steve and Amber
5 Nathalia and Alessandra

Grammar | possessive 's

4 a Which sentence is correct?

1 Nilza is Rafael mother.
2 Nilza is Rafael's mother.

b Make eight sentences about Amber and Rafael's family. Use 's.

> brother   daughter   father
> husband   mother   sister
> son   wife

Amber is Rafael's wife.

see Reference page 17

5 Who do the objects belong to? Look at the pictures and complete the gaps.

1 *Amber's* watch
2 _____ phone
3 _____ jacket
4 _____ wedding ring
5 _____ sunglasses
6 _____ handbag

Vocabulary | families

6 a Match the family words with the meanings.

1	mother and father	a	uncle
2	sons and daughters	b	grandmother
3	mother's or father's brother	c	nephew
4	mother's or father's sister	d	parents
5	mother's or father's mother	e	aunt
6	mother's or father's father	f	niece
7	brother's or sister's son	g	children
8	brother's or sister's daughter	h	grandfather

b Find the meanings of these words in a dictionary.

best friend   cousins   father-in-law
girlfriend   grandparents   stepbrother

7 Make three sentences about your family.

Kate is my best friend.

My brother's girlfriend is called Sophia.

Grammar | possessive adjectives

8 a 🔊 1.14 Heather is from Canada. Listen and find the mistakes. Circle the words that are wrong.

66 This is a picture of <u>my</u> family from Canada. This is my mom and this is my dad and this is my sister, Ben. <u>His</u> wife is Sheri and these are <u>their</u> two sons, Julia and Erica. This is my aunt, Margaret and my grandpa, Jack. They live in southern Ontario. This is my daughter, Emily. <u>Her</u> husband's name is Tom and their son's name is James. This is my brother, Jay. His grandmother's name is Shelley. And this is their dog. His name is Shadow. 99

b Complete the Active grammar box with the underlined words.

Active grammar

Subject pronouns	Possessive adjectives
I	_____
you	your
he	_____
she	_____
we	our
you	your
they	_____

see Reference page 17

9 Complete the sentences with possessive adjectives.

Clare is <u>our</u> sister. (we)

1 _____ teacher is English. (I)
2 Mr and Mrs Schegel are _____ parents. (they)
3 What is _____ homework? (we)
4 **A:** Are _____ grandparents from Madrid? (you)
   B: Yes, they are.
5 **A:** Are _____ sisters married? (she)
   B: No, they're single.
6 **A:** Is _____ boyfriend American? (you)
   B: No, he's Australian.
7 **A:** Is Tomas _____ brother? (he)
   B: Yes, he is.

Grammar | to be: questions

10 a Look at dialogues 4–7 in exercise 9 again. Complete the Active grammar box with *is* or *are*.

Active grammar

	he she it	American?	Yes,	he she it	_____ .
_____	we you they	American?	Yes,	we you they	_____ .

How old Where/What/ Who	am is are	I? he/she/it? we/you/they?

see Reference page 17

b Complete the questions and answers with *she*, *he*, *my*, *your*, *is* or *are*.

Mike: She's nice. Is she <u>your</u> mother?
Heather: No, (1) _____'s my sister-in-law, Ben's wife.
Mike: She's young! How old (2) _____ she?
Heather: Well, she (3) _____ 33.
Mike: And this man, is (4) _____ your uncle?
Heather: No, he's (5) _____ grandpa, Jack.
Mike: Where (6) _____ he from?
Heather: He (7) _____ from southern Ontario.
Mike: The girls are nice. Are they (8) _____ sisters?
Heather: No. They (9) _____ my nieces.

Speaking

11 Write the names of five people in your family. Show them to your partner. Ask and answer.

A: *Who's Elena?*   **B:** *She's my aunt.*
A: *Is she your mother's sister?*   **B:** *No, she's my father's sister.*

Vocabulary | jobs

1 Match the jobs with the photos.

an actor ☐ an architect ☐ a chef ☐
a computer programmer ☐ a dentist ☐
a doctor ☐ an engineer ☐ a farmer ☐
a lawyer A a sea captain ☐
a shop assistant ☐ a TV producer ☐

2 **a** 🔊 1.15 Listen to Mike and Helen. Which jobs do you hear?

b Listen again and complete the sentences.

1 Mike's _sister_ is in marketing; she's a _marketing director_.
2 His _____ is a TV producer.
3 His sister-in-law is a _____ .
4 His _____ is a farmer.
5 Helen's brother is a _____ .
6 Her other _____ is an engineer.
7 Her sister is in _____ ; she's a _____ .
8 Her _____ is a sea captain.

3 **a** Read the text. How many people in Cheryl's family work?

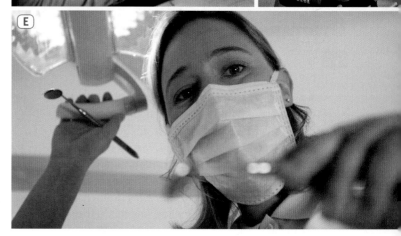

❝My name's Cheryl Rowland. I'm a doctor. I'm not a hospital doctor – I work with three other doctors in one office. My husband, Jeremy, is an architect but he isn't happy with his job now – he thinks it's boring. Our two sons are Liam and Ross; they're actors but they aren't in work at the moment; they're unemployed. My father's a dentist. He's 60 years old but he isn't retired. My mother's 63. She isn't really in work because she's retired now, but she's a shop assistant one day a week in a bookshop.❞

b Complete the sentences with the words in the box.

> 63 years old   happy at work
> ~~in a hospital~~   in work   retired
> unemployed

Cheryl's work isn't _in a hospital_.

1 Her husband isn't _____ .
2 Her mother isn't in work because she's _____ .
3 Her mother is _____ .
4 Her sons are actors but they aren't _____ .
5 Her sons haven't got jobs; they're _____ .

Grammar | a/an

4 **a** Look at the jobs in exercise 1 again. Complete the Active grammar box with a or an.

> ### Active grammar
>
> We use _____ before vowel sounds (a, e, etc.).
> He's _____ actor.
> We use _____ before consonant sounds (b, h, w, etc.).
> I'm _____ doctor.

see Reference page 17

b Write a or an.

_a_ student
1 ___ teacher
2 ___ aunt
3 ___ handbag
4 ___ family
5 ___ uncle
6 ___ iPod
7 ___ cousin

Pronunciation | /ə/

5 **a** 🔊 1.16 Listen to the pronunciation of *a* and *an*. Repeat the words.

b 🔊 1.17 Listen and repeat the jobs in exercise 1.

see Pronunciation bank page 148

Listening

6 🔊 1.18 Listen to four people at work. Talk about the jobs with your partner.

A: *I think 1 is a dentist.*
B: *No, I think she's a doctor.*

Grammar | *to be*: negative

7 Read about Cheryl in exercise 3a again and complete the Active grammar box.

Active grammar

I _____ not	We aren't
He _____	You aren't
She _____	They _____

see Reference page 17

8 Complete the sentences with the correct negative form of *to be*.

We *aren't* from the United States.

1   My sister _____ in work at the moment.
2   I _____ an assistant, I'm the director!
3   My cousins are twenty but they _____ at work.
4   Uncle John is old now but he _____ retired.
5   You _____ a teacher here. Are you a student?
6   I _____ unemployed; I'm retired.
7   I _____ a doctor, I'm a dentist!
8   A: I think they're architects.
     B: No, they _____ architects, they're engineers.

Speaking

9 **a** Guess other students' jobs. Use a dictionary.

A: *Are you a taxi driver?*   B: *No, I'm not a taxi driver.*
A: *Are you a ... ?*   B: *Yes, I am./No, I'm not a ...*

b Ask and answer questions about your partner's family or friends.

best friend   brother   father   mother   sister   uncle

A: *What's your brother's job?*   B: *He's an engineer.*
A: *Is your father a director?*   B: *No, he isn't. He's a dentist.*

Can do start and finish a basic conversation

1 **a** 🔵 1.19 Listen to six conversations and tick (✓) the expressions you hear.

Excuse me ... ☐ See you later. ☐ Bye. ☐
Hello. ☐ Hi. ☐ Good evening. ☐
Good morning. ✓ Good night. ☐
See you tomorrow. ☐ Goodbye. ☐
See you soon. ☐

b Listen again. Complete the How to... box.

> ### How to... start and finish a basic conversation
>
> Start : *Hello.*
>   : _____
>   : _____
>   : _____
>   : _____
> _____
> Finish : _____
>   : _____
>   : _____
>   : _____

2 **a** Match the questions with the answers.

1 Are you Czech? ☐ c
2 What's your job? ☐
3 Are you single? ☐
4 Where are you from? ☐
5 What's your name? ☐

a No, I'm not. I'm married.
b It's Dariusz.
c No, I'm not. I'm Italian.
d I'm from Łódź, in Poland.
e I'm a student.

b Write the answers to questions 1–5. Write about you.

3 **a** Complete the conversations with the expressions in the box.

> Excuse me, are you Krystof?
> ~~Hello Maria, I'm Clara.~~   I'm a teacher.
> I'm from Alicante.   Yes, I am. I'm from Warsaw.

1
Maria: Hello, I'm Maria.
Clara: *Hello Maria, I'm Clara.*
Maria: Pleased to meet you. Where are you from?
Clara: _____
Maria: Oh! Do you work there?
Clara: No, I'm a student.

2
Jordi: _____
Krystof: Yes, I am. What's your name?
Jordi: My name's Jordi. Are you Polish?
Krystof: _____
Jordi: What do you do?
Krystof: _____

b 🔵 1.20 Listen and check your answers.

4 Practise the conversations with a partner.

5 **a** Talk to other students. Find ...

1 a married student.
2 a student with two languages.
3 a student with the letter 'Y' in his/her name.
4 a student with a university degree.
5 a student from a different city.

b Tell the class your results.

Maria is married. She's a housewife.

Subject pronouns, possessive adjectives and possessive 's

There are eight subject pronouns in English. We use subject pronouns before verbs.

There are also eight possessive adjectives. We use possessive adjectives before nouns.

Subject pronouns			Possessive adjectives		
	I			*my*	
	you			*your*	
	he			*his*	
	she	*+ verb*		*her*	*+ noun*
	it			*its*	
	we			*our*	
	you			*your*	
	they			*their*	

Possessive adjectives and noun + *'s* have the meaning *belongs to* (for things). With people they show relationships.

*This is John's phone. This is **his** phone.*

*Kim is Steve's wife. Kim is **his** wife.*

Verb *to be*

➕	*I*	*am ('m)*	
	You	*are ('re)*	*German. / from Germany.*
	He/She/It	*is ('s)*	
	We/You/They	*are ('re)*	
➖	*I*	*'m not*	
	You	*aren't*	*Italian. / from Italy.*
	He/She/It	*isn't*	
	We/You/They	*aren't*	

❓						
Am	*I*			*I*	*am. ('m not.)*
Are	*you*	*American?*	*Yes, (No,)*	*you*	*are. (aren't.)*
Is	*he/she/ it*			*he/she/ it*	*is. (isn't.)*
Are	*we/you/ they*			*we/you/ they*	*are. (aren't.)*

In informal English we usually use the contracted forms:

'm = am, 's = is, 're = are, isn't = is not, aren't = are not

*I am British. = **I'm** British.*

*He is Brazilian. = **He's** Brazilian.*

*I'm not Italian. He/She/It **isn't** Italian. We/You/They **aren't** Italian.*

We don't use contracted forms in questions and short positive answers.

A: *Are you Russian?*

B: *Yes, I am.*

Wh- questions

We form *wh-* questions with a question word.

Who asks about a person.

What asks about a thing.

Where asks about a place.

How old asks about age.

Question word + *am/is/are* + subject pronoun.

***How old** is she?*

***Where** are you from?*

a/an

We use *a/an* to introduce singular nouns.

a teacher, a doctor, a car, an iPod, an address

We don't use *a/an* with adjectives.

She's unemployed.

a	before consonant sounds: *a burger, a handbag*
an	before vowel sounds: *an engineer, an uncle*

Key vocabulary

Family words

Male	Female
father	mother
husband	wife
son	daughter
brother	sister
uncle	aunt
nephew	niece
grandfather	grandmother
stepbrother	sister-in-law

Male or female

children   cousins   grandparents   parents

Jobs and work

actor   architect   chef
computer programmer   dentist   director
doctor   engineer   farmer   lawyer
sea captain   shop assistant   student
teacher   TV producer
retired
unemployed

 Listen to these words.

ACTIVE BOOK

 see Writing bank page 135

1 Review and practice

1 Choose the correct word in *italics*.

Excuse me. Is this *my/your* bag?

1 John is twelve and *his/her* sister is fourteen.
2 This is Mariana. She's *my/her* wife's best friend.
3 Mr and Mrs Silva are teachers and *they/their* children are students.
4 We are German. *Our/Their* parents are from Frankfurt.
5 Jennifer Lopez is American but *her/their* parents are from Puerto Rico.
6 My sister is married. *His/Her* husband is forty-three.
7 I am from Rio de Janeiro but *my/our* boyfriend is from El Salvador.
8 Tessa is married. *Her's/Tessa's* husband is Canadian.
9 Martin Sheen is a film star. Emilio Estevez and Charlie Sheen are *his/their* sons.

2 Make sentences.

Pilar and Esteban/Spain

Pilar and Esteban are from Spain. They are Spanish.

1 Elizabeth/the United States
2 Ivan and Katia/Russia
3 I/France
4 You/England
5 Pavlos/Greece
6 His camera/Japan
7 I/Poland

3 Complete the questions and answers. Use information from exercise 2.

A: (1) *Is* Elizabeth British?
B: No, she (2) *isn't*. She's (3) *American*.
A: (4) _____ Katia and Ivan from Mexico?
B: No, they (5) _____ . They (6) _____ from (7) _____ .
A: (8) _____ Pavlos (9) _____ Greece?
B: Yes, he (10) _____ .
A: (11) _____ his camera German?
B: (12) _____ , it (13) _____ . It's Japanese.

4 Write about you. Correct the false sentences.

I'm an English student.

That's right.

I'm from the United States.

No, I'm not from the United States. I'm from …

1 I'm seventeen years old.
2 My parents are doctors.
3 My best friend is a student.
4 Our teacher is British.
5 My mobile phone is German.
6 My brother/sister is married.

5 Complete the conversation with questions.

A: *Hi, what's your name?*
B: My name's Andreas Schmidt.
A: (1) _____
B: I'm from Germany.
A: (2) _____
B: I'm twenty-three.
A: (3) _____
B: I'm an engineer. ... This is David and Gina.
A: (4) _____
B: No, they're not my brother and sister. They're my cousins.
A: (5) _____
B: No, they aren't. They're British. My aunt is married to a British man.

6 Write *a* or *an*.

an American doctor

1 ____ email address
2 ____ Australian actor
3 ____ first name
4 ____ Polish student
5 ____ Japanese television
6 ____ Brazilian taxi
7 ____ Italian car
8 ____ English book

7 Find the jobs and family words in the word chains, and write them in the table.

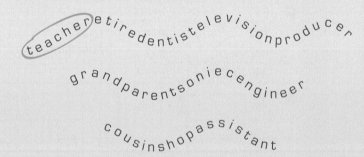

Jobs	Family
teacher	

8 Complete the sentences with family or job words.

1 Your nephew is your brother or sister's _____ .
2 Your mother's sister is your _____ .
3 Tom Cruise is an _____ .
4 Your mother-in-law is your husband's or _____ mother.
5 My 19-year-old cousin is a _____ at Oxford University.

2

Lead-in

1 a Which activities can you see in the photos?

> get home   get up   go to work   go to bed   leave home
> have breakfast   have dinner   have lunch   leave work

b Match the activities in exercise 1a with the parts of the day.

 1 in the morning *get up ...*   3 in the evening

 2 in the afternoon   4 at night

2 a 🔘 1.21 Listen and complete the times. Then match the times with the clocks.

What time is it?

1 It's *six* o'clock.

2 It's ten past _____ .

3 It's quarter past _____ .

4 It's twenty past _____ .

5 It's half past _____ .

6 It's twenty-five to _____ .

7 It's quarter to _____ .

8 It's five to _____ .

a `8:15`   b `1:35`

c `6:00`   d `4:55`

e `7:30`   f `2:10`

g `3:45`   h `3:20`

b 🔘 1.22 Listen and match the speakers with the photos.

Speaker 1 = photo _____   Speaker 3 = photo _____

Speaker 2 = photo _____   Speaker 4 = photo _____

19

Reading

1 **a** Look at the photo of Penny. What is her job?

b Match the labels with the photos A–D.

holiday rep and client ☐A   entertainment ☐
nightclub ☐   games at the swimming pool ☐

2 **a** Read the text and put Penny's activities in the correct order, 1–8.

Have lunch ☐   Take clients to a restaurant ☐
Get home ☐   Organise games at the pool ☐
Get up ☐1   Tell clients about parties ☐
Go to a nightclub ☐   Go to the hotels ☐

b Underline the times for each activity and use the information to complete the chart for Penny.

	Penny	You
1	*10 o'clock – get up*	
2	_____	
3	_____	
4	_____	
5	_____	
6	_____	
7	_____	
8	_____	
9	_____	

3 Work in pairs. Is this kind of holiday fun? Is Penny's job interesting?

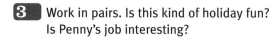

Just An Ordinary Day

Penny Hengrove works as a holiday rep for Fun Club holidays. She tells Lucy Brompton about her typical day.

P: I get up at about ten o'clock and go to the hotels at about eleven. I meet the clients at quarter past eleven and tell them about our parties, and I sell them tickets for excursions. I help them when they have problems. Then I have lunch at about two o'clock. But I don't eat lunch with the clients. I have lunch with the other reps.

L: And what do you do in the afternoon?

P: At half past three I go to the hotel pool and help the other reps with games. Fun Club holidays are for young people aged 18 to 30, so we organise competitions and games for them. It's great fun.

L: Do you play the games?

P: Oh no, I don't. They're only for the clients!

L: So, what do you do in the evening? Do you have dinner with the clients?

P: Yes, I do. I take them to a restaurant at quarter to eight and then to a nightclub at about half past ten. Sometimes we have special parties and entertainment.

L: When do you finish work?

P: Well, I leave the nightclub at about half past one in the morning. So I get home at about quarter to two. It's a busy life – but I have lots of fun!

Vocabulary | holidays

4 **a** Match the verbs with the nouns. Then check your answers with the text.

Verb	Noun
1 sell	a games
2 meet	b work
3 play	c clients
4 organise	d tickets
5 finish	e competitions

b We use the verb *have* with many different nouns. Look at the text and find five different words we use with *have*. Then complete the sentences.

We *have parties* on Saturday evenings – we sing and dance and eat lots of food.

1 In Spain we _____ very late, around 10 p.m.
2 Doctors can help you when you _____ with your health.
3 I enjoy parties. I always _____ !
4 I _____ in the office at 12:30 – just a sandwich.

Grammar | Present Simple: *I/you/we*

5 Look at the text again and complete the Active grammar box.

Active grammar

⊕
I meet the clients.
We _____ special parties.

⊖
I _____ eat lunch with the clients.

Yes/No questions
Do you have dinner with the clients?
_____ play the games?
Yes, I _____ .
No, I _____ .

Wh- questions
What do you do in the afternoon?
When do _____ work?

see Reference page 27

6 Match the questions with the answers.

1 Where do you work? `c`
2 What do you do at the school?
3 When do you have lunch?
4 Do you have lunch in a restaurant?
5 What do you do in the evening?

a I watch TV.
b No, I don't.
c I work at a school.
d At half past one.
e I'm a teacher.

7 **a** Complete the interview and write the job at the end.

A: When (1) *do* you get up?
B: At ten in the evening.
A: Do you work at night?
B: (2) _____ , I do.
A: What (3) _____ you do in the afternoon?
B: (4) _____ sleep.
A: (5) _____ do you have dinner?
B: I (6) _____ dinner at about eleven in the morning.
A: Do (7) _____ work in an office?
B: No, I (8) _____ .
A: Where (9) _____ you work?
B: I (10) _____ in a hospital.
A: So, what do you do?
B: I'm a _____ .

b 🔊 1.23 Listen and check your answers. Then practise the dialogue with a partner.

8 Complete the How to... box. Use the interview in exercise 7 for ideas.

How to... talk about your daily routine

Ask about routines	*What do you do in the morning/afternoon/evening?*
Answer	*I sleep.*
Ask about times	(1) _____ do you go to work? *What time* (2) _____ you _____ to work?
Answer	(3) _____ 11:00 in the evening.
Ask about places	(4) _____ do you work?
Answer	*I work* (5) _____ .

Speaking

9 **a** Complete the *You* column in the chart in exercise 2b. Write about your daily routine.

b Work in pairs. Ask your partner about their daily routine.

What do you do in the morning?
When do you go to work/school?
Do you work in an office?

c Is your daily routine on holiday the same or different? Ask and answer questions with your partner.

Reading

1 **a** Look at the people in the photos. What are their jobs?

b Read the texts quickly and check your answers.

c Match A–F on the photos with the underlined words in the texts.

A *wax model*   C _____   E _____

B _____   D _____   F _____

2 Write Jo, John or Jeanette.

This person ...

works under water. *Jeanette*

1 works in a museum.

2 thinks a lot at work.

3 starts work before eight o'clock.

4 listens to other people.

5 is very careful at work.

Vocabulary | verbs

3 Look at the verbs in red in the text. Then choose the correct verbs in *italics* in these sentences.

Jeanette cleans the tank and another diver (waits)/washes for her.

1 John *works/invents* at a theme park.

2 The people at the park *walk/talk* about the rides.

3 The people at the park *have/like* fun on the rides.

4 My brother *watches/washes* TV in the evening.

5 Every week Rob washes his car then he *cleans/dries* it.

6 My friend Sue *goes/leaves* to work at 6:00 in the morning.

7 Mary's mother *washes/cleans* the house every weekend.

8 Our teacher *works/checks* our homework every morning.

Grammar | Present Simple: *he/she/it/they*

4 Look at the verbs in the text again and complete the Active grammar box.

Active grammar

⊕		⊖	
he/she/it	*they*	*he/she/it*	*they*
goes	go	doesn't go	don't go
_____	_____	doesn't have	don't have
_____	invent	_____	don't invent
leaves	leave	doesn't leave	_____
talks	_____	doesn't talk	don't talk
_____	_____	doesn't watch	don't watch
_____	work	_____	don't work

see Reference page 27

Jo Kinsey has an interesting job. She's a hairdresser – but a very special hairdresser. Jo doesn't work at a hairdresser's; she works at Madame Tussaud's – the wax model museum. She goes to work at 7:30. In the morning she checks the models for dirty hair and in the afternoon she washes and dries their hair.

Jeanette Ewart is a cleaner, but in a very dangerous place. She cleans the shark tank in the zoo in her city. She swims under the water and cleans the tank. She also feeds the sharks three days a week. The sharks don't leave the tank, so Jeanette's very careful, but another diver waits by the tank and watches her. The visitors at the zoo watch her, too.

John Wardley is an inventor, but he doesn't invent boring kitchen equipment. He invents exciting rides for his theme park. He walks through the theme park and he listens to people when they talk about a ride. He wants to find out when they have fun on the rides. Then he invents new rides, and the engineers make them. John likes his work – his theme park is the best place to work!

5 **a** Complete the sentences with the correct form of a verb from the box.

> ~~clean~~   go   have   leave   like   play   talk
> wash   watch

My mother _cleans_ our house.

1 The teacher _____ in English in class.
2 Jake _____ his hair every morning.
3 Matt _____ his new job – it's very interesting.
4 Tracy _____ to work at 9:00 in the morning.
5 My brother _____ football on TV every evening.
6 Patrick _____ games on the computer at work.
7 Some engineers _____ dangerous jobs.
8 The shop assistants _____ work late.

b Change the sentences to make them negative.

My mother doesn't clean our house.

Pronunciation | Present Simple -s endings

6 **a** 🔊 1.24 Listen to three verbs. Do the endings sound the same? Listen again and repeat.

b 🔊 1.25 Listen and write the verbs in the table. Then repeat them.

/s/ walks	/z/ listens	/ɪz/ organises

c 🔊 1.26 Now listen to sentences 1–6 in exercise 5a. Repeat the sentences.

see Pronunciation bank page 148

Grammar | Present Simple: questions

7 **a** Complete the dialogue.

A: _Does_ Jeanette like her work?
B: Yes, she _does_. She loves it.
A: _____ she clean the shark tank?
B: Yes, she _____ , and she _____ the sharks.
A: _____ the sharks eat every day?
B: No, they _____ . They eat three times a week.
A: So … _____ Jeanette work every day?
B: No, she _____ . She _____ five days a week.

b 🔊 1.27 Listen and check your answers.

8 Choose the correct words to complete the questions in the Active grammar box.

> ## Active grammar
> 1 'Does/Do the sharks eat/eats every day?' 'No, they do/don't.'
> 2 'Does/Do Jeanette clean/cleans the tank every day?' 'No, she doesn't/don't.'
> 3 'Does/Do Jeanette like/likes her work?' 'Yes, she doesn't/does.'

see Reference page 27

9 **a** Complete the questions with the verbs in brackets.

Does Jo work every day? (work)

1 _____ John _____ his work? (like)
2 _____ your parents _____ DVDs? (watch)
3 _____ John _____ computer games? (invent)
4 _____ I _____ in my sleep? (talk)
5 _____ Anna _____ children? (have)

b Change the questions in exercise 9a. Ask and answer with a partner.

A: *Do you work every day?*
B: *Yes, I do./No, I don't.*

c Now ask and answer the questions about your family and friends.

Speaking

10 Doug Hitchens has a dangerous job – he cleans the windows on tall buildings. Talk about his daily routine.

Student A: look at page 129.
Student B: look at page 133.

Listening

1 **a** Tick (✓) the correct answer for you.

	Every day	Once a week	Once a month	Never
1 go shopping in supermarkets				
2 use local shops				
3 go to markets				

b In pairs, compare your answers.

A: *Do you go shopping in supermarkets?*

B: *Yes, every day.*

Jodie and Karl, fleamarket stallholders

2 **a** 🔵 1.28 Listen. What is a flea market?

b Listen again and choose the correct words.

1 Hell's Kitchen flea market is in the *UK/US*.

2 It's open *every day/two days a week*.

3 Jodie sells *clothes and shoes/cameras and phones*.

4 Jodie and Karl *like/don't like* the flea market.

c Do you go to flea markets? What kind of things do you buy in them?

Grammar | noun plurals

3 **a** Match the numbers with the things in the picture.

bags [3]   books ☐   cameras ☐   diaries ☐
DVD players ☐   laptops ☐   mobile phones ☐
MP3 players ☐   scarves ☐   shoes ☐   watches ☐

b 🔵 1.29 Listen and tick (✓) the things you hear.

4 Look at the plurals of the nouns in exercise 3a, then complete the rules in the Active grammar box.

Active grammar

We add *-s* to most nouns to make them plural.

We add ___ when the noun ends in *-ch, -s, -sh* or *-x*, e.g. *watch* → _____

We add ___ when the noun ends in *-y* (but take away the *-y*), e.g. *diary* → _____

When the noun ends in ___ , we change it to *-v* in the plural, e.g. *scarf* → _____

see Reference page 27

5 Look at the Lifelong learning box. Read the tip and complete the exercise.

Irregular plurals

❗ Use a dictionary to find irregular plurals:

person /ˈpɜːsən/ noun, plural *people* /ˈpiːpəl/

Find the plurals of these nouns. Use a dictionary.

address   bus   child   class   dictionary
family   man   niece   wife   woman

Lifelong learning

Vocabulary | adjectives (1): colour, opinion

6 **a** (Circle) eight colours, then find the colours in the picture in exercise 3a.

> bad   big   (black)   blue   brown   good
> green   grey   horrible   modern   nice
> old   old-fashioned   pretty   red   small
> ugly   useful   useless   white   yellow
> young

b Now put the other adjectives into pairs of opposites. *bad – good*

Grammar | this, that, these, those

7 **a** 🔵 1.30 Listen to Jodie and Karl. What things do they look at on Jane's stall?

b Listen again. Which adjectives from exercise 6a do you hear?

c Do Jodie and Karl like …
1 the belt?   4 the shoes?
2 the coat?   5 the bag?
3 the scarves?

8 **a** Listen again and complete the sentences with adjectives.

Now that's really _____ !

Look at those shoes. They're so _____ !

This is _____ !

These are _____ .

b Complete the Active grammar box with *this*, *that*, *these* and *those*.

> ### Active grammar
>
> | | near | far |
> |----------|----------|----------|
> | singular | _____ | _____ |
> | plural | _____ | _____ |

see Reference page 27

c Correct the underlined words in the sentences.
<u>These</u> is a car. *This is a car.*

1 What colour is <u>those</u>?   3 <u>Are</u> that your house?
2 <u>These</u> is very beautiful.   4 These <u>isn't</u> very old.

Pronunciation | /ɪ/ and /iː/

9 **a** 🔵 1.31 Listen to the vowel sounds. Repeat.
/ɪ/ this   /iː/ these

b 🔵 1.32 Listen and write the words in the table. Then listen again and repeat.

> big   clean   green   listen   niece   read
> sister   swim   teacher   think

/ɪ/ **this**	/iː/ **these**

see Pronunciation bank page 147

Speaking

10 Describe the photos and talk about them. Use the adjectives in exercise 6a.

A: *I think that dog's old.*
B: *Yes, and these are young.*
A: *They're very pretty. Do you like cats?*

A

B

C

1 Match the photos with the captions.

1 In the city ☐
2 In the mountains ☐
3 At the beach ☐

2 **a** 🔵 1.33 Listen and match the speakers with the photos.

Matt = photo _____
Wendy = photo _____
Gareth = photo _____

b Listen again. Which speaker(s) takes these things on holiday?

1 presents _____
2 a camera _____
3 sunscreen _____
4 a guidebook _____
5 games and books _____

c Which speaker(s) does these things on holiday?

1 go skiing _____
2 look at the sights _____
3 go to the beach _____
4 play games _____
5 read books _____

3 Look at the words in the box. Are they for a beach holiday, a city break, a holiday in the mountains, or all?

> camera   go sightseeing
> go skiing   guidebook   magazine
> museum   passport   suitcase
> sunbathe   sunscreen

4 **a** Complete the questionnaire with words from the box.

> do (x2)   go   time   what   when   ~~where~~   who   you

What do you usually do on holiday?

1 *Where* do you go on holiday?
2 _____ do you go with?
3 Where do _____ stay?
4 What _____ you take with you?
5 _____ do you get up on holiday?
6 What do you _____ in the day?
7 _____ do you do in the evening?
8 What _____ do you _____ to bed?

b Match the questions with these answers.

a My camera and a good book. ☑ 4
b To the beach. ☐
c At about ten in the morning. ☐
d Go on excursions or swim. ☐
e At about half past eleven. ☐
f Go to a nightclub or restaurant. ☐
g My friends. ☐
h In a hotel. ☐

5 **a** Work in pairs. Ask and answer the questions in exercise 4a and write the answers.

A: *Where do you go on holiday?*

B: *I go to my sister's house.*

b Tell the class about your partner's holiday routines.

Stefano goes to his sister's house in the city. He takes the bus. He goes with his wife ...

Present Simple

Positive and negative

	+	−
I We You They	work	don't (do not) work
He She It	works	doesn't (does not) work

I **work** in an office.

She **doesn't work** every day.

We use the Present Simple for daily routines and activities. With *I*, *we*, *you* and *they* the Present Simple positive form is the same as the infinitive. With *he*, *she* and *it* we add *-s* to the infinitive, but note these exceptions:

verbs ending -ch, -s, -sh, -x and -o	add -es	watch → watches go → goes
verbs ending consonant + -y	remove -y and add -ies	carry → carries

Note: verbs ending with a vowel + *-y* are regular: *play → plays*

The third person of *have → has*

Questions

Do Where do	I we you they	work?
Does When does	he she it	

In questions, don't add *-s* to the verb.

Note the short answers:

Yes, | I/we/you/they do.
he/she/it does.

No, | I/we/you/they don't.
he/she/it doesn't.

this, that, these, those

	Singular	Plural
near	this	these
far	that	those

What's **this**? | Do you like **these** shoes? | Look at **that** car! | **Those** bags are horrible.

Noun plurals

We add *-s* to nouns to make the regular noun plural:

*book → book**s**, picture → picture**s***

There are some special spelling rules:

nouns ending -ch, -s, -sh, -x	add -es	watch → watches address → addresses
most nouns ending -f	remove -f and add -ves	scarf → scarves knife → knives
nouns ending consonant + -y	remove -y and add -ies	diary → diaries city → cities

Note: nouns ending with a vowel + *-y* are regular: *day → days*

Some plural nouns are completely irregular: *child → children*

Key vocabulary

Personal possessions

bag belt book clothes coat diary digital camera DVD player laptop computer magazine mobile phone MP3 player scarf shoe watch

Basic verbs/verb phrases

Routines:

get up wash have breakfast eat leave home go to work/school start work work have lunch finish work get home have dinner · watch (TV) go to bed sleep

Note these phrases:

have breakfast/lunch/dinner/fun/problems/parties go to bed/a nightclub/a restaurant/school/work BUT go home

Other verbs:

check clean dry feed help invent like make meet organise play sell swim talk wait walk

  Listen to these words.

ACTIVE BOOK

---

  see Writing bank page 136

1 Look at the pictures and write sentences about Alvaro's day. Use the verbs and phrases in the boxes.

> ~~drive~~   eat   finish   go   read   watch

> a sandwich   his emails   television   to bed
> ~~to work~~   work

A   He drives to work at quarter past eight.

2 Complete the sentences with the correct form of the verbs in brackets.

She *finishes* work at five o'clock. (finish)

1 They _____ at ten o'clock on Sundays. (get up)
2 He _____ a good job. (have)
3 I _____ to English classes in the evening. (go)
4 She _____ the house in the morning. (clean)
5 We _____ football on Saturday afternoons. (play)

3 Now make the sentences in exercise 2 negative.

She doesn't finish work at five o'clock.

4 Put the words in the correct order to make questions.

to you work When go do ?

When do you go to work?

1 she afternoon What does do in the ?
2 have Where does lunch he ?
3 work in Do an you office ?
4 does finish he When work ?
5 What in you evening do do the ?

5 Find five incorrect plural nouns and correct them.

lunchs	✗ *lunches*	4	rides	_____
clients	✓ _____	5	watchs	_____
1 holidaies	_____	6	sharkes	_____
2 hotels	_____	7	zoos	_____
3 partys	_____	8	scarfs	_____

6 Complete the questions, then answer the questions using an adjective from the box.

> horrible   modern   old   ~~old-fashioned~~   pretty

1 'What's *this*?'
'It's a phone. It's *old-fashioned*!'

2 'What are _____ ?'
'They're _____ . They're _____ !'

3 'What's _____ ?'
'It's a _____ . It's _____ .'

4 '_____ _____ ?'
'_____ _____ _____ .
_____ _____ .'

5 '_____ _____ _____ ?'
'_____ _____ . _____
_____ .'

7 **a** Look at the 'personal possessions' vocabulary on page 27. Copy the table and write the objects.

Personal/Clothes	House/Home	Equipment
diary	*book*	*DVD player*

b Look at the 'routines' vocabulary on page 27. Write eight of the verbs in the order you do them during the day.

1 *get up*   2 *wash*   3 *have breakfast*

3

Lead-in

1 **a** Find six of the activities from the box in the photos.

> cook   go for a walk   go shopping   go to a concert
> go to the gym   listen to music   meet friends
> play football (or another sport)   play games online
> play the guitar (or another instrument)
> read a book or magazine   sunbathe   surf the Internet
> swim   text friends   watch TV or a DVD

b Answer the questions about the activities in the box.

1 Which activities do you usually do with other people?
2 Which activities do people do outside their house?
3 Which activities do people do inside their house?
4 Which of these activities do you do?

c Where do you do the activities in exercise 1a? Copy and complete the table.

At home	In the park	At the shops	At a club/ nightclub	At a sports centre/ swimming pool

2 **a** Write two more activities that you do in the table.

b Work in pairs. Ask and answer questions.

What do you do in your free time?

Where do you do it?   *When do you do it?*

c Tell the class about your partner.

Mark plays the piano. He plays at home in the evening.

3.1 | Lunchtime leisure

| Grammar | adverbs of frequency |
| Can do | talk about what you do in your free time |

(A)

(B)

(C)

(D)

Listening

1 🔘 1.34 Listen and match the speakers with the activities in the photos.

Stig = photo ____   Amber = photo ____

Matt = photo ____   Ailsa = photo ____

2 **a** Listen again and complete the table. You can sometimes tick (✓) two or three names.

		Stig	Amber	Matt	Ailsa
1	eats a sandwich				
2	eats in the canteen				
3	goes for a walk				
4	checks emails	✓			
5	goes to the gym				
6	reads a book/the news				
7	surfs the Internet				
8	goes shopping				

b Are the sentences true (T) or false (F)?

Stig goes to the canteen. ☐ F

1 Stig sometimes stays at his desk in the lunch hour. ☐

2 Amber works in the lunch hour. ☐

3 Matt sometimes leaves the office for lunch. ☐

4 Ailsa doesn't take the bus into the town centre. ☐

5 Ailsa goes to the gym in her lunch break. ☐

Grammar | adverbs of frequency

3 **a** Complete the sentences with verbs from the box. Check your answers with audioscript 1.34 on page 151.

> goes (x3)   has   ~~is~~   leaves   take   takes

1 Amber *is* often at her desk at lunchtime – she doesn't always _____ a lunch break.

2 Stig always _____ his desk. He usually _____ for a walk.

3 Ailsa often _____ the bus to town. She never _____ to the gym.

4 Matt sometimes _____ for a walk and occasionally _____ lunch in a café.

b Complete the diagram in the Active grammar box with *never*, *sometimes* and *usually*, then choose the correct answers.

Active grammar

Frequency

always _____ *often* _____ *occasionally* _____

↓   ↓   ↓   ↓   ↓   ↓

100% ──────────────────────────────→ 0%

We put adverbs of frequency *before/after* the verb *to be*.

We put adverbs of frequency *before/after* other verbs.

see Reference page 37

4 **a** Put the words in the correct order to make sentences.

sends emails   sometimes   Isabel   to her friends
Isabel sometimes sends emails to her friends.

1   often   We   go to concerts
2   cooks   occasionally   Lara   Chinese food
3   in the evening   football   usually   Jason   plays
4   in bed   My parents   read   never
5   always   I   go shopping   at the weekend
6   goes to the gym   in the morning   sometimes   Dan

b What about you? Change the sentences so they are true for you.

I occasionally cook Chinese food.

c Work in pairs. What do you do in your lunch break? What do your friends and colleagues do?

Reading

5 Read the blog. Make sentences about what Shane does in his lunch break.

work   *He never works in his lunch break.*

1   sleep   4   listen to music
2   leave the office   5   go shopping
3   use the computer

Home   **About Shane**   **Links**   **Contact**

In my lunch break

You know, I hear that some people sleep in their lunch break. Sleep in your lunch break – why? During the week I work for a magazine company – it's great fun and very busy, but I always take an hour for lunch, sometimes two (then I work until 7:00!). It's important to get out of the office. I always go on the Internet and go on Facebook for a few minutes, then I go out. On Monday I always go running or go for a walk, on Tuesday I usually do my homework (because I go to an evening class on Tuesday evenings). On Wednesday I often go shopping – some friends usually visit me on Wednesday evening so I get some food for the barbecue. I sometimes go to a concert on Thursday lunchtime and on Friday I always go for a long lunch with friends. I don't do a lot at the weekend – maybe go to the cinema on Saturday, then on Sunday I just relax and watch football on TV.

6 Write the days of the week in the correct order.
Monday, ...

Vocabulary | activities

7 **a** We use *go* with a lot of different activities. Write activities from the lesson in the word forks.

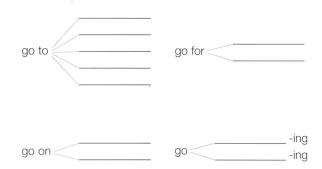

go to

go for

go on

go   -ing
             -ing

b Can you add any other words to the forks?

c Make simple word forks with *have*, *do* and *read*.

Speaking and writing

8 **a** Look at the questionnaire. Add six activities. Tick (✓) the things you do and write the day you do them.

Activity	You (when)	Your partner (when)
go out with friends	✓ (Friday)	
study		
play a sport		
go on the Internet		
_____		
_____		
_____		
_____		
_____		
_____		

b Work in pairs. Ask questions and complete the questionnaire for your partner.

A: *Do you go out with friends?*
B: *Yes, I always go out with friends at the weekend.*
     No, I never go out with friends.

9 **a** What do you do in your free time? Make a list.
Monday evenings – watch TV
Saturdays – read the newspaper/go shopping

b Write about your free time.

Vocabulary | sports and games

1 **a** Match the words with the pictures.

aerobics ☐   basketball ☐   chess ☐
judo ☐   rowing ☐   running ☐
skiing ☐   tennis ☐   windsurfing ☐
yoga ☐

b Write the activities in the table. Then check in the Reference on page 37.

do	go	play
aerobics	running	chess

c Work in pairs. Ask and answer questions.

A: *Do you do yoga?*

B: *Yes, I do.*

A: *When?*

B: *On Thursday evenings.*

LIVE THE DREAM!

Rebecca Romero is 29. She's British but her father is Spanish. She has a degree in sports science and English. And she's the second woman in history with two Olympic medals in two different sports, and the only British woman!

Reading

2 **a** Look at the photos. What sports can you see?

b Read the introduction to the text and complete the table.

Name	*Rebecca Romero*
Age	
Nationality	
Qualifications	
Achievements	

3 Read more about Rebecca and choose the correct words in *italics* to complete the sentences.

Rebecca has an Olympic silver medal in rowing from the Olympic Games in Athens, but silver isn't enough for her. She can't row now because of a back problem, but she can cycle, and she can cycle really fast. Her Olympic gold medal is in cycling, from the Olympic Games in Beijing, but Rebecca says she can't remember the medal ceremony at all!

Now Rebecca wants to win another Olympic medal, maybe in a different sport. She can't run or play sports like tennis, but perhaps skiing or windsurfing are possible. Can Rebecca do it? Can she live her dream?

Her silver medal is from *Beijing/Athens*.

1   Her silver medal is in *rowing/cycling*.

2   She doesn't row now because she *doesn't like it/has a bad back*.

3   Rebecca *remembers/doesn't remember* the medal ceremony in Beijing.

4   She wants to win a medal in a different sport, for example *skiing/tennis*.

Grammar | *can/can't*

4 **a** Tick (✓) the things Rebecca can do. Cross (✗) the things she can't do.

1	row	☐	3	run ☐
2	cycle fast	☐	4	play tennis ☐

b Complete the questions and answers with *can* or *can't*. Then complete the Active grammar box and answer the questions.

'What _____ Rebecca do?' 'She _____ cycle fast.'
'_____ she play tennis?' 'No, she _____ .'

Active grammar

⊕   *I/You/He/She/It/We/They* _____ *swim.*

⊖   *I/You/He/She/It/We/They* _____ *swim.*

❓   _____ *I/you/he/she/it/we/they swim?*

  Yes, I/you/he/she/it/we/they can.

  No, I/you/he/she/it/we/they _____ *.*

1 Do we use *do/does* to make questions and negatives? Yes/No

2 Do we add *-s* to *can* after *he/she/it*? Yes/No

see Reference page 37

c Which activities can you do? Which activities can't you do? Tick (✓) and cross (✗).

play chess ☐   play football ☐   play tennis ☐
ride a bike ☐   row ☐   run ☐   ski ☐   swim ☐

Pronunciation | /æ/, /ə/, /ɑː/

5 🔊 1.35 Listen. What can Jonny and Susie do? Tick (✓) the things they can do.

	Jonny	Susie
play the guitar	✓	✓
play the piano	☐	☐
sing	☐	☐
dance	☐	☐
play football	☐	☐
play tennis	☐	☐
ski	☐	☐
speak French	☐	☐
speak Spanish	☐	☐
ride a bike	☐	☐
drive a car	☐	☐

6 **a** 🔊 1.36 We say *can/can't* in different ways. Listen and repeat.

Can you dance?   Yes, I can.   No, I can't.
/ə/   /æ/   /ɑː/

b Work in pairs. Ask and answer questions about six things in exercise 5.

A: *Can Susie speak French?*   B: *Yes, she can.*
A: *Can Jonny drive?*   B: *No, he can't.*

see Pronunciation bank page 148

7 **a** Find out about your partner. Ask and answer questions about the activities in exercise 4c.

b Now ask your partner about languages and other abilities.

Speaking

8 **a** Work in groups. Find someone who ...

can ...
- speak three languages
- stand on their head
- write backwards
- move their ears
- play an unusual instrument
- make their own clothes

can't ...
- cook
- swim
- write with their right hand
- get up in the mornings
- send a text message
- use a DVD player

b Tell the class about your group.

Mobile Crazy!

1 There are now more than 4 billion mobile phones in the world. In the UK people send 78.9 billion text messages and 553 million picture messages every year. That's over 216 million text messages a day or 9 million an hour. In fact, the average mobile phone user sends about 20 text messages a day.

2 Now American fans of mobile phone texting can show what they can do at the US National Texting Championship. This year's champion is 15-year-old Kate Moore from Iowa. She sends 14,000 texts a month. Kate can even send a text message with her eyes closed!

3 Of course, some people hate mobile phones. Every year in London there is a special competition called The Mobile Phone Throwing Championships. In this event competitors throw their phones as far as they can. Some women can throw a phone over 50 metres, and some men can throw one over 95 metres. It's a lot of fun for mobile phone haters!

Reading

1 When do you use your mobile phone? Who do you call? Do you send text messages?

2 **a** Read the text quickly. Match the headings (a–c) with paragraphs 1–3.

a American Texting Championship ☐
b The phone throwing competition ☐
c Texting in Britain ☐

b Read the text again. Match the numbers (1–8) with the information (a–h).

1	4 billion		a	metres some men can throw a phone
2	78.9 billion		b	Kate's age
3	216 million		c	messages Kate sends every month
4	9 million		d	text messages a year in the UK
5	20		e	mobile phones in the world
6	14,000		f	messages an hour
7	15		g	messages a day for every user
8	95		h	messages a day

c Do you think the information in the text is surprising, or not?

3 **a** How do you use your mobile phone? Tick (✓) the things you do.

surf the Internet ☐
take photos ☐
listen to music ☐
send texts ☐
send pictures ☐
play games ☐
translate words ☐
make phone calls ☐
download ring tones or music ☐
watch videos ☐
use maps or GPS ☐
do calculations ☐

b Compare with other students. Find out how many students in your class use each phone feature.

Vocabulary | numbers

4 🔊 1.37 How do we say these numbers? Match the numbers with the words in the box. Then listen and check your answers.

6 *six*   16   60   600   601   660
6,000   6,616   60,000   600,000
6,000,000   6,000,000,000

> six̶   six billion   six hundred
> six hundred and one   six thousand
> six hundred and sixty   sixty
> six hundred thousand   six million
> six thousand, six hundred and sixteen
> sixteen   sixty thousand

Pronunciation | word stress

5 **a** 🌐 1.38 Listen. <u>Underline</u> the main stress.

six<u>teen</u>   <u>six</u>ty   fourteen   forty

b 🌐 1.39 Listen. <u>Underline</u> the number you hear.

1	fourteen	forty
2	eighteen	eighty
3	seventeen	seventy
4	thirteen	thirty
5	nineteen	ninety
6	sixteen	sixty

c Test your partner. Say a number. Your partner points to the number he/she hears.

see Pronunciation bank page 148

Listening

6 **a** 🌐 1.40 Listen. Match the names with the messages.

Damian	☐	Benson Cameras	☐
Jane	1	Steve Henshaw	☐
Mary Wilde	☐		

b Listen again and complete the messages with one word, a number or a time. How does Mary say *88* in the phone number?

1
Message for: *Tony*
From: _____
Message:

Meet outside the
_____ at 7:50.

2
Message for Mandy from
Steve Henshaw.
Please _____ him –
068 919 _____

3
Message for Michael
_____:
Carol at Benson Cameras
– your new _____ is
there. Can you go and get
it this _____? Shop is
open 9:00 _____.

4
Why don't we
meet for _____
this evening?
8:25 at the
restaurant in
Green Street?
Call me in the
_____. Damian

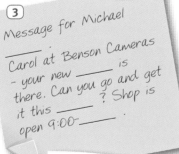

5
Brandon Travel Agency
Message for: _____ Renton
From: Mary Wilde
Number: 713 _____ 8834
Message:

Please _____ her.

7 **a** 🌐 1.41 Number the sentences in the correct order. Then listen and check.

OK. What's your number?	☐
OK. Bye.	☐
She isn't here right now. Can I take a message?	☐
Hello.	1
Yes, please ask her to phone Jeffrey.	☐
It's 011 908 5561.	☐
Hello, can I speak to Laura, please?	☐

b Work in pairs and practise the dialogue.

8 Complete the How to... box.

How to... use the phone; take and leave a message

Answer the phone	*Hello.* *(This is) 908 934 782.*
Take a message	*She isn't here right now. Can I (1) ____ a message?* *Sorry, can you repeat that?* *What's your (phone) number?*
Leave a message with a person	*Please (2) ____ her to call me.* *My (3) ____ is 909 541 323.*
Leave a voicemail message	*(Informal) Hi, John. (4) ____ Ana here. Can you call me?* *(Formal) Good morning. (5) ____ is Michael Brown. I'd like to leave a (6) ____ for Mrs Brinley.*
End the call	*Thanks./OK. Bye./Goodbye.* *See you there/later.*

Speaking

9 Make some phone calls.

Student A: turn to page 129.

Student B: read the notes below.

Call 1   Your name is Carla. Phone Student A. You want to speak to Jason. Your number is 990 675 3551.

Call 2   Your number is 899 054 782. Answer the phone and start the conversation. (Sylvia isn't here today. Take a message for her.)

Call 3   Your name is Mr/Mrs Grey. Phone Student A. You want to speak to the manager. Your number is 07733 89105.

Call 4   You work for Sunshine Holidays. Answer the phone and start the conversation. (Mr Preston is on holiday. Take a message for him.)

3 | Communication

1 **a** Match the abilities (1–10) with the jobs (a–j). Use a dictionary if necessary.

Abilities	Jobs
1 speak foreign languages	a sports teacher
2 design buildings	b taxi driver
3 play sports	c artist
4 drive	d carpenter
5 repair computers	e mechanic
6 play a musical instrument	f photographer
7 draw and paint	g tourist guide
8 repair cars	h musician
9 use a camera	i architect
10 make things in wood	j computer technician

b Work in pairs. Add three more abilities and jobs to the list.

2 Read the text. What is a skills exchange? Do you have one in your town?

BARTON SKILLS EXCHANGE

Do you live in Barton?
Can you drive?
Can you teach a foreign language?
Can you cook?
If so, join Barton's Skills Exchange and help other people – they can help you, too.
Your town needs you!

3 **a** Read the information about Carmen and Brian. Complete the skills exchange notes about them.

Carmen Lopez is thirty-two years old. Her phone number is 0206 331 212. She can speak Spanish and German. She can paint and draw. She likes the Internet. She takes digital photos and she changes them on her computer. She can't drive. She goes to the hospital on Friday mornings and she wants a driver.
Brian Winter's phone number is 577 894 505. He can do a lot of things. He can repair cars and engines, and he can repair houses. He makes furniture in wood and metal. He loves computers and he can repair them.
He has a big house and he doesn't like cleaning, so he needs a cleaner.

b 🔊 1.42 Listen and complete the notes for Dario and Lizzie.

Name: Carmen Lopez
Phone number: 0206 331 212
What she can do:
What she needs:
SKILLS EXCHANGE

Name: Brian Winter
Phone number:
What he can do:
What he needs:
SKILLS EXCHANGE

Name: Dario
Phone number:
What he can do:
What he needs:
SKILLS EXCHANGE

Name: Lizzie
Phone number:
What she can do:
What she needs:
SKILLS EXCHANGE

4 Work in pairs. Match the four people in the skills exchange.

Carmen can take the photos for Dario's sister.

5 **a** Organise a skills exchange in your class. Interview two students and complete the notes.

A: *What do you need?*
B: *A teacher – my English is very bad!*
A: *What can you do?*
B: *I can cook good food – I'm a chef.*

Name:
Phone number:
What he/she can do:
What he/she needs:
SKILLS EXCHANGE

Name:
Phone number:
What he/she can do:
What he/she needs:
SKILLS EXCHANGE

b Now compare your notes with other students. Can you match people in your class?

3 | Reference

Adverbs of frequency

Common adverbs of frequency are:

0% ——————————————→ 100%

never occasionally sometimes often usually always

We use adverbs of frequency with the Present Simple to describe how regularly or how often something happens.

*We **often** go to the gym in the evenings. (= three days a week)*

*I **always** go for a walk at lunchtime. (= every day)*

We put adverbs of frequency after the verb *to be* but before other main verbs.

*The children **are usually** in bed at eight o'clock.*

*The children **usually go** to bed at half past seven.*

can/can't

Can is a modal verb. We use modal verbs before other verbs.

The negative of *can* is *cannot*, but we usually use the short form *can't*.

I You He She It We You They	can can't (cannot)	sing.

Modal verbs do not change their form after *he*, *she* or *it*.

*He **can play** the piano.*

We use *can* and *can't* to talk about ability. We use *can* to talk about things we are able to do, and *can't* to talk about things that we are not able to do.

*I **can sing** but I **can't dance**.*

Note: when we talk about the skill or ability, we don't say *go running* or *go swimming*; we use *run*, *swim*, etc.

*I **can swim**. I **go swimming** on Mondays.*

We use *can* + *you* + infinitive to make requests – when we want someone else to do something.

***Can you take** a message?*

play, do, go + activities

We use *play* + noun for games, and for sports we usually do in teams.

e.g. *play football, play chess*

We use *do* + noun for activities we can do alone (not in a team).

e.g. *do aerobics, do yoga*

We use *go* with activity verbs that end in *-ing*.

e.g. *go swimming, go running*

Key vocabulary

Days/parts of the week
Sunday   Monday   Tuesday   Wednesday
Thursday   Friday   Saturday
at the weekend   during the week

Activities
cook   drive (a car)   go for a walk   listen to music
meet friends   ride a bike   sing   study   sunbathe
Collocations:
do aerobics/judo/yoga
go rowing/running/shopping/skiing/windsurfing
go on Facebook/the Internet
go to the cinema/a concert/the gym
play basketball/chess/football/games/sports/tennis
play the guitar/the piano
read a book/a magazine/the news
watch TV/a DVD/a video

Numbers

6	six
16	sixteen
60	sixty
600	six hundred
6,000	six thousand
60,000	sixty thousand
600,000	six hundred thousand
6,000,000	six million
600,000,000	six billion

Technology/phones
Verbs:
call   check emails
download (ring tones, music, videos)   phone
send (a message/picture)   surf (the Internet)
text (friends)
Nouns:
email   picture/text message
texting   voicemail

 Listen to these words.

ACTIVE BOOK

---

 see Writing bank page 137

1 Make sentences about Malcolm. Use adverbs of frequency or a negative.

live in a nice house (not)

Malcolm doesn't live in a nice house.

sleep in the park (usually)

Malcolm usually sleeps in the park.

1   have a job (not)
2   have an address (not)
3   go to work in the morning (never)
4   eat in restaurants (never)
5   have lunch in a café (occasionally)
6   meet friends in the park (sometimes)
7   Malcolm's days/be/boring (always)
8   Malcolm/like his life (not)

2 Write four sentences about the activities that you and your friends do together. Choose from the box. Use adverbs of frequency.

> eat in restaurants   go shopping   go to concerts
> go to nightclubs   go to the cinema
> go to the gym   listen to music
> play computer games   play sport   watch TV

We occasionally eat in restaurants.

3 Write a sentence with *can* and *can't* about the things below. Choose from the box.

> check spellings   drive   play computer games
> play football   play music   run
> send picture messages   send text messages
> sleep all day   swim   think

Young children

can play computer games but they can't drive.

1   Computers
2   Sharks
3   Mobile phones
4   Dogs

4 Find eight mistakes in the text and correct them.

> ⠀⠀⠀⠀⠀⠀⠀*can*
> Andreas ~~cans~~ do a lot of things. He likes sports
> and he can plays basketball and football but
> he no can play tennis. He don't like tennis. He
> likes rock music and he play the guitar in shows.
> He sing too, but he doesn't dances. He can't
> plays the piano.

5 Complete the puzzle with SIX days of the week and one other part of the week, to find the seventh day.

			↓					
			W					
		T						
	M							
		S						
			D					
			A					
			Y					

6 Complete the diary with the correct verbs.

> Monday _____
> ⠀⠀⠀*play football with the boys*
> 1 _____ *to the cinema (evening)*
> Tuesday _____
> 2 _____ *Jack and Ellie for lunch*
> 3 _____ *cycling in the park*
> Wednesday _____
> 4 _____ *to the gym*
> 5 _____ *emails and* _____ *on Facebook*
> Thursday _____
> 6 _____ *holiday pictures to Alison*
> 7 _____ *Elbow's new CD for Sam*
> Friday _____
> 8 _____ *yoga with Jane (morning)*
> 9 _____ *swimming with the girls*
> Saturday _____
> 10 _____ *shopping*
> Sunday _____
> 11 _____ *Harry's DVD*

7 Underline the wrong word in the lists.

1	**play**	chess	<u>judo</u>	tennis
2	**go on**	the Internet	Facebook	a nightclub
3	**go to**	a DVD	a concert	the gym
4	**do**	aerobics	yoga	running
5	**go**	cycling	skiing	reading
6	**watch**	music	the TV	a film
7	**read**	a book	the Internet	a magazine
8	**play**	the piano	football	swimming

Lead-in

1 **a** Match the words from the box with the pictures.

> apples   beef   bread   cheese   chicken   eggs   fish   milk
> pasta   rice   strawberries   tea   tomatoes   watermelon

b Do you know any other food words?

2 **a** We use the words in the table to measure food, drink and money. Put the words in the correct column.

litres   dollars   grammes   euros   kilos   cents

Food	Drink	Money

b Can you add any more words to the table?

3 **a** Match the pictures below with the words from the box.

> cash machine ☐   coin ☐   credit card ☐   note ☐   receipt ☐

b Which pictures show cash? When do you use cash/credit cards?
Where do you buy food? How do you pay for it?

A

B

C

Reading

1 **a** Match the words with the pictures.

rice ☐   bananas ☐   hot dogs ☐

b In which countries do people eat these things?

2 **a** Read the text quickly. Match each family with the food pictures and check your answers to exercise 1b.

b Read the text again and tick (✓) the correct answers.

Which family ...	Toro	Merton	Esteban
1 eats a lot of fish?			
2 eats fresh fruit?			
3 has a ration book?			
4 eats at fast food restaurants?			
5 doesn't have time to cook?			
6 has dinner together?			

Listening

3 **a** 🔘 **1.43** Listen to three people talk about food in different countries. Tick (✓) the countries you hear.

Canada ☐   Britain ☐   Iran ☐   Brazil ☐   Finland ☐

b Listen again. Which speaker(s) talk about these food words?

	Speaker 1	Speaker 2	Speaker 3
dried fruit	☐	☐	☐
lamb	☐	☐	☐
black beans	☐	☐	☐
rice	☐	☐	☐
seafood	☐	☐	☐

4 Work in pairs and discuss the questions.

1 Is your family like any of the families in the texts?

2 What food do people in your country eat?

3 What's your favourite food?

Grammar | countable and uncountable nouns

5 **a** Look at the pictures in exercise 1 and answer the questions.

1 Which food can you count?

2 Which food can't you count?

Eating around the world

The Toros live in Tokyo, Japan. Yamada Toro lives with his wife, Keiko, and his children Yoshi and Haruna. He works in an office. Keiko cooks breakfast before Yamada leaves for work at 7:00 a.m. They have dinner together at home in the evenings. They eat a lot of fish and rice. Keiko cooks all the meals for her family.

Steve and Corinne Merton and their children, Larry and Courtney, live in New York. They are a typical American family. Steve and Corinne both work and they don't usually have time to cook, so they like convenience food. The children eat a lot of hot dogs, burgers and cola. They eat at fast food restaurants once a week.

Julio Esteban, his wife Manuela and their children, Maria and Pedro, live in Havana. Cuba is a tropical country so they eat a lot of fresh fruit – pineapples, watermelons and bananas. Families in Cuba have ration books. These show how much food the family can buy every month.

b Here is the Merton family shopping list. Choose the correct words in *italics* to complete the sentences.

1 The red words are *countable/uncountable* nouns.

2 The blue words are *countable/uncountable* nouns.

12 hot dogs	orange juice
12 burgers	18 bananas
bread	4 pizzas
milk	rice

c Choose the correct words in *italics* in the Active grammar box.

Active grammar

1 *Uncountable/Countable* nouns

• They have singular and plural forms.

• We can use numbers in front of them.

2 *Uncountable/Countable* nouns

• They do not have plural forms.

• We cannot use numbers in front of them.

see Reference page 47

Grammar | *much/many/a lot of*

8 **a** Read the sentences. Are the underlined words countable or uncountable?

We eat a lot of <u>seafood</u>.

We don't eat much <u>fast food</u>.

We don't eat many <u>takeaways</u>.

The children eat a lot of <u>burgers</u>.

b Look at the red words in the sentences. Then complete the Active grammar box with ticks (✓) and crosses (✗).

Active grammar

	+ countable noun	+ uncountable noun
(how) much	☐	☐
(how) many	☐	☐
(not) a lot of	☐	☐

We usually use *much* and *many* in questions and negatives, but not in positive sentences.

---

see Reference page 47

9 **a** Cross out the words in *italics* that are incorrect.

1 How *much/many/a lot of* coffee do you drink every day?

2 I don't eat *much/many/a lot of* meat these days.

3 How *much/many/a lot of* bananas do you want?

4 Do you drink *much/many/a lot of* water?

5 Do people in your country eat *much/many/a lot of* burgers?

6 My family eats *much/many/a lot of* eggs every week.

b Complete the sentences with words from the box.

a lot   coffee   many   much   six   tomatoes

A: How (1) _____ rice do you buy each week?

B: I don't buy (2) _____ of rice, really. I don't like it.

A: Oh! How many (3) _____ do you buy?

B: About (4) _____ .

A: How much (5) _____ do you buy?

B: I usually buy just one jar of coffee.

A: How (6) _____ pineapples do you get?

B: Oh, only one.

10 Work in pairs. Ask questions about your partner's weekly diet and food shopping. Make notes and tell the class.

How much ... do you buy?

Do you eat a lot of ... ?

6 Four of these sentences have mistakes. Find the mistakes and correct them.

1 I don't like rices.

2 Do you eat breads?

3 Can I have six bananas, please?

4 I drink orange juices with my breakfast.

5 Do you like milks in your coffee?

Vocabulary | food

7 **a** Look at audioscript 1.43 on page 152 and <u>underline</u> the food words. Then complete the words in the table. Use a dictionary.

Meat	Seafood	Vegetables	Others
beef	fish	potatoes	n_____
p_____	l_____	b_____	s_____
h_____	s_____		
l_____			
d_____			

b Work in pairs. How many more food words can you add to each column?

Vocabulary | containers

1 a Look at the picture and match A–H with the containers in the box.

> bag A   bottle ☐   box ☐   can ☐
> carton ☐   jar ☐   packet ☐   tube ☐

b Now match the containers (1–8) with the things they can contain (a–h).

1	bag	a	juice
2	bottle	b	eggs
3	box	c	water
4	can	d	coffee
5	carton	e	toothpaste
6	jar	f	crisps
7	packet	g	rice
8	tube	h	cola

c What other things can you buy in these containers in your country?

Listening

2 Look at the extract from a TV guide. Work in pairs and discuss the questions.

1 What is the TV programme about?
2 Who introduces the programme?
3 Which food in the bins is healthy? Which food is unhealthy?

3 a ⬤ 1.44 Listen to the first part of the TV programme. Label the bins in the picture 1 or 2.

b Listen again. Write the food and drink you hear in the correct column.

Healthy food	Unhealthy food
fruit	*cola*
vegetables	*pizza*

4 Work in pairs and discuss the questions.

1 Do you agree with Laurence about the diets of the two families?
2 Are these types of food healthy or unhealthy?

> rice   chocolate   red meat
> hot dogs   oranges   salad

Bin ☐   Bin ☐

Tonight's choice: *In the rubbish bin*

Your rubbish can tell us about your life!

Tonight this popular series looks at the diet of two ordinary families. They bring their food rubbish from one week into the studio and Doctor Laurence Redburn examines it. He then discusses with the families what is good and bad about their diets. Messy, but really interesting TV! *Don't miss it.*

Channel 6, 9:00 p.m.

Grammar | *a/an*, *some* and *any*

5 Look at the extracts from the show. Complete the Active grammar box with *a/an*, *some* or *any*.

> 'We have some cans ...' 'We have a bottle ...'
> 'Do they eat any vegetables or any fruit?'
> 'They eat some pasta ...'

Active grammar

Noun	Singular countable, e.g. *bottle*	Plural countable, e.g. *cans*	Uncountable, e.g. *fruit*
➕	_____	_____	_____
➖	*a/an*	*any*	*any*
❓	*a/an*	_____	_____

see Reference page 47

6 **a** Complete the conversation between Laurence and Mrs Clark (Bin 2) with *a/an*, *some* or *any*.

L: This bin is very interesting, Mrs Clark. Do you eat (1) _____ fast food?

Mrs C: Well, we occasionally eat (2) _____ pizza.

L: Mmm, you eat a lot of vegetables ...

Mrs C: Oh, yes, we eat (3) _____ vegetables every day, and (4) _____ fruit.

L: You clearly eat fish. Do you eat (5) _____ meat?

Mrs C: Well, my husband and I don't eat (6) _____ meat, but the children sometimes eat (7) _____ burger. They like burgers a lot.

L: What about drinks. Do you drink (8) _____ coffee?

Mrs C: No, we don't like it, but we always have (9) _____ jar of coffee in the cupboard, for visitors.

L: I see. Well, thank you, Mrs Clark. Your family has (10) _____ very healthy diet!

b 🔵 1.45 Correct the underlined mistakes in this paragraph, then listen and check.

66 We eat <u>any</u> pizza once a week ... and the children eat <u>a</u> burgers. And, yes, we sometimes drink <u>any</u> coffee, and the children drink <u>some</u> can of cola once or twice a week, but we don't drink <u>some</u> tea, and we drink a lot of water – about ten litres a week. We also eat a lot of vegetables every day, and we eat <u>a</u> meat and chicken. We don't eat <u>some</u> sweets or chocolate – that's good, isn't it? 99

Pronunciation | /æ/ and /ʌ/

7 **a** 🔵 1.46 Listen to the vowel sounds in these words. Can you hear the difference?

pasta   some
/æ/   /ʌ/

b 🔵 1.47 Listen to these words. Is the vowel sound /æ/ or /ʌ/? Repeat the words.

salad   butter   lamb   apple   lunch   carrot

see Pronunciation bank page 147

Vocabulary | adjectives (2): feelings

8 **a** Match the pictures with the adjectives.

fit ☐   healthy ☐   hungry ☐   thirsty ☐   tired ☐   unhealthy ☐

b Which adjectives have a positive meaning? Which have a negative meaning?

c Use the adjectives above to complete the sentences.

1 When I watch TV late at night I feel _____ the next day.

2 Are you _____ ? Do you want a drink?

3 I'm _____ ! Let's get a burger!

4 We don't do much exercise so we aren't very _____ .

5 I don't eat a lot of chocolate because it's _____ .

Speaking

9 **a** Look at the quiz about diet. Complete the column for you.

Quiz: How healthy are you?

How much/many do you eat/drink?

✗ = I don't eat/drink any   ? = some   ✓ = a lot

	you			your partner		
	✗	?	✓	✗	?	✓
1 burgers						
2 crisps						
3 water						
4 salad						
5 biscuits						
6 coffee						
7 fruit						
8 milk						
9 fruit juice						
10 chocolate						
11 cola						
12 cheese						

b Work in pairs. Ask and answer questions and complete the column for your partner.

A: *How many burgers do you eat?*

B: *I don't eat any burgers./I eat some burgers./I eat a lot of burgers.*

c Look at page 129 and tell your partner about his/her diet.

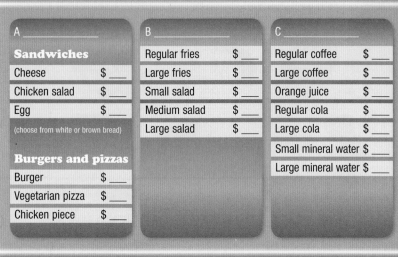

A _____	B _____	C _____
Sandwiches	Regular fries $ ___	Regular coffee $ ___
Cheese $ ___	Large fries $ ___	Large coffee $ ___
Chicken salad $ ___	Small salad $ ___	Orange juice $ ___
Egg $ ___	Medium salad $ ___	Regular cola $ ___
(choose from white or brown bread)	Large salad $ ___	Large cola $ ___
Burgers and pizzas		Small mineral water $ ___
Burger $ ___		Large mineral water $ ___
Vegetarian pizza $ ___		
Chicken piece $ ___		

Listening and speaking

1 Work in pairs and look at the photo of the diner. Discuss the questions.

1 Do you eat at fast food restaurants? Which?
2 Where is your favourite restaurant?

2 **a** 🔘 1.48 Listen to a dialogue in a restaurant. Who orders these things? Write J for Jenny and S for Sam.

cheese sandwich ☐   fries ☐   salad ☐
coffee ☐   water ☐

b Listen again and complete 1–4 in the bill below.

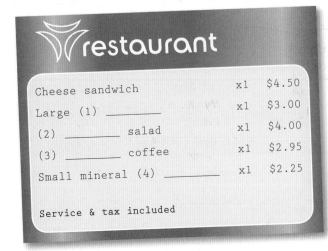

restaurant

Cheese sandwich	x1	$4.50
Large (1) _____	x1	$3.00
(2) _____ salad	x1	$4.00
(3) _____ coffee	x1	$2.95
Small mineral (4) _____	x1	$2.25

Service & tax included

3 🔘 1.49 Listen and answer the questions.

1 What does the waitress bring first?
2 How does Sam ask for the price of the meal?
   _____ _____ _____ that?
3 What is the total for the bill?
4 How does Sam pay for the meal?

4 **a** Look at the menu from the diner. Match the headings with A–C.

Drinks   Main dishes   Side orders

b Work in pairs.

Student A: turn to page 129.
Student B: ask your partner questions to complete the menu.

How much is a burger?

5 **a** Match 1–7 with a–g.

1	What	a	much is that?
2	I'd like	b	pay by credit card?
3	Jenny, what would	c	can I get you today?
4	Do you	d	a cheese sandwich, please.
5	Sam, do	e	have salads?
6	How	f	you like?
7	Can I	g	you want some juice?

b Look at audioscripts 1.48–1.49 on pages 152–153 and check your answers. Then complete the sentences in the How to... box.

How to... order food in a restaurant

Ask about the menu	(1) _____ you have salads?
Say what you want	I'd (2) _____ a cheese sandwich, please. I'll have a coffee.
Ask about prices	How (3) _____ is that?
Ask about payment	(4) _____ I pay by credit card?

c Use some of the words from exercises 5a and 5b to complete the conversation.

A: Hello, what (1) _____ I get you today?

B: (2) _____ like a vegetarian burger, please.

A: Any side orders?

B: (3) _____ you have salads?

A: No, we don't. Do you (4) _____ some fries?

B: OK. Small fries.

A: Anything to drink?

B: Yes, I'll (5) _____ an orange juice, please.

A: OK.

B: How (6) _____ is that?

A: That's €10.95.

B: (7) _____ I pay by credit card?

d Work in pairs and practise the dialogue.

Grammar | object pronouns

6 **a** Match the sentences (1–5) with the speech bubbles (A–E).

1 'A medium salad for **you**, sir.' ☐

2 'No, they're not for **us**.' ☐

3 'Two vegetarian pizzas? I really like **them**.' ☐

4 'No, the salad's for **her**.' ☐

5 'A large cup of coffee for **him** and a small glass of mineral water for **me**.' ☐

b Read the speech bubbles again and complete the Active grammar box.

Active grammar

Subject pronouns	Object pronouns
I	*me*
he	_____
she	_____
it	*it*
we	_____
you	_____
they	_____

see Reference page 47

7 **a** Choose the correct words in *italics*.

1 The coffee is for *I/me* and the water is for *she/her*.

2 'Is that our waitress?' 'No, it isn't *her/them*.'

3 Do I like cheeseburgers? Yes, I love *it/them*!

4 My brother doesn't eat meat. The salad's for *her/him*.

5 Excuse me. Can you bring *us/we* a menu?

b Complete the sentences with object pronouns.

1 'Is this for you?' 'No, it isn't for _____ , it's for my friend.'

2 I don't eat many vegetables; I don't like _____ .

3 We live in a big house. My grandmother lives with _____ .

4 My mobile phone is great. I use _____ every day.

5 'Is this sandwich for _____ ?' 'Yes, it's for me.'

Speaking

8 Work in groups of three. Use the menu in exercise 4a.

Student A: you are a waiter/waitress. Take the customers' order.

Students B and C: you are customers at the restaurant. Look at the menu, choose the things you want and order a meal.

1 a 🔵 1.50 Listen. What does the woman ask for? Tick (✓) the blue boxes.

apples	☐☐	fish	☐☐
bananas	☐☐	melon	☐☐
beef	☐☐	milk	☐☐
carrots	☐☐	potatoes	☐☐
cheese	☐☐	tomatoes	☐☐
chicken	☐☐	water	☐☐

b Listen again. What things can she buy? Tick (✓) the red boxes.

c Listen again. How much of these things does the woman buy?

apples _____ beef _____
fish _____ cheese _____
milk _____

How much does she pay for all her shopping?

2 Do we usually use *kilos*, *grammes* or *litres* when we buy these things?

carrots coffee cola fruit juice
lamb mineral water potatoes
sugar

3 Listen to the conversations again and complete the How to... box.

How to... go shopping at a market

Offer help	*Can I (1) _____ you?*
Ask for things	*I'd (2) _____ three bananas ...* *I (3) _____ some fruit.*
Give things	*(4) _____ you are.*
Ask the price	*(5) _____ is that?*
Give the price	*(6) _____ 18 euros.*

4 a Work in groups of three.

Student A: You are a shopper. Choose six things from this unit and write your shopping list. You have 40 euros for all your shopping. Ask the shop assistants and try to buy all the things on your list. How much do you pay?

Student B: You are a shop assistant. You sell fruit, vegetables and drinks. Choose six things from this unit for your shop. Write them down and write a price next to each one, e.g. coffee – 3 euros for 250g coffee.

Student C: You are a shop assistant. You sell meat, fish, cheese, milk and butter. Choose six things from this unit for your shop. Write them down and write a price next to each one, e.g. milk – 1 euro for a litre.

b Do your roleplay. Look at the audioscript on page 153 if necessary.

c Change roles and do the roleplay again.

Countable and uncountable nouns: *much/many/a lot of*

Countable nouns	Uncountable nouns
Things that we can count. *1 banana, 2 bananas*	Things we can't count. *rice, salt*
They have singular and plural forms. *apple, apples*	They do not have plural forms. *~~rices~~*
We can use numbers in front of them. *25 bananas*	We cannot use numbers in front of them.* *~~2 rices~~*
We use *many* in questions and negatives. *I don't eat **many** apples.*	We use *much* in questions and negatives. *I don't drink **much** milk.*
We use *how many* to ask questions. ***How many** bananas do you buy every week?*	We use *how much* to ask questions. ***How much** water do you drink every day?*
We can use *a lot of* with countable and uncountable nouns. *Do you eat **a lot of** burgers/cheese?*	

* Show the quantity (*how much/many*) of countable and uncountable nouns by using another noun (e.g. *a bag*) or a measurement (e.g. *kilos*) + *of* in front of the noun. ***A bag of** bananas.* ***A glass of** water.* ***A litre of** water.*

a/an, *some* and *any*

Singular countable nouns

We use *a/an* before singular countable nouns when there is only one of the noun.

⊕	We have a car.
⊖	We don't have a car.
?	Do you have a car?

Plural countable nouns

We use *some* and *any* to talk about a number of something, when we don't know how many, or the number isn't important.

We usually use *some* in positive statements, and *any* in negative statements and questions.

We use *some* and *any* with plural countable nouns.

⊕	We have **some** magazines.
⊖	We don't have **any** magazines.
?	Do you have **any** magazines?

Uncountable nouns

We also use *some* and *any* with uncountable nouns.

⊕	We have **some** cheese.
⊖	We don't have **any** cheese.
?	Do you have **any** cheese?

Object pronouns

We use subject pronouns (see page 17) before verbs, and object pronouns after verbs.

Subject pronouns	*I he she it we you they*
Object pronouns	*me him her it us you them*

He loves her.   He loves them.   She loves him.   They love me!

Key vocabulary

Food

Dishes: burger fries hot dog pizza salad sandwich

Meat and fish: beef chicken duck ham lamb lobster pork scallops seafood

Fruit and vegetables: apple banana beans carrot dried fruit pineapple potato strawberry tomato (water)melon

Drinks: coffee cola fruit/orange juice milk tea water

Other: biscuits bread butter cheese chocolate crisps eggs nuts pasta rice spices sugar

Containers: bag bin bottle box can carton jar packet tube

Money: cash machine coin credit card note receipt

Adjectives for physical and emotional states: fit healthy/unhealthy hungry thirsty tired

 Listen to these words.

ACTIVE BOOK

 see Writing bank page 138

4 Review and practice

1 Match the sentence halves.

1	I usually buy a	a	tomatoes for this recipe.
2	We often get ten	b	of chocolates to his girlfriend every Saturday.
3	She puts 100 grammes	c	of milk every day.
4	I drink a carton	d	pizza on Friday evening.
5	We need a can of	e	bags of crisps at the supermarket.
6	He takes a box	f	of cheese in the cheeseburger.

2 Choose the correct words in *italics*.

How *much* / *many* oranges do you eat?

1 How *much* / *many* students come to your lesson?
2 She drinks three litres of *waters* / *water* every day.
3 Let's have *two* / *two kilos* of those nice brown eggs for breakfast.
4 How *much* / *many* money do you have in your pocket?
5 How *many* / *much* sugar do you eat every week?

3 Amanda phones her husband, but he doesn't answer. Complete her message with *a*, *some* or *any*.

'Hello John. Please listen to this message. Can you go to the shops and get some things for dinner? We need (1) _____ fish, and (2) _____ box of eggs. I think we have (3) _____ potatoes, but we don't have (4) _____ coffee. Do we have (5) _____ carrots? Can you check? Please buy (6) _____ cheese, and I'd like (7) _____ carton of orange juice. That's it. Oh ... we don't have (8) _____ butter – can you get some? Thanks. See you later.'

4 Replace the underlined words with pronouns and rewrite the sentences.

Mr Bosgrove takes my friend and me to work in his car.

He takes us to work in his car.

1 My mother and I go shopping with Julia and Carla every Saturday.
2 My sister gets up before my brother and me.
3 David and Serena don't take the children on holiday.
4 My uncle uses the computer every day.
5 My friend and I have lunch with Maria every Tuesday.

5 Complete the dialogue with the correct pronouns.

A: Hello, Mrs Lovett. How are you?
B: Oh, hello Sonia. (1) _____'m fine, thanks.
A: How's your husband?
B: (2) _____'s fine. He works in the supermarket now.
A: Yes, I know. I see (3) _____ when I do my shopping. And how are the twins, Jake and Jerry?
B: Oh, (4) _____'re very well.
A: Do they go to school on the bus?
B: No. I take (5) _____ with (6) _____ in the car every morning.
A: Who is their teacher?
B: It's Mrs Moore. Do you know (7) _____ ?
A: Yes, I do. (8) _____ lives in our street. She always says 'Hello' to (9) _____ .

6 Put the letters in the correct order to write the food words.

hcsdwina		*sandwich*	
1	crie	r	_____
2	errbug	b	_____
3	eabrd	b	_____
4	onermwalte	w	_____
5	otmotsea	t	_____
6	ckechin	c	_____
7	ilmk	m	_____
8	apzzi	p	_____

7 Which container do we usually use for these things?

coffee		*jar*
1	water	_____
2	butter	_____
3	rubbish	_____
4	biscuits	_____
5	cola	_____

8 Use adjectives to complete the sentences.

1 I want to be *healthy* so I eat a lot of salad and fruit.
2 I'm _____ . I want to go to bed now.
3 Are you _____ ? Do you want a glass of water?
4 Don't smoke. It's _____ .
5 Carol goes to the gym every day. She's very _____ .
6 I'm _____ . Do you have any biscuits?

A

B

C

Lead-in

1 **a** Match the types of house in the photos with 1–4 below.

1 detached house 2 terraced houses 3 apartments 4 villa

b Now match the types of houses with these descriptions.

a a home in a building with lots of others ☐
b a big house with a garden, often near the sea ☐
c a house with no others joined to it ☐
d a house with another house on each side ☐

2 Where can you do these activities? Match the rooms with the activities.

> ~~cook~~   eat   have a shower   keep things you don't use   sleep
> watch TV   work

> attic   bathroom   bedroom   dining room   ~~kitchen~~   living room
> shower room   study

Cook – You can cook in the kitchen.

3 Look at the compass and answer the questions.

1 What is in the north of your country? (the centre/the south/the west/the east)
2 Which part of your country do you live in? Where is your capital city?

4 **a** What's important to you about your home?

1 type of house   2 number/type of rooms   3 location (where it is)

b Where would you like to live? Why?

49

Grammar *there is/there are*

Can do talk about your home

Reading

1 What kind of home do you live in? Do you like your home? Why/Why not?

2 **a** Look at the text quickly. What is unusual about each home?

b Read the text and match the features with the house.

1 It is ...
a by lake. ☐
b not hot during the day. ☐
c near a town. ☐

2 It has ...
a a room at the top of the house. ☐
b a room below the house. ☐
c a room to work in. ☐

c Do you like these houses? Which one do you prefer?

Vocabulary | homes

3 **a** Write words from the text in the correct column.

Type of building	Rooms	Other features	Adjectives describing house
detached house	bathroom	garden	beautiful

b Find out about your partner's home.

Do you live in a house or an apartment? Is it detached? Does it have a garden? Is it near the town? etc.

4 Look at the Lifelong learning box. Read the tip and complete the exercise.

Personalise it!

When you want to learn new words, it is useful to write them in a personal sentence, e.g.

shower room – *We have a bathroom and a shower room in our house.*

Write sentences about your home, using each of these words.

1 central heating
2 solar panels
3 cellar
4 double glazing
5 patio

Unusual homes for sale

1 Luxurious three-bedroomed home

This beautiful old windmill in the south of England is next to open parkland but near a busy town. It has three bedrooms, a bathroom and shower room, large kitchen/dining room and a living room. There is also a cellar under the kitchen, and a garden and patio outside.

2 Unusual detached house

Near a pretty village in the Italian countryside, between the towns of Locorotondo and Martina Franca, this house with an unusual roof is very private. The small windows mean that the house feels cool all day, but you can also relax in the light, sunny garden behind the house. Inside, there are five bedrooms, two bathrooms and a study. There's also central heating and double glazing in part of the house.

3 Eco-villa by a lake

This lovely eco-friendly home is on an island in Georgian Bay, Canada. In front of the villa lies the bay, which is part of Lake Huron. The villa has one bedroom in the attic, a bathroom, a kitchen, a dining room and a living room with a small library. On one side of the roof there are solar panels, which provide all the hot water. There isn't a garage.

Grammar | *there is/there are*

5 Look at the text and complete the Active grammar box with *'s, is, isn't, are* or *aren't*.

Active grammar

	Singular	Plural
➕	There's a garden. (There is)	There _____ five bedrooms.
➖	There _____ a garage.	There aren't any solar panels.
❓	_____ there a cellar?	_____ there any windows?
	Where is there a library?	How many rooms _____ there?
	Yes, there is. No, there _____ .	Yes, there _____ . No, there aren't.

see Reference page 57

6 Complete the questions with *is there* or *are there*. Answer the questions about the houses on page 50.

Are there two bedrooms in the windmill?

No, there are three bedrooms in the windmill.

1 How many bedrooms _____ in the eco-villa?
2 _____ central heating in the detached house?
3 _____ a cellar in the eco-villa?
4 How many bathrooms _____ in the detached house?
5 _____ solar panels on the windmill?

Vocabulary | prepositions of place

7 Find the prepositions below in the text and write them under the pictures.

> behind   between   in   in front of   near
> next to   on   under

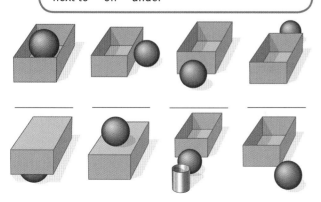

_____   _____   _____   _____

_____   _____   _____   _____

8 **a** Think about your dream home. Make notes about it.

modern apartment, three bedrooms, patio ...

b Now tell your partner about your dream home.

There are three bedrooms in my dream home ...

Listening

9 **a** Jon Nott wants to buy the house in Italy. Can you answer some of his questions? Make notes.

a ☐ Is there air conditioning?
b ☐ Are there many shops in the village?
c ☑ 1 How many bedrooms does it have?
d ☐ Is there a garden?
e ☐ Is the house near a village?
f ☐ Is there only one bathroom?
g ☐ How much is the house?
h ☐ Are there any schools in the area?

b 🔊 1.51 Listen. Number Jon's questions in the correct order in the boxes.

c Listen again and answer all the questions.

Speaking

10 Work in pairs.

Student A: look at the information on page 129.
Student B: You want to buy a holiday villa in Spain. Student A has the details. Ask questions to find out these things about the villa:

1 how big?   4 garden/terrace?
2 how many rooms?   5 where (near shops, etc.)?
3 other features?   6 price?

Do you want to buy the villa?

Now answer Student A's questions about the apartment below.

For Sale

Stunning apartment in Manhattan

100 square meters

two bedrooms, two bathrooms

living room, kitchen

dining room
(can be another bedroom/study)

central heating

two large terraces, front and back

Central Manhattan – very near shops, restaurants, theaters

$950,000

5.2 To have and have not

Vocabulary | furniture and equipment

1 **a** In pairs, look at the two rooms. Which room do you prefer? Why?

b Match these objects with the pictures.

bed ☐   chair ☐   coffee table ☐
cooker ☐   cupboard ☐
dining table ☐   dishwasher ☐
fridge ☐   lamp ☐
microwave ☐   plant ☐
sofa ☐   TV [1]
washing machine ☐

c What else can you see in the pictures? Write two or three more things in the table.

Room A	Room B

2 Use words from exercise 1 to complete the word maps.

fridge —  **equipment**

_____   _____

dining table — **furniture**

_____   _____

mobile phone —  **personal possessions**

_____

Listening and speaking

3 **a** 🌐 1.52 Pete Morgan wants to get home insurance. Listen to his conversation with an insurance agent. Which picture on page 52 shows Pete's apartment?

b Listen again. Tick (✓) the things Pete has got and cross (✗) the things he hasn't got.

chairs ☐   coffee table ☐   cooker ☐
dining table ☐   fridge ☐   garden ☐   house ☐
laptop computer ☐   microwave ☐
mobile phone ☐   music system ☐   sink ☐
sofa ☐   studio apartment ☐   terrace ☐   TV ☐

4 **a** You also need insurance. Think of five important or valuable possessions. Make a list.

b Compare your list with other students.

My five things are my wedding ring because it's made of gold; my family photos – they're valuable because …

Grammar | *have got*

5 **a** 🌐 1.53 Listen to part of the conversation again and complete the gaps.

Agent: Have you *got* your own house?
Pete: No, I _____ . I _____ got a modern studio apartment in the centre of town, but it's rented.
Agent: _____ it got a garden?
Pete: No, it _____ got a garden, but it _____ got a small terrace.

b Complete the Active grammar box.

Active grammar

➕	I/We/You/They	_____	got
	He/She/It	's	
➖	_____	haven't	got
	He/She/It	_____	
❓	_____	I/we/you/they	got … ?
	_____	he/she/it	
	Yes, No,	I/we/you/they	have. _____ .
	Yes, No,	he/she/it	has. hasn't.

see Reference page 57

6 **a** Correct the sentences about Pete which are not true.

He's got three children. ✗ *He hasn't got any children.*
1 He's got a house.
2 He's got an apartment in the centre of town.
3 He's got a kitchen.
4 He's got a laptop computer.
5 He hasn't got any chairs.
6 He's got a garden.

b Make questions from the prompts. Then write true short answers.

you/a sister?

Have you got a sister? No, I haven't.
1 you/apartment?
2 your home/garden?
3 your home/attic?
4 you/a dishwasher?
5 you/a big sofa?
6 your home/a garage?
7 you/a pet?
8 you/a bicycle?

Pronunciation | /æ/ and /ɒ/

7 **a** 🌐 1.54 Listen to the underlined sounds. Which sound is different?

He's g<u>o</u>t a lapt<u>o</u>p, a c<u>a</u>t and a w<u>a</u>tch.

b 🌐 1.55 Listen. Underline the word you hear.
1 hot   hat
2 on   an
3 top   tap
4 pocket   packet

see Pronunciation bank page 147

Speaking and writing

8 Work in pairs. Ask and answer the questions in exercise 6b with your partner. Think of other questions about your home and possessions. Find things that …
1 your partner has got but you haven't got.
2 you've got but your partner hasn't got.
A: *Have you got a sister?*
B: *No, I haven't, but I've got two brothers.*

9 Write a paragraph about your partner's home, possessions and family.

Mariela lives in a house with a garden. She's got two sisters. She's got a sofa and a coffee table in the living room, but she hasn't got a dishwasher.

5.3 World class

Grammar modifiers (*very, quite, really*)

Can do describe where you live

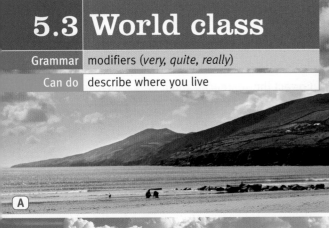

Listening and reading

1   **a**   Match the places with the photos. There are two extra words.

mountains ☐   desert ☐   forest ☐   hills ☐
city ☐   lake ☐   river ☐

b   Which countries are in the photos?

2   **a**   Read about two countries. What is the same and what is different between them?

Argentina has got mountains but Ireland ...

Do you want to travel before university?

Here's some information to help you decide where to go ...

Valentina from Buenos Aires writes ...
Argentina is not only a hot country; there are some very cold parts, too. Because the south is near Antarctica it's often very cold, especially in the mountains. There are very high mountains in all of Argentina – the Andes. In the south they meet the sea, and are really lovely. *More ...*

Jane from County Kerry tells us ...
Ireland is a beautiful country – very green and fresh. Unfortunately, this is because it's also a very wet country – it gets a lot of rain. Ireland has a lot of pretty, low hills; they're certainly not mountains! In some places in the west the hills come right down to the beach, so it's possible to sunbathe and look at the hills at the same time. *More ...*

Click to listen to information about other countries:

Spain   Poland   Greece   Japan

b   🔊 1.56   Listen to four people talking about their countries. Match five of the countries from this exercise and exercise 2a with the photos. Then check your answers to exercise 1b.

3   **a**   Read and listen again. Make notes about the places in the table.

	Place	Landscape	Which part?
1	Argentina	_____	south
2	Ireland		_____
3	_____	desert	_____
4	_____	beautiful lakes	_____
5	Kefalonia	_____	_____
6	_____	_____	west

b   Make sentences with *There's* or *There are*.

There's a famous desert in the south of Spain.

Vocabulary | adjectives (3): places

4   **a**   Which adjectives can we use with *desert*? Add two adjectives from the box to the word map.

hot ——— desert
_____   _____

beautiful   busy   cold   dry
famous   green   high   ~~hot~~
huge   long   low   noisy
popular   wide

b   Make word maps for *mountain, island, forest, beach, hill, river* and *city*.

Pronunciation | main stress

5 🔊 1.57 Listen to the words and answer the questions.

river   desert

1   How many syllables do the words have?
2   Underline the syllable with the main stress.

6 **a** Look at the Lifelong learning box. Read the tip and complete the exercise.

Use your dictionary...

❗ Use your dictionary to find how many syllables there are in a word.

two: moun–tain   three: beaut–i–ful

Use your dictionary to find out where the main stress is.

<u>moun</u>tain   /ˈmaʊntɪn/
<u>beau</u>tiful   /ˈbjuːtɪfəl/

Use your dictionary to mark the syllables and underline the main stress on these words.

<u>riv</u>–er   <u>des</u>–ert   detached   famous
luxurious   noisy   popular

Lifelong learning

---

b 🔊 1.58 Listen and check your answers.

see Pronunciation bank page 148

Grammar | modifiers

7 **a** 🔊 1.59 Listen and complete the sentences with *quite*, *really*, *very* or *not very*.

1   It's _____ hot and dry.
2   It's _____ popular now with people from other countries, too.
3   Kefalonia is a _____ green island.
4   It's _____ busy and noisy, and it's _____ friendly.

b Write the correct modifiers next to the thermometer in the Active grammar box.

Active grammar

_____ hot, _____ hot
hot
_____ hot
_____ hot

40° 30° 20° 10°

---

see Reference page 57

8 Make sentences.

Russia/big   *Russia is very big.*

1   Britain/big   4   Mexico City/busy
2   Mount Everest/high   5   Canada/cold
3   The Amazon/long   6   Spain/cold

9 In pairs, make sentences about your country and other countries. Use *quite*, (*not*) *very* or *really* in each sentence.

A: *In Russia there are some very big lakes.*
B: *Yes, and I think there are some really big lakes in Canada, too. We have some hills in Belgium, but they're not very high.*

Listening and speaking

10 **a** 🔊 1.60 Listen to Megan talking about her country. Where does she come from? Does she like it?

b Which things does she talk about?

1   where she comes from ☐
2   what her village is near ☐
3   where her parents live ☐
4   where her brothers and sisters live ☐
5   the landscapes in different parts of Wales ☐
6   jobs in Wales ☐
7   what she likes about her country ☐
8   what she doesn't like about her country ☐

11 **a** Prepare to talk about your country. Make notes about the answers to the questions. Use the How to... box and audioscript 1.60 on page 153 to help you.

1   Where do you live now?
2   Do you come from a town or village? Where is it near?
3   What kind of landscape is there in your country? Where is it?
4   What do you like/not like about your country?

How to... talk about where you come from/live

Say where you come from/live	*I'm from ... . I live in ...*
Say what kind of place it is and where it's near	*It's a ... place, and it's near ...*
Describe the landscape	*There is/are ... in the south/north of ...*
Give your opinion	*I like/don't like ... because ...*

---

b Tell your partner about your country.

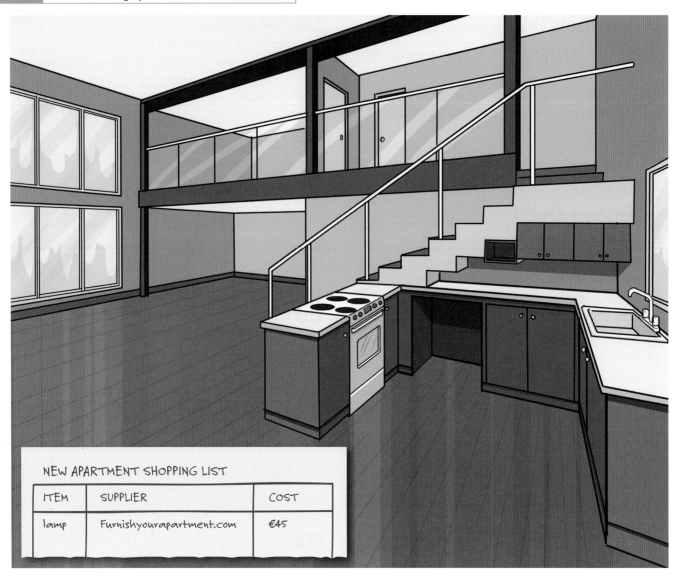

NEW APARTMENT SHOPPING LIST

ITEM	SUPPLIER	COST
lamp	Furnishyourapartment.com	€45

1 Look at the picture. What has the apartment got? What hasn't it got?

2 **a** What furniture and equipment does the apartment need? Choose ten things. Use a dictionary if necessary.

bed ☐   bookshelves ☐   CD player ☐   chair ☐
coffee machine ☐   computer ☐   cupboard ☐
desk ☐   dining table and chairs ☐   dishwasher ☐
DVD recorder ☐   lamp ☐   microwave ☐
MP3 player ☐   sofa ☐   TV ☐
vacuum cleaner ☐   washing machine ☐

b Compare your list with another student. Agree on ten important things and put the things in order, 1–10 (1 = very useful, 10 = not very useful).

3 **a** Work with other students and buy things for the apartment. You each have information from a different place, but you've only got €1,000!

Are there any sofas in your list?

How much do they cost?

What have we got? What do we need now?

Student A: you have information from the Internet. Turn to page 129.

Student B: you have a catalogue. Turn to page 133.

Student C: you have this information from a local shop.

Davis Electrical

★ TODAY'S BARGAINS! ★

Home cinema (DVD recorder and flat screen TV)
ONLY €600
Combination DVD player and TV €225
MP3 player €200
Washing machine €330
CD player €195
Italian coffee machine €150
Laptop computer €450
Vacuum cleaner €125
Dishwasher €250

b When you finish, compare your list with other groups.

there is/there are

	Singular	Plural
+	There's ... (There is)	There are ...
−	There isn't ... (There is not)	There aren't ... (There are not)
?	Is there ... ? Where is there ... ?	Are there ... ? How many ... are there?
	Yes, there is. No, there isn't.	Yes, there are. No, there aren't.

We use *there is* (+ a singular noun) and *there are* (+ a plural noun) to talk about people or things for the first time. We often use them to describe places.

Use *there's, there isn't* and *there aren't* when you speak.
***There's** a huge forest in the west.*

Use *There's*, not *There are*, to introduce a list of singular objects.
***There's** a swimming pool, a lake and a restaurant at the holiday village.*

have got

	I/We/You/They	He/She/It
+	've got (have got)	's got (has got)
−	haven't got (have not got)	hasn't got (has not got)
?	Have ... got?	Has ... got?
	Yes, we have. No, I haven't.	Yes, it has. No, she hasn't.

We usually use the contracted forms: *'s got, 've got, hasn't got, haven't got*.

There are no contracted forms for questions.
***Have you got** a DVD player?*

We often use short answers when we answer *have got* questions.
A: *Have you got a television?*
B: *Yes, I have./No, I haven't.*

We use *have got* to talk about our possessions and family/friends. Don't use *have got* in very formal English.
*I**'ve got** two sisters.*
*They**'ve got** a sports car.*

Modifiers

The words *(not) very, quite* and *really* are modifiers. We put them in front of an adjective to make it stronger or weaker.

We use *very* and *really* to make the adjective stronger.
*This car is **very**/**really** expensive!*

We use *quite* or *not very* to make the adjective weaker.
*This car is **quite** expensive.*
*This car **isn't very** expensive.*

Key vocabulary

Adjectives and places
a hot, dry desert
a busy, noisy city
a long, wide river
a beautiful lake
a high mountain
a low hill
a lovely beach
a green forest
a popular island

Landscapes
bay   beach   city   desert   forest   hill   island
lake   mountain   river   sea

Types of home
apartment   detached house   studio
terraced house   villa   windmill

Rooms and parts of a house
attic   bathroom   bedroom   cellar
dining room   garage   garden   kitchen
library   living room   roof   shower room
study   window

Features of a house
air conditioning   central heating
double glazing   patio   solar panels   terrace

Furniture
bed   bookshelves   chair   coffee table
cupboard   desk   dining chairs/table   sofa
table

Equipment and possessions
CD player   coffee machine   cooker
dishwasher   DVD recorder   fridge   lamp
laptop computer   microwave   mobile phone
MP3 player   music system   plant   sink   TV
vacuum cleaner   washing machine

 Listen to these words.
ACTIVE BOOK

 see Writing bank page 139

1 Look at the floor plan and complete the dialogue with the correct form of *there is/isn't* or *there are/aren't*.

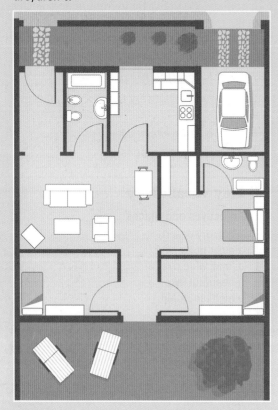

A: Good morning. Can you give me some information about the house on Chandos Road?

B: Yes, of course. It's a very nice, big apartment. (1) *There are* three bedrooms, ...

A: (2) _____ a bathroom with each bedroom?

B: No, (3) _____ . The main bedroom has got a bathroom, and then (4) _____ one other bathroom in the apartment.

A: OK. Is the kitchen big?

B: Yes, it is, and it's got a lot of equipment.

A: What about the dining room?

B: Ah, well, (5) _____ a dining room. But (6) _____ a large living room with a dining area.

A: I know there's a garden, but (7) _____ any terraces?

B: No, (8) _____ , I'm afraid.

A: And finally, (9) _____ a garage?

B: Yes, (10) _____ a garage at the front of the house.

2 Write negative sentences.

We've got an apartment in London.

We haven't got an apartment in London.

1 I've got a video camera.
2 She's got a mobile phone.
3 They've got a lot of money.
4 Their car's got a CD player.
5 England's got a lot of mountains.

3 Write questions and short answers.

Simon/sports car? No, _____ .

Has Simon got a sports car? No, he hasn't.

1 Rachel/laptop computer? Yes, _____ .
2 they/big house? No, _____ .
3 your apartment/garden? No, _____ .
4 Kelly/washing machine? Yes, _____ .
5 Spain/desert? Yes, _____ .

4 Complete the sentences with modifiers. You choose the modifier.

English is *quite* easy to learn.

1 My town/city is _____ beautiful.
2 People in my country are _____ friendly.
3 My country is _____ popular with tourists.
4 My diet is _____ healthy.
5 My home is _____ noisy.

5 Write the things from the box in the rooms where you usually find them. Some things can go in two or three rooms.

> bed   bookshelves   CD player   chairs
> coffee table   cooker   cupboard   dishwasher
> fridge   music system   sofa   table   TV
> washing machine

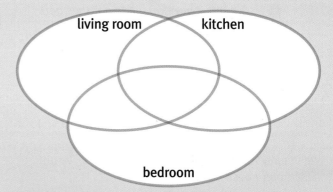

6 Match the words in the box with the places on the map (A–J).

> a bay   a beach   a city   a desert   a forest
> an island   a lake   mountains   a river   the sea

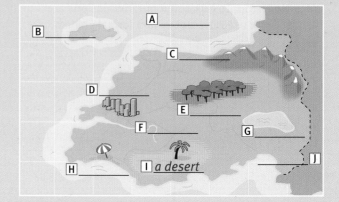

Lead-in

1 **a** Look at the photos. Which places in the box can you see?

> art gallery   bank   bar   bus station   café   cinema
> factory   hospital   library   museum   post office
> restaurant   school   (train) station

b Check the meanings of the other words with a partner.

c 🔊 1.61 Listen to the words from exercise 1a. How many syllables does each place have? Practise saying the words.

art–gal–le–ry = 4   bank = 1

2 What do you do in the places in exercise 1? Ask and answer questions.

A: *What do you do in an art gallery?*

B: *You look at paintings.*

3 **a** Where can you buy these things (1–6)? Match them with the shops (a–f).

1	some aspirin	a	a newsagent's
2	a dictionary	b	a supermarket
3	pens and paper	c	a department store
4	food and drink	d	a stationer's
5	clothes, bags, ...	e	a bookshop
6	a magazine	f	a chemist's

b What else can you buy in these shops?

Grammar	Past Simple of *to be*: all forms; Past Simple of regular verbs: positive
Can do	talk about the past

Reading

1 **a** What are the places in the photos? Read the text and check your answers.

b Match the places with *now* and *in the past*.

		now	in the past
1	Oxford Castle	an office	a sailing ship
2	The Musée d'Orsay	a restaurant	a station
3	The Smolny Institute	an art gallery	a prison
4	The *Moshulu*	a hotel	a school

c Do you know any of these places, or places like them?

Changing Buildings

You live in an apartment now, but was it an apartment fifty years ago? Buildings often change during their life. Maybe it wasn't an apartment, but a school or a station ...

Oxford Castle is an old building in the centre of Oxford, England. In the twentieth century it was a prison, but now it is a shopping centre and a luxurious hotel! You can sleep in the old prison cells.

The Musée d'Orsay in Paris was a station in the early twentieth century. It was the main station for trains from Paris to the south-west of France. It is now a really beautiful art gallery.

In the twentieth century the *Moshulu* was a sailing ship, for carrying food and other things all around the world. But now it is a luxury restaurant in Philadelphia, in the US.

Grammar | Past Simple of *to be*

2 Read the text again. Choose the correct words in the rules in the Active grammar box, then complete the table.

Active grammar

We use *is* and *are* to talk about <u>now/the past</u>.
We use *was* and *were* to talk about <u>now/the past</u>.

	I/He/She/It	We/You/They
+	was	_____
−	_____	weren't
?	_____ I/he/she/it?	Were we/you/they?
	Yes, I/he/she/it was.	Yes, we/you/they _____ .
	No, I/he/she/it _____ .	No, we/you/they weren't.

see Reference page 67

3 These sentences about the places in exercise 1 are all false. Make them true.

The Smolny Institute is a school.

No it isn't. It was a school but now it's offices.

1 The Musée d'Orsay was a bus station.
2 Oxford Castle was a shopping centre.
3 The *Moshulu* was a sailing ship in the nineteenth century.
4 The Musée d'Orsay is a prison.

The Smolny Institute in St Petersburg is now the office of the Governor of the city. It was a school for rich girls in the nineteenth century, and the offices were classrooms. Then it was Lenin's home for a few months in 1917.

Listening

4 a 🔊 1.62 Listen to Jason and Angeles. They talk about the two buildings above. Match the speaker with the building.

Jason: ___   Angeles: ___

b Which building does each sentence describe, the Hoover Building or the Reina Sofia?

1 It was a hospital.
2 It was a factory.
3 It changed to a supermarket about thirty years ago.
4 A family member worked there.

5 Complete the sentences with words from the box, then listen again to check.

> equipment   factory   modern art   Reina Sofia

1 They planned the Hoover Building as a _____ . Jason's grandfather worked there. He produced electrical _____ .
2 The _____ is Angeles' favourite gallery – she studied _____ .

Grammar | Past Simple of regular verbs: positive

6 Find the Past Simple of these verbs in exercise 5, then match them with the rules in the Active grammar box.

> produce   ~~worked~~   study   plan

Active grammar

1 add -ed to most regular verbs, e.g. *worked*
2 add -d to verbs that end in -e, e.g. _____
3 remove -y and add -ied to verbs that end in -y, e.g. _____
4 when a verb ends in vowel + one consonant, we usually double the consonant, e.g. _____

7 a Look at audioscript 1.62 on page 154. <u>Underline</u> the Past Simple verbs and write them in the table.

+ -ed	+ -d	remove -y, + -ied	double consonant

see Reference page 67

b Make sentences in the Past Simple from the prompts.

Doctors/work/in the Reina Sofia hospital
Doctors worked in the Reina Sofia hospital.

1 The Hoover Factory/produce/vacuum cleaners
2 Alicia/study/at the Sorbonne
3 My brother/start/a new job yesterday
4 My mother/marry/my father in 1977
5 The prison/change/to apartments in 2002
6 My father/stop/work at the age of sixty

Pronunciation | Past Simple endings

8 a 🔊 1.63 Listen to the Past Simple endings of the verbs. Do they sound the same?

worked   opened   started

b 🔊 1.64 Listen and write the verbs in the correct column. Then repeat them.

> changed   lived   looked   planned
> produced   studied   visited

/t/ worked	/d/ opened	/ɪd/ started

see Pronunciation bank page 148

c Read a sentence from exercise 7b. Your partner listens and checks your pronunciation.

Speaking

9 In pairs, talk about another two buildings that are different now from in the past.

Student A: look at the information on page 130.
Student B: look at the information on page 133.

10 Are buildings in your city different now? Tell your partner about changes from the past to now.

Home | Hotels | Flights | Restaurants | Holiday Rentals | Holiday Ideas | Write a Review

City breaks | Search

City break reviews – *give your opinion!*

Dublin

(*from Manolo Sanchez, Spain*)

★ ★ ★ ★ **Great trip, bad weather**

Fantastic city! Perfect for a city break. We left Dublin yesterday after a three-night break – we flew there on Friday morning. The airport is 12km outside the city centre so we arrived at lunchtime. It's really lively, noisy, full of tourists, but exciting. We spent hours in the old streets and in Phoenix Park. It rained all day Sunday so we went to the National Gallery.

Dubai

(*from Susanna Lloyd, UK*)

★ ★ ★ **Good shops, not a lot of culture**

My husband took me to Dubai for my birthday last year. I loved it – it has great markets and shops – shoe shops and jewellers; we bought our wedding rings there! The hotel was modern and luxurious. We spent a lot of money but it was a good break.

New York

(*from Christiane Gautier, France*)

★ ★ **Noisy, expensive**

I went to New York with some friends last month. There's a lot to see and do but we met some very unfriendly people. We visited the Museum of Modern Art – that's great, and we saw a lot of expensive clothes shops and department stores. We ate in some famous restaurants but the food was awful!

Havana

(*from Alvin Parmiter, USA*)

★ ★ ★ ★ ★ **Wonderful break!**

Havana is amazing – so different from our cities. We had a short break there a few weeks ago. We walked around all weekend; the buildings are beautiful. The restaurants and shops aren't great – but we bought some interesting cigars in a newsagent's! I really want to go back there for a week!

Reading

1 **a** Look at the text. What type of website is it from?

b Read the text quickly. Which people have these opinions?

1 I like the shopping there, especially the jewellery.

2 The people aren't friendly and the food isn't good.

3 I'm interested in looking at buildings.

4 I love busy, noisy cities, but I don't like rain!

2 Read the text again and answer these questions.

1 Why was Manolo in a gallery all day Sunday?

2 Susanna bought something special in Dubai – what?

3 Did Christiane like the food in New York? Why/Why not?

4 Does Alvin like Havana? How do you know?

3 **a** Find expressions in the text with the word *break*. Match them with these meanings.

1 small holiday (two expressions)

2 great holiday (two expressions)

3 town holiday

b Look at the expressions with *break*. What do you think they mean?

1 coffee break

2 winter break

3 lunch break

4 weekend break

5 take a break

4 You and your partner want a city break. Which city from the text do you want to go to? Why?

Vocabulary | places in a city, shops

5 **a** Write the words from the box in the table.

> airport   building   clothes shop
> department store   gallery   hotel   jeweller's
> market   museum   newsagent's   park
> shoe shop

Shopping	Places in/near a city

b Add more words to the table.

6 Match places from exercise 5 with the descriptions.

1 you can buy a lot of different things here, but not food
2 you can stay in a room here
3 you can walk here and relax in good weather
4 you can buy magazines, sweets and cigars here
5 you can see famous paintings here
6 you can buy food and other things here; it's often outside

Grammar | Past Simple: irregular verbs

7 **a** Look at the verbs in the Active grammar box. Find the past forms of the verbs in the text and write them in the table.

> ### Active grammar
>
> | Infinitive | Past form |
> |---|---|
> | leave | left |
> | fly | flew |
> | spend | _____ |
> | go | _____ |
> | take | _____ |
> | buy | _____ |
> | meet | _____ |
> | see | _____ |
> | eat | _____ |
> | have | _____ |

b Complete the text with past forms of the verbs in the Active grammar box.

Last weekend I (1) _went_ to Lucerne, in Switzerland for a short break. It was fantastic! We (2) _____ there from Heathrow Airport on Friday morning. The town is really pretty. On Sunday we (3) _____ a bus trip around the lovely lake and we (4) _____ some very interesting sights. We (5) _____ some really friendly people and we (6) _____ some delicious food, but we (7) _____ a lot of money because it's a very expensive town. We (8) _____ on Sunday, but I really want to go back there one day!

see Reference page 67

8 **a** Find these time expressions in the text on page 62.

yesterday   last year   last month   a few weeks ago

b Number the time expressions 1–7 (1 = close to now).

an hour ago	☐
at eight o'clock last night	☐
last Saturday evening	☐
last Sunday afternoon	☐
six hours ago	☐
ten minutes ago	1
yesterday at midday	☐

c Now write three true sentences and three false sentences about yourself. Use a verb from the Active grammar box and a time expression. Your partner guesses True or False.

A: *I went to Las Vegas on holiday last year.*
B: *False!*
A: *No, it's true! I went to the US for the summer.*

Speaking

9 Write down the name of the last city you visited. Make notes about what you liked/didn't like.

10 Work in pairs. Tell your partner ...

1 what you liked about the city. Why did you like it? What did you do and see there?
2 what you didn't like about the city. Why didn't you like it?

6.3 New citizens

Grammar Past Simple: questions and negatives

Can do talk about past events in your life

Reading and listening

1 **a** Look at the photo. Which city does it show?

    a New York **b** Mumbai **c** London

    b Where do you think the people come from?

2 **a** Read the text quickly and check your answer to exercise 1b.

    b Read the text again and match the people with the cities.

1	British and Irish	a	San Francisco
2	Korean	b	New York
3	Portuguese	c	London
4	Chinese	d	Los Angeles
5	Indian	e	Frankfurt
6	Turkish	f	Paris

    c Answer the questions.

What happened …

    1 in 1809?

    2 in the 1960s and 70s?

    3 in the middle of the nineteenth century?

    4 in the 1980s and 90s?

3 Find these words in the text and use them to complete the sentences.

> citizen   culture   foreign
> immigrants   tradition   workers

    1 Italians moved to New York and took their food and ____ to the city: pizzas, spaghetti and art.

    2 Chinese farm ____ moved to America in the nineteenth century.

    3 In California there are many ____ from Mexico.

    4 In my country we give presents for New Year. It's an old ____ .

    5 My uncle married a woman from Vancouver and became a Canadian ____ .

    6 The students in my school speak fifteen different ____ languages.

4 Do you have people from different countries in your home town? Where did they come from and when did they arrive?

Modern Cities

People in big cities often come from other places. People move to cities to get jobs or to find a better life, and many of them come from other countries. They often bring their culture, music and food with them. Visitors to London are often surprised to see so many Indian shops and restaurants. But there are over a million Indians living in the UK and the first Indian restaurant opened in London in 1809 – a time when pizzerias and hamburger restaurants didn't exist!

Many European cities have large numbers of immigrants. There are Portuguese people in Paris and Turkish workers in Frankfurt. They mostly arrived in the 1960s and 70s. But American cities have a very long tradition of new citizens from foreign countries. For example, San Francisco has more Chinese people than any city outside Asia. The city is famous for its Chinese restaurants. A lot of Chinese people went to California in the middle of the nineteenth century, but they didn't work in restaurants, they worked on farms and in factories. And New York, of course, is well known for its British and Irish citizens. The city has an Irish newspaper and its most important holiday is St Patrick's Day – the national day of Ireland. In the 1980s and 90s many Koreans moved to the US, especially to Los Angeles. In fact there is a large area in the centre of Los Angeles that is called 'Koreatown'.

5 **a** 🔊 1.65 Listen to two interviews. Which cities do Sean and Meera live in?

    b Listen again. Who said it? Write S (Sean) or M (Meera).

    1 I'm Irish-American. ☐

    2 Rich Indians sent their children to school in England. ☐

    3 My parents moved here when I was five. ☐

    4 I'm a New Yorker! ☐

    5 It was very hot. ☐

    c Correct the mistakes in three of the sentences.

Sean was born in ~~Ireland~~. *New York*

    1 Sean grew up in New York.

    2 American citizens went to Ireland in the 1840s.

    3 Meera didn't go to school in India.

    4 Meera's family went to London in the 1990s.

    5 Meera went to India for her cousin's birthday.

    d Look at audioscript 1.65 on page 154 and check your answers to exercise 5c.

Grammar | Past Simple: questions and negatives

6 Read the sentences in the Active grammar box. Choose the correct <u>underlined</u> words and complete the rules.

Active grammar

Did you grow up in the USA?

Where did your family come from?

To make questions in the Past Simple we use *did* and the *past form/infinitive* of the verb.

They didn't work in restaurants, they worked on farms and in factories.

To make negatives in the Past Simple we use *didn't* and the *past form/infinitive* of the verb.

Did you grow up in the US? – Yes, I did.

Did you go to school in India? – No, I didn't.

To make short answers in the Past Simple we use:

'Yes, I/you/he/she/it/we/they <u>do/did</u>.' and

'No, I/you/he/she/it/we/they <u>didn't/don't</u>.'

---

see Reference page 67

7　**a** Make past tense questions from the prompts.

Heather/grow up/in New Brunswick

Did Heather grow up in New Brunswick?

1 Heather/go/to English school/in New Brunswick
2 Heather/leave/home/in 2005
3 she/meet/her partner/in Canada
4 Stig/go/to school/in Norway
5 Stig/study/economics at university
6 he/become/an economics teacher

b 🔊 1.66 Now listen to Heather and Stig talk about their lives. Answer the questions in exercise 7a.

c Correct these false statements.

Stig grew up in the US.

Stig didn't grow up in the US.

1 Heather went to school in London.
2 People used cars in the sixteenth century.
3 Beethoven painted the *Mona Lisa*.
4 Marco Polo owned a mobile phone.
5 I watched a DVD last night.
6 My parents moved to Los Angeles.

Vocabulary | time expressions

8　**a** Complete the sentences with time expressions from the box.

> in 1492　　in the 1960s　　in those days
> in the nineteenth century　　when I was five

1 Men often had long hair ____ .
2 I first went to school _____ .
3 Columbus discovered America _____ .
4 I didn't have my apartment in the 1990s. I lived with my parents _____ .
5 Women wore long dresses _____ .

b Complete the expressions. Then finish the sentences with true information about you, your family or your country.

1 _____ 2001 we ...
2 In the sixteenth _____ my country ...
3 When I _____ a small child, I ...
4 In _____ 1990s my family ...

Pronunciation | contrastive stress

9　**a** 🔊 1.67 Listen and <u>underline</u> the stressed words in the answers.

1 **A:** Were you born in London?
　B: No, I was born in Mumbai.
2 **A:** Did you visit Venice?
　B: No, we visited Rome.
3 **A:** Was it nice?　**B:** No, it was horrible.

b Ask and answer questions using the table.

Like	Visit	Was it
coffee? (✗ tea)	the cinema? (✗ the theatre)	small? (✗ big)
rice? (✗ pasta)	Russia? (✗ Poland)	new? (✗ old)
bikes? (✗ cars)	your uncle? (✗ my brother)	good? (✗ bad)

A: *Do you like coffee?*　**B:** *No, I like tea.*

see Pronunciation bank page 148

Speaking and writing

10　**a** Find out about your partner's past life. Ask questions and make notes.

When/Where were you born?　Where did you grow up?　When did you start school? Where did you go to school?

b Write a paragraph about your partner's life.

Antonio was born in Spain in 1989. His family moved to Italy when he was six ...

6 | Communication

1 Discuss these questions.

1 Do you shop in department stores? Which ones?

2 Why are department stores useful?

3 When did you last go to a department store? What did you buy? Why? How much did it cost?

4 How can you go from one floor to another in a department store?

2 a ● 1.68 Listen to customers asking for information in a department store and complete the store guide.

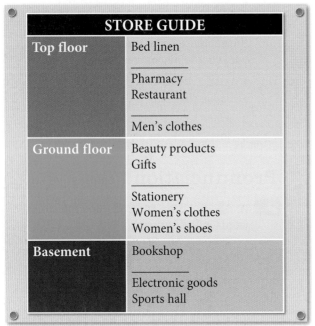

STORE GUIDE	
Top floor	Bed linen
	_____
	Pharmacy
	Restaurant
	_____
	Men's clothes
Ground floor	Beauty products
	Gifts
	_____
	Stationery
	Women's clothes
	Women's shoes
Basement	Bookshop
	_____
	Electronic goods
	Sports hall

b Listen again (or look at audioscript 1.68 on page 154) and complete the How to... box.

How to... shop in a department store

Ask where something is	Where (1) _____ men's shoes?
	Which floor is that on?
Ask for something	(2) _____ a store guide?
	Can (3) _____ a copy, please?
Ask about prices	How (4) _____ is that?
	How much are they?

c In pairs, ask and answer about where to find things. Use the information in the store guide.

> aspirin CD player computer dictionary
> football pencil sofa women's jeans

A: *Where can I find a sofa?*

B: *In the furniture department on the top floor.*

3 Work in pairs.

A pairs: you work in a gift shop. Turn to page 130.

B pairs: you are customers. It is the end of term next week and you want to buy your teacher two presents. Decide how much you want to spend, then look at the categories below and decide on two suitable presents.

- travel guidebooks
- DVDs
- chocolates
- gifts (wallets, diaries, address books)
- stationery (pens, pencils, notebooks)

B1: *I think she'd like a guidebook to New York and a box of Swiss chocolates.*

B2: *Good idea! ...*

Write down the things you want to buy then talk to different A pairs and find the things you want.

Excuse me, have you got any Swiss chocolates?

How much are they?

Can I have a box?

Past Simple

We use the Past Simple to talk about actions and situations in the past. The actions and situations are finished.

*My hair **was** red when I was a girl, but it's grey now.*

to be

⊕	I/He/She/It was	We/You/They were
⊖	I/He/She/It wasn't (was not)	We/You/They weren't (were not)
❓	Was I/he/she/it?	Were we/you/they?
	Yes, I/he/she/it was.	Yes, we/you/they were.
	No, I/he/she/it wasn't.	No, we/you/they weren't.

*She **was** tired last night.*
*They **weren't** at the cinema yesterday.*
***Was** Karin at the office on Monday? No, she **wasn't**.*
***Were** the musicians good? Yes, they **were**.*
*Where **were you** last night? I **was** at home.*

Regular verbs: positive

Make the Past Simple of most regular verbs by adding *-ed* to the verb.

*work → work**ed**, watch → watch**ed**, listen → listen**ed***

Note the spelling rules:

Verbs that end in ...	Rule	Examples
-e	add -d	liv**ed**, chang**ed**
consonant + -y	remove -y and add -ied	stud**ied**, carr**ied**
one vowel + consonant	repeat consonant and add -ed	plan**ned**, stop**ped**

Negative

Did + not + infinitive

*The tourists **did not visit** all the museums.*

In informal English, we use the contracted form *didn't*.

*They **didn't** work in restaurants.*

Questions

Wh- questions

Wh- word + did + subject pronoun + infinitive

***When did you finish** work yesterday?*

Yes/No questions

Did + noun/subject pronoun + infinitive

***Did you study** at university?*

Short answers

Yes, I/he/she/it/we/you/they did.
No, I/he/she/it/we/you/they didn't.
***Did** you **study** at university? Yes, I **did**.*

Irregular verbs

Many common verbs in English have an irregular past form, i.e. they do not end in *-ed* in the past.

*have → had   We **had** a lovely meal in the restaurant.*

*go → went   Sara **went** to Amsterdam on a weekend break.*

*take → took   Paul **took** a lot of photos in India.*

*see → saw   I **saw** the Mona Lisa when I went to Paris.*

There are no general rules for the formation of the Past Simple of irregular verbs. See page 149 for a list of irregular Past Simple forms.

These verbs are irregular only in the positive. They form the negative and questions like regular verbs, with *did* + the infinitive.

> ### Key vocabulary
>
> **Places in/near a town/city**
> airport   (art) gallery   bank   bar   building   bus station   café   cinema   factory   hospital   hostel   hotel   library   market   museum   park   post office   power station   restaurant   school   station
>
> **Shops**
> bookshop   chemist's   clothes shop   department store   jeweller's   newsagent's   shoe shop   shopping centre   stationer's   supermarket
>
> **Time expressions**
> (two years) ago
> in 1809
> in the 1960s and 70s
> in the nineteenth century
> in those days
> last night/week/month/year
> last (Sunday) morning/afternoon/evening
> yesterday
>
> Listen to these words.
> ACTIVE BOOK

 see Writing bank page 140

1 Write the Past Simple form of the verbs in the correct column.

> ~~carry~~ change close decide finish live
> look marry move own plan start
> stop want

+ ed	+ d	– y + ied	+ consonant + ed
		carried	

2 There are ten mistakes in the text. Find and correct nine more.

This is a photo of my great-grandparents – my
mother's grandparents. They ~~live~~ *lived* in the middle of
the last century. They was lovely people. My great-
grandfather works in a car factory and he ownd a
car when most people didn't know about them. My
great-grandmother was very beautiful when she
were a girl. She marryed my great-grandfather when
she was only 17. She didn't work – she stays at home
and looked after the children. My great-grandfather
stoped work when he was 65, then every day they
walked to the park and my great-grandmother
always carries a little bag with sandwiches for their
lunch. She died in 1983, when she was only 73, and
after three months my great-grandfather dieed too –
he didn't want to live without her.

3 Complete the text with the correct Past Simple form of the verbs in brackets.

> Natasha Richardson died on Wednesday in New
> York. She _was_ (be) only 45. She died a few days after
> she (1) _____ (have) a skiing accident in Canada.
> She was the daughter of British actress Vanessa
> Redgrave. She (2) _____ (spend) her childhood in
> England and (3) _____ (make) her first film when
> she was only four years old. She (4) _____ (meet)
> her husband, the Irish film star Liam Neeson, in
> 1994 and (5) _____ (leave) England. She
> (6) _____ (go) to the US and starred in many
> successful shows in New York.

4 Make Past Simple questions and answers from the prompts.

Albert Einstein/understand/mathematics? (✓)
Did Albert Einstein understand mathematics?
Yes, he did.
Charles Darwin/French? (✗ British)
Was Charles Darwin French?
No, he wasn't. He was British.

1 Pablo Picasso/Spanish? (✓)

_____

2 Mozart/play/the guitar? (✗ the piano)

_____

3 President Kennedy/Russian? (✗ American)

_____

4 the Hoover Building/a factory/80 years ago? (✓)

_____

5 Alexander Graham Bell/invent/the computer?
(✗ the telephone)

_____

5 Use the clues to complete the crossword with shops and places in a town.

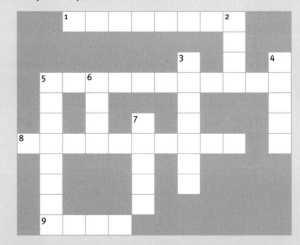

Across
1 You can buy travel guides, maps and books here.
5 You can buy different kinds of food here.
8 A _____ shop sells pens, pencils and paper.
9 You can often find handbags at a _____ shop.

Down
2 A nice place to sit outside and read.
3 My favourite paintings are in the local art _____ .
4 There are many different parts in a department
_____ .
5 You can start a journey from your town's bus and
train _____ .
6 You can send things from a _____ office.
7 A good place to sleep when you're away from home.

Lead-in

1
  a Complete the descriptions of the people in the photos with letters A–G.

  1 _____ has got blue eyes.
  2 _____ has got long fair hair.
  3 _____ has got dark skin.
  4 _____ has got short grey hair.
  5 _____ has got a beard.
  6 _____ is slim.
  7 _____ is young.
  8 _____ is bald.
  9 _____ is tall.
  10 _____ is short.
  11 _____ wears glasses.
  12 _____ has got a moustache.

  b 🔊 2.01 Listen and compare your answers.

2
  a Look at the people in the photos. Find someone you think looks …
  1 pretty   2 friendly   3 unfriendly   4 handsome

  b Compare your answers with a partner.

3 Work in pairs.
  Student A: describe a person from the photos.
  This person's got dark hair and wears glasses. She looks friendly.
  Student B: find the person.

Girls solve jigsaw puzzle and become rich!

One morning last year, schoolgirls Rachel Aumann and Maisie Balley set off for school as usual. Halfway there, they picked up a tiny piece of paper from the ground.
5 When they looked at it, they saw that the piece of paper was part of a banknote. They noticed some other pieces of banknotes on the ground, but where did they come from? Then Rachel and Maisie noticed a bag in a rubbish bin. They pulled out the bag from the bin and checked it – it had
10 thousands of pieces of banknotes in it. The two 12-year-olds went to school and told their teachers. Then, after school, they took the bag to the police station and handed in the money.

The police kept the money for six months. During that time
15 no one asked for it, so the police gave back the money to the girls. For the next few months the girls, with Rachel's stepfather Peter, spent time every evening matching the numbers on the pieces, and they put together a lot of the banknotes. They now have £1,200 in £10 notes, but they
20 think there's another £800 in the pieces of £5 and £20 notes. Whose money was it? The girls have no idea, but they're happy that it belongs to them now! Rachel wants to keep her money for when she goes to university, but Maisie wants to go shopping right now!

Reading

1 Look at the headline and the photo. What is a jigsaw puzzle?

2 Read the text. What was the jigsaw puzzle?

3 Read the text again. Put the events in the correct order.

a The police returned the pieces of banknotes to the girls. ☐

b They went to school. ☐

c They handed the pieces of banknotes in to the police. ☐

d They saw a bag in a bin, with thousands of pieces of banknotes in it. ☐

e The girls noticed a piece of paper and picked it up. ☐

f The girls now have £1,200. ☐

g Rachel and Maisie were on their way to school. ☐1

h The girls matched the pieces of £10 notes. ☐

4 Look at the Lifelong learning box. Read the tip and complete the exercise.

Understanding a story

❗ When you read a story, these steps can help you understand it:

1 identify the main events
2 find the meaning of new words
3 understand the details

You can try to work out the meaning of new words. Look at this example, with *set off* (line 3):

Is *set off* a noun, verb or adjective?	*verb*
Which words come before it?	*Rachel and Maisie*
Which words come after it?	*for school*
Can you guess the meaning?	*went to, left home*

Now work out the meaning of these words:

1 *ground* (line 7)   2 *told* (line 11)   3 *belongs to* (line 22)

Lifelong learning

5 What did you think of the story? Choose two or three adjectives and tell your partner. Why did you choose these adjectives?

> boring   different   exciting   great   horrible
> interesting   nice   unusual

Vocabulary | phrasal verbs

6 **a** Some verbs have two parts. Read the text again and find the missing words.

set *off*

1 pick ____   3 pull ____   5 give ____
2 look ____   4 hand ____   6 put ____

b Write the verbs from exercise 6a under the correct picture.

_____   _____

_____   _____

_____   _____

_____

c Complete the sentences using some of the verbs and the pictures in exercises 6a and b.

1 _____ _____ that burger. It's huge!
2 Can I _____ _____ this wallet?
3 I always _____ _____ rubbish from the ground.
4 Here's some glue. We can _____ _____ the pieces and glue them.
5 Kevin and Mary _____ _____ very early yesterday morning.

Grammar | articles

7 **a** Look at the sentences from the text, then complete the sentences in the Active grammar box with *a/an* or *the*.

They picked up a tiny piece of paper ... they saw that the piece of paper was part of a banknote.

Rachel and Maisie noticed a bag in a rubbish bin. They pulled out the bag from the bin ...

> **Active grammar**
>
> We use *a/an* and *the* in different ways. When we talk about something for the first time, we put _____ before the noun. When we mention it again, we put _____ before the noun.

see Reference page 77

b Choose the correct word in *italics*.

1 The girls went to *a/the* school in Brighton. *A/The* school is for 11 to 18-year-olds.
2 They took *a/the* bag from *a/the* rubbish bin. *A/The* bag was full of banknotes. We don't know why *a/the* bag was in *a/the* bin.
3 There was *a/the* story like this in the newspaper last week, but *a/the* story was about two boys.

8 **a** Complete the story with *a/an* or *the*.

❝One day last year my friend and I were on our way to work when we heard (1) ___ sound. It was (2) ___ sound of an unhappy child, and we noticed (3) ___ little boy outside (4) ___ house on the other side of the road. We spoke to (5) ___ boy and he told us that he went to school without his homework, so he came home to get it but his mother and father were out. His mother had (6) ___ mobile phone with her, but when we called it, (7) ___ phone was off. Then we asked the little boy for his father's number, but he didn't know it, so we told him to go back to school and tell his teacher. During the conversation, (8) ___ little boy's mother arrived. We went into (9) ___ house with her and she gave us (10) ___ cup of tea, and then we went to work. We were an hour late! ❞

b Work in pairs. Retell the story in your own words.

Speaking

9 **a** Work in pairs to tell a story.

Student A: look at page 130.

Student B: look at page 133.

b Do you have an interesting story to tell other students?

Reading

1 Marianne is twenty-two. She comes from New Zealand, but is at university in Brazil. Work in pairs and discuss the questions.

1 Where is the beach in the photo?
2 What is the connection between Marianne and the beach, do you think?

2 **a** Read the email and check your answers to exercise 1. Then answer the questions.

1 What did Marianne do a month ago?
2 Who does she live with now?
3 What does she do in the afternoon?

To: Carol
Cc:
Subject: How are you?

Hi Carol

A Thanks for your email about all my friends in New Zealand!

B Everything's fine here. I arrived in Rio de Janeiro a month ago to start my course and then I moved in with my host family. They live in a big apartment near the beach in Ipanema.

C The family is very nice. Mr and Mrs Silva are middle-aged and very friendly. They've got three children. Tina's my age, she's got dark hair and she's pretty. She's tall, like me. João is the middle one; he's fifteen. He's quite short and he's very tanned from playing football in the sun! Carlos is the young one. He's lovely, and he laughs all the time, but he isn't very slim.

D Every morning I go to college. The classes are really interesting, especially the literature ones. I usually go to the beach in the afternoon. The beach here is beautiful and the sea is warm. There's a really handsome man on the beach. He watches me every day. He looks nice but, as you know, I'm quite shy - so I don't look at him!

E Write to me soon and tell me all your news.

Love
Marianne

---

b Match the statements with paragraphs A–E.

1 Marianne describes her host family. [C]
2 She asks Carol to do something. ☐
3 She thanks Carol. ☐
4 She describes what she does. ☐
5 She writes about where she lives. ☐

c Read the email again. Match the people with the adjectives.

1	Mr and Mrs Silva	a	tanned, short
2	Tina	b	handsome, nice
3	João	c	friendly, middle-aged
4	Carlos	d	dark, pretty
5	the man on the beach	e	tall, shy
6	Marianne	f	young, not very slim

3 Look at the Lifelong learning box. Read the tip and complete the exercise.

Opposite adjectives

❗ A good way to remember adjectives is in pairs with opposite meanings.

old – young

Find adjectives in exercise 2c with the opposite meaning.

pale – *tanned*
1 fair – _____
2 confident – _____
3 horrible – _____
4 unattractive – _____ / _____
5 tall – _____

Lifelong learning

Vocabulary | adjectives (4): people

4 **a** Put the adjectives from exercises 2c and 3 in the correct column(s).

Appearance					Age	Personality
body	face	skin	hair	height		
		tanned				

b Can you add any more adjectives to the table?

c Complete the How to... box with these words: *appearance*, *personality* and *age*.

How to... describe people

(1) _____	he's the young one, she's middle-aged
(2) _____	she's got dark hair, he's quite short, he looks nice
(3) _____	he's lovely, they're very friendly

d When we describe someone's personality we often give an example of the things they do:

He's lovely, and he laughs all the time.

In pairs, think of an example of what people with these personalities do. Think about people you know.

> confident   friendly   horrible   nice   shy
> unfriendly

Grammar | pronoun *one/ones*

5 **a** Read the sentences in the Active grammar box and match the <u>underlined</u> words with the meanings (a–d). Then choose the correct words in *italics*.

Active grammar

1 *They've got three children ... João is the middle <u>one</u>.*

2 *The classes are really interesting, especially the literature <u>ones</u>.*

a) classes   b) class   c) children   d) child

- We use *one* to replace <u>singular/plural</u> nouns when we write them a second time.
- We use *ones* to replace <u>singular/plural</u> nouns when we write them a second time.

see Reference page 77

b Replace the <u>underlined</u> words in these sentences with *one* or *ones*.

1 I don't like green pens. Do you have any red <u>pens</u>?

2 Did you buy a cheap watch or an expensive <u>watch</u>?

3 Don't get that DVD. I've got that <u>DVD</u> at home.

4 Do you want a pizza? Those cheese <u>pizzas</u> look nice.

c Read this paragraph. Find four more words you can change to *one* (or *ones*).

66 When I was a child I lived in three different
houses. The first h̶o̶u̶s̶e̶ *one* was lovely. The second
house was quite small, but it was in a nice location.
The third house wasn't very nice but there were six
bedrooms. I used the bedroom on the second floor.
The other bedrooms were on the first floor. 99

Listening

6 **a**   2.02 Listen to Marianne talking to her friend about the man on the beach and look at the photos. Which man is Marianne talking about?

b Listen again. How does she describe him? Make notes.

He's really friendly.

Speaking

7 **a** Work in pairs. Describe one of the other men in the photos. Can your partner guess which one it is?

He's ...   He looks ...   He's got ...

b Think of someone in your class, or a famous person. Describe him/her to your partner but don't say his/her name. Can your partner guess the person?

Reading and listening

1 **a** Do you have any special holidays in your country? When are they? Do you give presents? What do you give?

b Read the text quickly and find the names of three special days.

Special gifts and special days

In many countries there is a tradition of giving gifts on special days during the year. For example, in China parents give their children money on New Year's Day. They put the money in small red envelopes called 'Lai-See'. Red is the colour of good luck.

Russians give presents to their wives, mothers and sisters on International Women's Day. That's on 8th March. They usually give candy, chocolates or beautiful yellow flowers called mimosas. People often give flowers to their mothers on Mother's Day. That's a special day in many countries, but it isn't on the same day. In most European countries it's on the second Sunday of May, but in Spain and Portugal it's on the first Sunday in May.

The Japanese have an interesting tradition of giving presents in the middle of the year. The present is called 'Ochugen' and people give it on 15th July. They usually give gifts of food or sweets to people that help them during the year.

c Read the text again and answer the questions.

1 When is Mother's Day in Spain?

2 What do Japanese people give on 15th July?

3 What colour are mimosa flowers?

4 Why do Chinese people put presents in red envelopes?

2 **a** ⏺ 2.03 Listen to Heather talk about two special days in Canada. Tick (✓) the activities she talks about.

	Canada Day	Halloween
people dress up in costumes	☐	☐
there is a parade	☐	☐
people give children candy	☐	☐
everyone has the day off work	☐	☐
children play 'trick or treat'	☐	☐

b Now match some of the activities with the photos.

c Do you have special days like these in your country? What do people do?

Vocabulary | ordinal numbers and months

3 **a** Read the text again and look at audioscript 2.03 on page 154 to fill in the red lines in the table. Then complete the black lines.

1st _____	6th _____	11th _____	20th *twentieth*
2nd _____	7th _____	__ *twelfth*	22nd *twenty-second*
3rd *third*	__ *eighth*	13th _____	30th _____
4th *fourth*	__ *ninth*	14th *fourteenth*	31st _____
5th *fifth*	10th _____	__ *fifteenth*	

b ⏺ 2.04 Listen and check your answers. Then repeat.

4 Choose the correct words in *italics*.

1 My birthday is on the *first/one* of October.
2 Our new house has got *three/third* bedrooms.
3 In Greece, Mother's Day is on the *second/two* of February.
4 This is my *three/third* holiday this year!
5 It's Lucy's *nine/ninth* birthday on Saturday.

5 **a** Find the names of three months in the text in exercise 1b.

b Number the months in the correct order (1–12).

September ☐   August ☐   October ☐   April ☐
March ☐   December ☐   February ☐   July ☐
January ☐1   May ☐   November ☐   June ☐

c Work in pairs. Say these dates.

25th July   14th August   11th October
3rd January 1911   21.4.99   31.12.2010

d In pairs, ask and answer these questions.

1 When is your birthday?
2 What dates are holidays in your country?

Grammar | possessive pronouns

6 **a** Jane has got some presents for her friends. Match the words in the box with the pictures.

clock ☐A   diary ☐   DVDs ☐   handbag ☐
trainers ☐   umbrella ☐

A   B   C
D   E   F

b 🔊 2.05 Jane went to work this morning. Her husband phoned and asked about the presents. Listen and match the presents with the people.

Davy: _____   Tara: _____
Jane's parents: _____   Gordon: _____

7 **a** Look at the sentences. Match the underlined words (1–2) with the meanings (a–b).

1 A: The trainers. Are they Davy's?
   B: Yes, the trainers are his.
2 A: There's an umbrella on the table.
   B: It's ours!

a it belongs to us ☐   b they belong to him ☐

b Look at the audioscript on page 155 and complete the Active grammar box.

Active grammar

Possessive adjectives	Possessive pronouns
my	____
his	____
her	____
its	*its*
our	____
your	____
their	____

see Reference page 77

8 Rewrite the sentences. Use a possessive pronoun (and a verb if necessary) to replace the phrases in *italics*.

These aren't my CDs, they *belong to Jane*.
These aren't my CDs, they're hers.

1 Excuse me. Is this *your bag*?
2 Use the blue pen; the red one *belongs to me*.
3 Is this *Maria's watch*?
4 The house next to the church *belonged to them*.
5 Are these sandwiches *for us*?
6 That wasn't her phone number, it was *John's*.
7 They weren't our dogs, they were *Bob and Jo's*.
8 *Does* this *belong to your brother*?

Pronunciation | /θ/

9 **a** 🔊 2.06 Listen to the *th* sound /θ/ in the word *birthday*. Is it the same as the sound in *brother* or *bathroom*?

b 🔊 2.07 Listen. Underline the word you hear.

1 free   three   4 first   thirst
2 sink   think   5 tree   three
3 sick   thick

c 🔊 2.08 Listen. Do you hear the sound /θ/? Tick (✓) for yes, cross (✗) for no. Listen and repeat.

1 ☐   2 ☐   3 ☐   4 ☐   5 ☐   6 ☐   7 ☐   8 ☐

see Pronunciation bank page 147

Speaking

10 Talk to your classmates. Find a student/students with:

1 a birthday in the same month as yours.
2 the first and last birthdays of the year.
3 a birthday this month.
4 a birthday next month.
5 a birthday last month.

ARRIVALS

1 Look at the picture. Where are the people?

2 a 🔊 2.09 Listen to two people talking. What is Isabel's problem?

b Listen again and complete Geoff's notes.

> Mr Schäfer
> age – _____
> height – about _____ tall
> hair – _____ brown (but maybe _____ now?), quite _____
> body type – _____
> skin – very _____
> eyes – ?????
> other features – has a _____, wears _____

c Look at the picture. Which man is Mr Schäfer?
He's the one on the left/right/with ...

3 Listen again and complete the questions in the How to... box.

How to... ask about appearance and personality

Appearance	*What does he/she (1) _____ like?*
	How (2) _____ is he/she?
	What (3) _____ is his/her skin/hair?
	(4) _____ he/she have long or short (5) _____ ?
	(6) _____ he/she thin?
	What (7) _____ are his/her eyes?
Personality	*What's he/she (8) _____ ?*

---

4 Work in pairs. You need to meet someone at the airport.

Student A: turn to page 130.
Student B: turn to page 134.

Articles

We use *a/an* (see Unit 1, Reference page 17) when we talk about something for the first time.

*There's **a** theatre in our town.*

*I know **a** really good dentist.*

*Julie's got **a** lovely little dog.*

We use *the* when we talk about the thing/person again.

*Some really good actors work in **the** theatre.*

*He's **the** dentist my parents go to.*

*She takes **the** dog to work with her every day!*

Phrasal verbs

Some verbs in English have two or three parts, usually a verb and a preposition. These verbs are very common. The phrasal verbs in Unit 7 are *look at, give back, hand in, pull out, put together, set off* and *pick up*.

Other phrasal verbs in Units 1–6 are *find out, get up* (Unit 2) and *look after* (Unit 6).

*I **handed in** my homework late this week.*

*Umut **gets up** at 5 a.m. to go to work.*

Pronoun *one/ones*

We use *one* or *ones* to avoid repeating a noun. Use *one* after *this, that* or an adjective.

A: *Do you want the black pen or the blue **one**?*

B: *That **one** over there – the blue **one**.*

Use *ones* to replace plural nouns. Use *ones* after *these, those* or an adjective.

A: *Did you buy the brown shoes or the black **ones**?*

B: *I bought the black **ones**.*

A: *Great. Those **ones** are really nice.*

Possessive pronouns

Possessive pronouns show who something belongs to. We use possessive pronouns in the place of a possessive adjective and a noun. (See also page 17.)

*This is **my coat**. = This is **mine**.*

Subject pronoun	Possessive adjectives	Possessive pronouns
I	*my*	*mine*
he	*his*	*his*
she	*her*	*hers*
it	*its*	*its*
we	*our*	*ours*
you	*your*	*yours*
they	*their*	*theirs*

*That book **is John's** (book).*
*That book is **for John**.* = *That book is **his**.*
*That book **belongs to John**.*

Ordinal numbers

We use these numbers with nouns and when we talk about dates.

*My **first** child was a boy.*

*The **third** of September/September the **third**.*

We can write dates in different ways.

3 September   3rd September   September 3rd

1	first	18	eighteenth
2	second	19	nineteenth
3	third	20	twentieth
4	fourth	21	twenty-first
5	fifth	22	twenty-second
6	sixth	23	twenty-third
7	seventh	24	twenty-fourth
8	eighth	30	thirtieth
9	ninth	31	thirty-first
10	tenth	40	fortieth
11	eleventh	50	fiftieth
12	twelfth	60	sixtieth
13	thirteenth	70	seventieth
14	fourteenth	80	eightieth
15	fifteenth	90	ninetieth
16	sixteenth	100	one hundredth
17	seventeenth		

We often write ordinal numbers like this:

first = 1st   second = 2nd   third = 3rd   fourth = 4th
fifth = 5th, etc.

Key vocabulary

Describing words

Appearance

Body   (not very) short/slim/tall

Skin   dark   fair   pale   tanned

Hair   dark   fair   grey   long   short   bald*

*We say *He's bald*, not *He's got bald hair*.

Age   middle-aged   old   young

Opinion   attractive   handsome   pretty

Others   has got a beard/moustache
has got blue eyes   wears glasses

Personality

confident   friendly   horrible   lovely   nice   shy
unfriendly

Months

January   February   March   April   May   June
July   August   September   October   November
December

 Listen to these words.

ACTIVE BOOK

 see Writing bank page 141

1 Complete the gaps with *a/an* or *the*.

Send Chat Attach Address Fonts Colors Save As Draft

To: Sammy
Cc:
Subject: Madrid

Hi Sammy

Madrid is great! I love it here. I moved into (1) _____ new apartment last week. It's (2) _____ apartment I told you about in my last email, do you remember? It's quite small but it's got (3) _____ big terrace. I can sit on (4) _____ terrace in the evening and enjoy (5) _____ nice cool drink! There's a small kitchen and (6) _____ bathroom. (7) _____ bathroom hasn't got (8) _____ bath, but it's got a nice big shower.

2 Use a word from Box A and a word from Box B to complete the sentences.

Box A   ~~hand~~ give look pick put set

Box B   at back ~~in~~ off together up

Please *hand in* your completed forms to the tour guide.

1 Can you _____ _____ the pieces of the broken vase? It's my favourite one!

2 _____ _____ your rubbish, please. Don't leave it on the floor.

3 Can you _____ _____ my dictionary? I want to finish my homework.

4 **A:** I don't know the answer.
   B: _____ _____ your grammar book for help.

5 We always _____ _____ early but there are a lot of cars on the roads at weekends, so we're often late.

3 Read the dialogue. Find seven words you can change to *one* or *ones*.

A: There are so many sofas here, Philip. Which <u>sofas</u> do you like?   *ones*
B: Well, I like the brown <u>sofa</u>.   *one*
A: No, it's ugly. What about the red sofa?
B: It's OK.
A: Fine. Now, chairs. Do you like modern chairs?
B: Yes. I like those big chairs in the corner.
A: The metal chairs?
B: Yes.
A: Yes, they're quite nice. But how about this chair?
B: No, I don't like that chair. It isn't very attractive.
A: Well, I don't like this shop. Let's go to a different shop.

4 Match questions 1–7 with the questions (a–h) with the same meaning.

1 Does this bag belong to you?
2 Is this his?
3 Is this Mary's MP3 player?
4 Are these our letters?
5 Are these theirs?
6 Is this present for me?
7 Are these mine or yours?
8 Does this umbrella belong to us?

a Are these ours?
b Is this hers?
c Is this mine?
d Do these books belong to them?
e Is this yours?
f Is this ours?
g Are these my keys or your keys?
h Does this belong to Mr McBride?

5 Complete the sentences with ordinal numbers. The numbers in the box are clues.

    1   8   9   ~~16~~   18   25

Abraham Lincoln was the <u>sixteenth</u> president of the United States.

1 August is the _____ month of the year.
2 Christmas Day is on the _____ of December.
3 Neil Armstrong was the _____ man on the Moon.
4 British people can vote after their _____ birthday.
5 The _____ series of *Friends* was the last one.

6 Match the people with the descriptions. Be careful, two of the descriptions do not match the photos.

 A
 B

 C
 D

1 She's old and she's got grey hair.
2 He's bald and middle-aged.
3 She's young and slim and she's got fair hair.
4 He's short. He's got grey hair and a beard.
5 She's old and she isn't very slim; she's got dark hair.
6 He's tall and he's got dark hair and a beard.

(A)

(B)

(C)

(D)

Lead-in

1 **a** Check the meanings of these words in a dictionary. Which photo are they in? Write A, B, C or D.

> boots *B*   coat ☐   dress ☐   gloves ☐   hat ☐
> jeans ☐ ☐   pullover ☐   scarf ☐   shorts ☐   skirt ☐
> suit ☐   T-shirt ☐   tie ☐

b Can you name any other clothes in the photos?

2 When do we wear clothes like these? Match the clothes with one or more of the seasons (spring, summer, autumn, winter).

3 Match the clothes adjectives (1–6) with their meanings (a–f).

1	formal	a	don't fit closely, not small
2	casual	b	not thick or heavy
3	tight	c	tidy, in good condition
4	light	d	for important events, for business
5	loose	e	comfortable and informal
6	smart	f	feel small, fit closely

4 **a** 🔵 2.10 Listen to people talking about clothes and complete these sentences.

1 I think _____ are uncomfortable.

2 You can't wear jeans to a _____ business meeting.

3 _____ shirts and pullovers look good.

4 Winter _____ are usually warm and comfortable.

b Do you agree or disagree with the statements above?

Grammar	Present Continuous
Can do	describe what people are doing now

Listening

1 Look at the photos of three festivals.

   1   There are two photos from each festival. Match the pairs.

   2   Where do these festivals take place?

2 **a** 🔊 2.11 Listen and check your answers to exercise 1. Match the reporters (Anna, Justin and Pam) with the photos.

   b Match the people with the photos.

a Mariachi group	☐
dancers in colourful costumes	☐
Whitney	☐

   c Match the people with the activities. Listen again to check.

1	Anna	a	is cooking Caribbean food.
2	The dancers	b	is sitting in the town square.
3	Whitney	c	isn't queuing for the theatre.
4	Justin	d	are all playing together.
5	The guitarists	e	is having a good time.
6	The spectators	f	are wearing colourful costumes.
7	Pam	g	is reporting from Finland.
8	Mika	h	aren't just listening to the music.

3 Work in pairs and discuss the questions.

   1   Are there any well-known festivals in your town/country? What are they? When do they take place?

   2   Do you go to festivals? Do you like them? Why/Why not?

   3   Is your country famous for a kind of music or dancing like mariachi or flamenco?

Grammar | Present Continuous

4 **a** Look at the sentences in exercise 2c and complete the Active grammar box.

Active grammar

➕	➖	❓
I'm dancing.	I'm not dancing.	Am I dancing?
He/She/It _____ cooking.	He/She/It _____ cooking.	Is he/she/it cooking?
You/We/They _____ playing.	You/We/They _____ playing.	Are you/we/they playing?

Yes,	I am. he/she/it is. we/you/they are.	No,	I'm not. he/she/it isn't. we/you/they aren't .

Speaking

7 Play a game. Mime an activity from the box at the bottom of the page. Your classmates guess the activity.

A: *Are you swimming?* B: *Yes, I am.*

8 Look at the picture. What's happening? Where is it?

b Choose the best ending for the sentence.

We use the Present Continuous when we talk about activities that ...

1 happened yesterday/in the past.
2 are happening now.
3 happen every day.

c Complete the rule.

To form the Present Continuous we use the verb _____ + the *-ing* form of the main verb.

d Write the *-ing* forms.

1 verb + *-ing*	cook → *cooking* watch → _____ play → _____
2 verb *-e* + *-ing*	have → _____ move → _____ dance → _____
3 verb + consonant + *-ing*	sit → _____ clap → _____

see Reference page 87

5 **a** Make sentences from the prompts.

he/play/the guitar

He's playing the guitar.

1 all the people/have a good time
2 she/not dance/now
3 they/wear/traditional costumes
4 we/read/an interesting book
5 I/wear/a coat
6 I/not study/any languages/at the moment
7 we/not write/an exercise
8 what/you/do/at the moment?

b Change sentences 4–7 so they are true for you, then answer question 8.

Pronunciation | sentence stress

6 2.12 Listen to the sentences. <u>Underline</u> the stressed syllables. Then listen again and repeat.

1 She's dancing. 3 Are you listening?
2 They're talking. 4 We aren't leaving.

see Pronunciation bank page 148

9 **a** 2.13 Match the descriptions (a–d) with the parts of the picture (1–4). Then listen and check your answers.

1 at the front   a people are watching the dancers
2 at the back   b there are buildings
3 on the left   c two women are dancing
4 on the right   d musicians are playing

b Now complete the How to... box.

> ### How to... describe a picture
>
> | Place | *At the* (1) _____ / _____ *of the picture ...*
(2) _____ *the left /* _____ *of the picture ...* |
> |---|---|
> | People/
things | *Two women* (3) _____ *dancing.*
(4) _____ *are some buildings*
Some musicians are playing.
(5) _____ *are some people watching.* |

10 In pairs, find the differences between two pictures.

Student A: look at the picture on page 131.
Student B: look at the picture on page 134.

> cook cycle dance drink eat laugh
> play a guitar run sit sleep swim
> teach use a computer walk write

Grammar	position of adjectives
Can do	talk about what you wear

 A

 B

 C

 D

 E

STREET FASHION

Fashion is always changing. Sometimes it's difficult to know what is fashionable and what isn't! We talked to five young people about their ideas of 'fashion' and gave them a fashion rating.

This is Simon. He's wearing scruffy old jeans and a tight T-shirt. Simon says he likes comfortable old clothes – he isn't interested in fashion. In the summer he wants to feel cool, so he wears thin shirts and he never wears jackets or coats.

Fashion rating ★ ★

What about Tara? She's wearing a formal suit. Tara likes fashion, but she works in an office, so she can't wear fashionable clothes very often. She likes formal clothes because she looks slim in them.

Fashion rating ★ ★ ★

Sunny loves traditional Indian clothes. Here she's wearing a beautiful silk sari – she looks lovely. Sunny doesn't like Western fashion. She loves bright colours and luxurious materials.

Fashion rating ★

Danny's from Canada. It's very cold in the winter in Canada, so Danny often wears thick wool pullovers and warm jackets. He likes fashionable clothes but he wants to be comfortable and warm! Today he's wearing a grey jacket, smart brown trousers and leather shoes. Danny is young but we think he looks middle-aged!

Fashion rating ★

Karen thinks fashion is only for rich people. She can't afford to buy designer clothes because she doesn't have a lot of money. She buys a lot of her clothes at second-hand shops. Karen only wears natural materials. Today she's wearing a second-hand leather jacket, a short cotton skirt and brown boots.

Fashion rating ★ ★ ★ ★ ★

Reading

1 Read the text quickly and write the names under the pictures.

2 **a** Match the clothes with the people in the pictures A–E.

boots ☐   jacket ☐   jeans ☐   pullover ☐
sandals ☐   sari ☐   shoes ☐   a skirt ☐   a suit ☐
sunglasses ☐   trainers ☐   trousers ☐

b Work in pairs and discuss the questions.

1 Do you like the clothes in the pictures?
2 Do you think the clothes are fashionable?

c Read the text again and complete the sentences.

1 _____ thinks fashionable clothes are expensive.
2 _____ doesn't like cool, thin clothes.
3 _____ doesn't like boring colours.
4 _____ likes clothes for the office.
5 _____ doesn't like feeling hot.

3 Work in pairs. What is your opinion of fashion? Do you follow fashion, or do you like to be comfortable?

Vocabulary | clothes

4 a Read the text again and find the opposites of these words.

smart – scruffy

1 thin _____   4 dark _____
2 cold _____   5 unfashionable _____
3 loose _____   6 man-made _____

b Find these words and phrases in the text and match them with the meanings.

1 cotton   a a soft expensive material
2 wool   b material made from a plant
3 leather   c material from animal hair
4 silk   d material from animal skin

Grammar | position of adjectives

5 a Look at the sentences from the text and answer the questions.

She looks lovely.
Danny is young.
Here she's wearing a beautiful silk sari.
He's wearing smart brown trousers.

1 Which adjectives describe facts?
2 Which adjectives describe the writer's opinion?

b Now complete the rules in the Active grammar box.

> ### Active grammar
>
> We usually put adjectives *after/before* nouns.
>
> When we have two adjectives before a noun we put opinions *after/before* facts.
>
> We put adjectives *after/before* the verbs *be* and *look*.

see Reference page 87

6 Use words from the box to write labels for the pictures.

> beautiful   ~~black~~   ~~boots~~   brown   cotton   dress
> expensive   ~~old~~   scruffy   shoes   Swiss   watch

old black boots

7 Put the words in the correct order to make sentences.

designer expensive I are think clothes
I think designer clothes are expensive.

1 dress she's a silk wearing beautiful
2 looks that smart suit
3 expensive clothes second-hand aren't
4 love my wool pullover comfortable I
5 jeans fantastic look your
6 always Mario cotton T-shirts wears nice

8 Work in pairs. Describe what another student in your class is wearing. Use four or five adjectives. Your partner guesses who you are describing.

X is wearing blue jeans, a smart white T-shirt and ...

Speaking

9 a What kind of dresser are you? Work in pairs. Interview your partner to complete the questionnaire.

What kind of dresser are you?

A How often do you ...
1 wear jeans?
2 wear a suit?
3 wear trainers?
4 buy clothes on the Internet?

B Put these in order of importance, 1–5.
I wear clothes ...
   to be comfortable.
   to be fashionable.
   to be like my friends.
   to make me look slimmer/taller, etc.
   to be warm/cool because of the weather.

C What do you usually wear ...
1 at home?
2 at the weekend?
3 to work?
4 to interviews?
5 to visit your relatives?
6 in hot weather?

b Tell the class about your partner's answers. What kind of dresser is your partner, do you think?

Grammar	Present Simple and Present Continuous
Can do	talk about the weather

Vocabulary | the weather

1 Match the symbols with the weather descriptions.

1 It's foggy. *E*   5 It's snowing. ☐
2 It's warm. ☐   6 It's cold. ☐
3 It's sunny. ☐   7 It's raining. ☐
4 It's windy. ☐   8 It's cloudy. ☐

2 **a** 🔊 2.14 Listen to some people talking about the weather in their countries. Underline the weather words in exercise 1 that you hear.

b Listen again and complete the summaries.

Scotland In the south it's quite (1) _____ and sunny, but in the north there's still (2) _____ on the mountains.

Canada It's not that warm. It's 15 (3) _____ and really (4) _____ today.

Norway It's late (5) _____ and today it's warm and (6) _____ .

Brazil This morning it was really (7) _____ and sunny but now it's (8) _____ .

c What's the weather like in your country today?

Pronunciation | /ɒ/ and /əʊ/

3 **a** 🔊 2.15 Listen to these words. Is the vowel sound the same in all four?

cold   hot   foggy   snowing

b 🔊 2.16 Listen to these word pairs. Are the vowel sounds the same or different?

1 cold   gold   3 snow   hot
2 top   told   4 not   lot

c 🔊 2.17 Listen. Is the sound /ɒ/ (not) or /əʊ/ (cold)?

see Pronunciation bank page 147

Reading

4 Work with a partner and discuss the questions.

1 What's happening in the photos?
2 Which cities are they?
3 What time of year is it?
4 Is the weather usually like this in these cities?

5 **a** Read the text quickly and match it with one of the photos.

Extreme Weather

Many people say the climate is changing. It certainly seems that there are more extremes of weather these days. There are several examples of unusually hot and cold conditions in Europe from the last few years.

Recently there was an extreme summer heat wave in Greece. Temperatures in Athens reached 46° Celsius and fifteen people died because of the heat. There were power cuts because so many people turned on their air conditioners. As a result, thousands of people spent the evenings in complete darkness.

The south of Britain usually has a mild winter, but last year it was extremely cold. It snowed in London and the temperature remained below zero for several weeks, so the snow didn't melt. Because of the snow and ice the buses and trains stopped, so a lot of people didn't get to work.

b Read the text again and answer the questions.

1 How hot was Athens recently?

2 Why was it dark in the evenings?

3 How long was the temperature below 0°C in London?

4 Why didn't some people get to work?

6 Find the words (1–6) in the text and match them with their meanings (a–f).

1 mild   **a** change from solid to liquid

2 heat wave   **b** when there is no electricity

3 heat   **c** machines that make the air cold

4 power cuts   **d** a short period of very hot weather

5 air conditioners   **e** the noun from 'hot'

6 melt   **f** not extreme, not very hot or cold

7 Look at the Lifelong learning box. Read the tip and complete the exercise.

Nouns and adjectives

Lifelong learning

! You can often work out the meaning of a word from its parts, e.g. *darkness* is the noun from *dark*. A lot of nouns from adjectives end in *-ness*.

Which adjectives do these nouns come from?

1 tiredness   4 sickness

2 happiness   5 baldness

3 fitness   6 craziness

Grammar | Present Simple/Present Continuous

8 **a** 🔊 2.18 Listen to a phone conversation. Why isn't Luke working today?

b Listen again. Are the statements true or false?

1 Luke is phoning Jan from his office.

2 In London, lots of people are staying at home today.

3 It hardly ever snows in New York.

4 It's raining in London.

5 Jan hates rain.

c Work in pairs and discuss the questions.

1 Jan says she likes snow. Why?

2 Do you like winter weather? What's the weather like in your country in winter?

3 Do you think the weather is changing?

9 **a** Look at these extracts from the conversation. Underline the verbs in the Present Continuous and circle the verbs in the Present Simple.

The underground isn't working today.

It snows all through the winter in New York.

The trains and buses aren't running.

You always phone in the evenings.

b Complete the rules in the Active grammar box.

Active grammar

1 Use this tense for actions happening now. _____

2 Use this tense for actions that happen often, every year, etc.

_____

---

see Reference page 87

10 Choose the correct form of the verbs in the sentences.

1 At the moment it *rains/is raining*.

2 We never *take/are taking* the bus to work.

3 I always *carry/am carrying* my umbrella in winter.

4 It's hot so Kevin *doesn't wear/isn't wearing* a coat today.

5 We *study/are studying* a new tense in the English class.

6 My parents *don't drink/aren't drinking* coffee after 6:00 p.m.

11 **a** Write what the people usually do and what they are doing today.

1 Peter – drive/sunbathe

Peter usually drives a bus. Today he's sunbathing.

2 Laura – walk to work/drive her new car

3 Sally – clean the house/play football

4 Anna – wear jeans/wear a dress

b In pairs, check your answers. Ask and answer questions about the pictures.

A: *Is Laura walking to work today?*

B: *No, she isn't. She's driving her new car.*

Can do | describe problems and ask for solutions

(A)

(B)

(C)

(D)

(E)

(F)

1 **a** Which pictures are ...

1 in a hotel? 2 in a shop? 3 at home?

b Match the phrases with pictures A–F.

	picture
It isn't working.	☐
It doesn't fit.	A
a receipt	☐
a refund	☐
to repair something	☐
an exchange	☐

2 🔘 2.19 Listen to three dialogues and match them with the pictures. Write 1, 2 or 3 next to the correct pictures.

3 **a** Listen again and complete the How to... box.

How to... describe problems and ask for solutions

Ask for help	Excuse me. (1) _____ you help me?
Explain the situation	I (2) _____ this yesterday. It's very (3) _____ in here.
Explain the problem	There's a (4) _____ with the air conditioning. It (5) _____ fit. It (6) _____ working.
Ask for a solution	Can I (7) _____ it? I'd (8) _____ a refund. Can you send somebody to (9) _____ it?

b Read audioscript 2.19 on page 156 and check your answers.

c In pairs, use the audioscript to practise the dialogues.

4 Work in pairs.

Student A: turn to page 131.

Student B: look at the information below.

Student B

Roleplay 1

You bought an Ace Technology C100 computer at Computer Central in Danby Street, Dublin yesterday. You paid €1,250. But the screen is broken and the computer isn't working. You want to exchange it for another one.

Roleplay 2

You are a shop assistant. Your shop doesn't give refunds, but you can exchange things.

Roleplay 3

You are staying at an expensive hotel. It's the middle of winter and it's very cold. There is central heating in your room but it isn't working. Phone reception and ask for somebody to repair it.

Roleplay 4

You work for Anglo Airlines. There are some seats on Sunday's flight to Athens. They cost €250 each. You can give refunds or use the refund as part of the cost of a new ticket.

Present Continuous

We make the Present Continuous with a present form of the verb *to be* and the *-ing* form of the main verb.

⊕	I	'm (am)	staying at home today.
	He/She/It	's (is)	
	We/You/They	're (are)	
⊖	I	'm not (am not)	staying at home today.
	He/She/It	isn't (is not)	
	We/You/They	aren't (are not)	
❓	Am	I	staying at home today?
	Is	he/she/it	
	Are	we/you/they	
	Yes,	I am. he/she/it is. we/you/they are.	No,	I'm not. he/she/it isn't. we/you/they aren't.

The main verb in the Present Continuous is in the *-ing* form. Make this form by adding *-ing* to the base form of the verb, but note:

With verbs that end in *-e*, remove *-e* and add *-ing*.

dance → *danc**ing***

With verbs of one syllable that end in one short vowel + consonant, repeat the consonant and add *-ing*.

clap → *clap**ping***

Use the Present Continuous to describe actions that are happening now, at the moment of speaking:

***I'm looking for** your hat right now.*

Present Simple and Present Continuous

We use the Present Simple to talk about routines: what we do every day/year, and to talk about facts.

We use adverbs and expressions of frequency with the Present Simple.

*We always **have** a pizza on Friday evenings.*

We use the Present Continuous to talk about actions happening now, at or around the moment of speaking.

We use phrases like *at the moment* and *right now* with the Present Continuous.

*We're **having** our pizza now so we can't talk to you at the moment.*

Position of adjectives

We put adjectives in front of nouns.

a young man   ~~a man young~~

Adjectives are the same for singular and plural nouns.

*a **young** man   two **young** men*

We can use more than one adjective in front of a noun. When we do this we put opinion adjectives (e.g. *beautiful, expensive, nice*) before fact adjectives (e.g. *silk, Swiss*).

*a **beautiful silk** dress*

*an **expensive Swiss** watch*

We use adjectives after the verbs *be* and *look*.

*That watch is **expensive**.*   ~~That watch expensive is.~~

*Her jacket looks **lovely**.*   ~~Her jacket lovely looks.~~

Key vocabulary

Clothes

boots   coat   dress   gloves   hat   jacket   jeans   pullover   sandals   scarf   shirt   shoes   shorts   skirt   suit   sunglasses   tie   trainers   trousers   T-shirt

Materials

cotton   leather   silk   wool
natural/man-made materials

Clothes adjectives

casual   comfortable   dark   fashionable   formal   heavy   informal   light   loose   scruffy   smart   thick   thin   tight   warm

Weather

Good weather:

It's sunny.   It's hot.   It's warm.   It's cool.

Bad weather:

It's raining.   It's snowing.   It's cold.   It's cloudy.   It's windy.   It's foggy.

heat   heat wave   mild

 Listen to these words.

ACTIVE BOOK

---

 see Writing bank page 142

8 Review and practice

1 **a** Write the -*ing* form of these verbs.

come   coming

1	clap _____	7	study _____
2	make _____	8	swim _____
3	plan _____	9	use _____
4	read _____	10	wait _____
5	ride _____	11	write _____
6	sit _____	12	carry _____

b Complete Sandra's email to her friend with verbs from exercise 1a in the Present Continuous.

To: Geena
Cc:
Subject: Thanks!

Hi Geena
Thanks for your email. I'm sitting in Luigi's café with my laptop at the moment. Do you remember Luigi's? We had a really good meal here in March. I (1) _____ this email from here because I (2) _____ for Jacob. He's at college at the moment; he (3) _____ art. He (4) _____ a computer in his art classes and he really enjoys it – he (5) _____ some amazing pictures on the computer. There's a travel guide to Canada on the table – do you know why? I (6) _____ it because Jacob and I (7) _____ a visit to Canada! Really! We want to...

2 Write questions and answers.

sun/shine ✗ (rain)

Is the sun shining? No, the sun isn't shining. It's raining.

1 you/read/good book ✓
2 you/study German ✗ (English)
3 she/cook dinner ✗ (prepare tomorrow's lunch)
4 he/work at home today ✓
5 they/play tennis ✗ (basketball)

3 Each sentence has a mistake. Find the mistake and correct it.

lovely red
Emily's wearing a ~~red lovely~~ dress today.

1 The new James Bond film exciting looks.
2 I bought a leather fashionable jacket yesterday.
3 The weather very hot is today.
4 You awful look in those old jeans.
5 Our teacher is a middle-aged friendly woman.
6 I gave my girlfriend a red beautiful scarf.

4 Read the paragraph. Then write sentences in the Present Simple or the Present Continuous.

Amélie is a computer programmer. She works in a big, formal office. She has one hour for lunch. Today is her office summer excursion – every year they take their clients out for the day and buy them a big lunch. Today they are at a football match.

use/computer
Amélie usually uses a computer.
take/photos/match
She's taking photos of the football match today.

1 wear/formal business suit
2 wear/jeans and a T-shirt
3 talk/to people in the office
4 talk/to clients at the match
5 have/sandwich for lunch in the office
6 have/big meal in a restaurant

5 Complete the sentences with suitable clothes.

I wear shorts and a T-shirt when it's sunny.

1 I wear _____ when it's snowing.
2 I wear _____ when it's raining.
3 I wear _____ for a country walk.
4 I wear _____ when I go to parties.
5 I wear _____ when I go to work.
6 I wear _____ for formal meetings.

6 Describe the weather in the photos.

It's spring. It's ...

Lead-in

1 **a** Put the letters in the correct order. Then match the art forms to the photos.

1 S C I U M _____ ☐   3 R E T H E A T _____ ☐
2 M I L F _____ ☐   4 A N I G N I P T _____ ☐

b Look at the words and phrases in the box. In pairs, name one example of each.

> ballet   cartoon   classical music   comedy   dance   horror   literature
> modern art   novels   opera   painting   plays   poetry   rock music

2 **a** Copy the word map and add the words and phrases from the box in exercise 1. Then compare your answers with a partner.

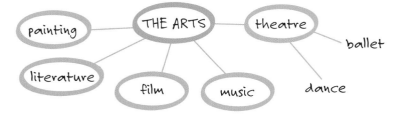

b 🔊 2.20 Listen to Ailsa and Amber doing exercise 2a. Do you agree with their decisions?

c Add more words to your word map if you can.

3 Work in groups. Discuss the questions. What or who is your favourite ...

• film?   • book?   • play?   • opera or ballet?   • classical composer?   • poem?
• painting?   • group or singer?

Reading

1 Work in pairs and discuss the questions.

1 What's in the news today?

2 How do you usually get the news?

2 **a** Match the photos (1–5) with the names of the news sources in the table.

	fast	easy	detailed	exciting	cheap	convenient
Newspapers			✓			
The radio						
The TV						
The Internet						
Mobile phone						

b Read the text quickly. Which news sources do the people like?

Fuad likes newspapers and ...

c Read the text again and tick (✓) the correct adjectives in the table in exercise 2a.

Vocabulary | news sources

3 **a** Complete the phrases with verbs from the box.

> go   listen to   read
> read   use   watch

1 _____ a blog

2 _____ a news programme

3 _____ newspapers

4 _____ online

5 _____ the radio

6 _____ Twitter

b Work in pairs and discuss the questions.

1 Do you read (or write) a blog?

2 How often do you go online?

3 Do you use Twitter?

Is the Internet today's news source?

- **37 percent of Americans regularly go online for news, especially when the news is important: 70 percent used the Internet during the last presidential election.**

- **34 percent read a newspaper or listen to the radio.**

- **29 percent watch a daily news programme on TV.**

Are you surprised? Why is Internet news so popular? Have your say here.

It isn't the same in my country – we don't all have computers, so we read newspapers or listen to the radio. I think they're great – newspapers are detailed and give you a lot of information, and the radio is convenient – you can listen to it while you're driving, in bed, even in the bath. They're easy ways to get news – <u>easier than</u> using a computer, and of course they're cheaper than computers!

Fuad

I believe the Internet is taking away TV's audience. In my opinion, the Internet is <u>better than</u> TV because it's <u>faster</u>, and it's quite detailed. You can go online to look at news stories or read a blog. TV is better than the Internet for some things, I agree, and I watch a news programme every day. TV is <u>more exciting than</u> some other news sources because it's visual. I think TV news feels <u>more realistic than</u> newspapers or radio news for that reason.

Katie

No – this is all wrong! TV, newspapers, computers ... they're all old-fashioned. I get my news on my mobile phone – the main news stories, sports news, film news. I also use Twitter a lot – that's how I found out about that plane crash on the Hudson River, before the TV or Internet had the story! Mobiles are really fast now, and convenient, because I have my phone with me all the time.

Magnus

Grammar | comparison of adjectives

4 Look at the underlined words in the text and complete the Active grammar box.

Active grammar

Adjective	Comparative	
fast	faster	than
easy	_____	than
realistic	_____	than
exciting	_____	than
good	_____	than
bad	worse	than

Write comparative adjectives next to the rules.

1 Add *-er* to adjectives with one syllable only: *faster*
2 With adjectives that end in *-y*, remove the *-y* and add *-ier*: _____
3 With longer adjectives, we use *more* before the adjective: _____
4 Some adjectives have irregular comparatives: _____

---

see Reference page 97

Pronunciation | /ə/ in comparatives

5 a ● 2.21 Listen to these phrases and underline the syllables with /ə/. Listen again and repeat.

1 eas*ier* <u>than</u>   3 colder than
2 faster than   4 healthier than

b Write sentences comparing these things. Then read your sentences to a partner. Do you agree with each other?

1 Iceland/Egypt/cold   3 fruit/chocolate/healthy
2 maths/English/easy   4 a Ferrari/a Fiat/fast

see Pronunciation bank page 148

6 Make sentences using the comparative form of these adjectives: *good, useful, exciting, interesting, modern.* Give your own opinion.

Newspapers Mobile phones	are		
The radio The TV The Internet	is	*more exciting*	than ...

The TV is more exciting than newspapers.

Listening and speaking

7 a ● 2.22 Listen to Nick and Petra talking about news. Who thinks the following? Write N (Nick) or P (Petra).

1 The number of Americans using the Internet is amazing. ☐
2 The same number of people use the Internet for news in the UK and the US. ☐
3 Younger people use the Internet. ☐
4 Newspapers are better than other news sources. ☐

b Listen again and complete the sentences in the How to... box. Use audioscript 2.22 on page 156 to help you.

How to... give your opinion

Ask for an opinion	*What do you think of ... ?* *Do you (1) _____ (that) ... ?*
Give a positive opinion	*I (2) _____ (that) .../* *I (3) _____ (that) ...* *I find it/that (amazing)!*
Give a negative opinion	*I (4) _____ think (that) ...* *I don't (5) _____ it (surprising).*
Use an 'opinion' phrase	*In (6) _____ opinion, (it's better) ...*

---

8 In pairs, talk about the topics in 1–4 below. Give your opinion and ask your partner's opinion. Use adjectives from the box to make comparisons.

> bad   cheap   exciting   expensive   fast   good   interesting   lively   modern   noisy   popular   relaxing

1 entertainment: TV, cinema, theatre, concerts
2 music: pop, classical, rock, opera
3 sports: football, tennis, motor racing, athletics
4 books: novels, poetry, plays, history books

A: *What do you think of rock music?*
B: *I don't like it. I think it's noisy. I like classical music because it's more relaxing than rock music.*
A: *Really? I don't think so. In my opinion, rock music is more exciting.*

Vocabulary | films

1 **a** Match the films in the photos with the types of film in the box.

> an action/adventure film   a cartoon
> a comedy   a documentary
> a horror film   a love story   a musical
> a science fiction film   a thriller

A = _____ B = _____ C = _____ D = _____

b Think of one film of each type in the box.

The Indiana Jones films are action films.

c Which of the types of film are/can be ...

• sad? • exciting? • violent? • clever?
• funny? • scary? • romantic?
• happy? • interesting?

2 What types of films do you like/not like? Why? Use the adjectives in exercise 1c and others.

I don't like horror films because they're usually scary and violent.

Listening

3 **a** 🔘 2.23 Listen to an interview and match the films with the opinions.

> An Inconvenient Truth ☐   Casino Royale ☐   Chicago ☐
> Little Miss Sunshine ☐   No Country for Old Men ☐
> Slumdog Millionaire ☐   The Lives of Others ☐

1 the best film in the last ten years
2 the most exciting film
3 the biggest surprise
4 the best foreign film
5 the most violent film
6 the funniest film
7 the freshest musical for a long time

b Listen again and correct the mistakes about the films.

1 A lot of people think the *Harry Potter* series were the best films.
2 In Mariela's opinion, *Casino Royale* has the best photography.
3 *An Inconvenient Truth* is a thriller.
4 Javier Bardem played a good man in *No Country for Old Men*.
5 Mariela loves musicals.

c Match the words with their meaning.

1	bad guy/villain	a	a famous prize in the film world
2	Oscar	b	the person an actor plays in a film
3	scene	c	a person who talks or writes about films
4	character	d	part of a film or play
5	film critic	e	an unpleasant or violent person in a film

4 Do you know the films Mariela talked about? What do you think of them?

Grammar | superlative adjectives

5 a Look at this sentence. Choose the best ending, 1, 2 or 3.

It was the best film in the last ten years.

It was ...

1 better than some of the other films.
2 better than all of the other films.
3 worse than all of the other films.

b Complete the table in the Active grammar box with superlative adjectives from exercise 3a. Then choose the correct words in *italics*.

Active grammar

Adjective	Superlative
bad	the *worst*
big	the *biggest*
exciting	the _____
fresh	the _____
funny	the _____
good	the _____
violent	the _____

To make the superlative, we add *-est*/*-er* to one-syllable adjectives and we put *more*/*most* before longer adjectives.

---

see Reference page 97

6 a Complete these sentences with superlatives.

Harrison Ford is ____ (exciting) film star.
Harrison Ford is *the most exciting* film star.

1 Owen Wilson is ____ (funny) actor.
2 Johnny Depp is ____ (scary) actor these days.
3 Meryl Streep is ____ (good) actress.
4 Brad Pitt is ____ (handsome) star.
5 Angelina Jolie is ____ (beautiful) actress.
6 Tom Hanks is ____ (romantic) actor.

b Change the sentences to give your opinion.

I think that Daniel Craig is the most exciting film star.

Reading and speaking

7 Work in groups of three. Read some facts about films. Then ask and answer questions to complete this table.

longest film	
most expensive film	
earliest film with sound	
most successful cartoon	
richest film star	
youngest Oscar winner	
most romantic love story	
scariest horror film	
worst villain in a film	

Student A: read the text on page 131.
Student B: read the text on page 132.
Student C: read the text below.

A: *What's the longest film?*
B: *It's The Cure for Insomnia. It's 87 hours long!*

Movie madness

The youngest Oscar winner is Tatum O'Neal. She won the Oscar for her part in *Paper Moon*, a film from 1973. In the film, she played opposite her real father, Ryan O'Neal. She didn't win the Oscar for Best Actor, but the one for Best Supporting Actor.

Obviously, different people find different types of film scary, but many people agree that the scariest film is *Psycho*, by Alfred Hitchcock, from 1960. A young actress called Janet Leigh played the main character – this was the first film where the main character died only a short way into the film!

Cartoons are always popular. The most successful cartoon ever was *Shrek 2*. It made $129 million in its first five days! Before that, the most successful cartoon was *Finding Nemo*.

8 Work in pairs and discuss these questions.

1 How many films in exercise 7 do you know?
2 What do you think is ...
- the best film ever?
- the most exciting action film?
- the most romantic love story?
- the funniest comedy?
- the scariest horror film?
- the most boring film?

Art or Vandalism?

In the year 2000 strange paintings appeared on the sides of buildings in Bristol and London. These weren't drawings by bored teenagers; they were funny and very artistic. But who was the artist? Nobody knew.

Over the next few years more and more of these amazing pictures appeared. Usually, people hate graffiti: they think it is ugly and unattractive, just a form of vandalism. And of course it's illegal. But this work was different. Some of the paintings were funny, some were frightening, but they were always interesting and original.

Some people said the artist was called 'Banksy'. But who was Banksy? It became a huge mystery and several newspapers tried to find out Banksy's real identity. It was fantastic publicity for the artist and his work became famous in America and Australia. In 2007 a gallery in London sold one of his wall paintings for $576,000. In 2009 Bristol City Art Gallery organised an exhibition of his work. More than 300,000 visitors came to the exhibition. But nobody knew Banksy's real name, not even the manager of the gallery. Of course, some people think it is shocking that paintings on the sides of buildings can be 'art'. But these days almost anything is art!

Reading

1 Look at the photos. What can you see? Which of these things do you think is art?

2 **a** Read the article quickly and match it with one of the photos.

b Read the text again and decide if these statements are true (T) or false (F).

1 Banksy did his first wall painting in 2007. ☐
2 His paintings are sometimes scary. ☐
3 People can't buy Banksy's paintings. ☐
4 Nobody knows Banksy's real name. ☐
5 Everybody agrees that Banksy's work is art. ☐

c Find the words in the text and match them with their meanings.

1	graffiti	a	show where you can see paintings
2	vandalism	b	pictures and words on walls
3	illegal	c	bad, very surprising
4	original	d	damaging buildings or other things
5	exhibition	e	new, different from other things
6	shocking	f	not allowed

3 Look at the photos and discuss the questions.

1 Do you think Banksy's paintings are art or vandalism? Why?
2 The text says these days almost anything is art. Do you agree? Can you think of any examples?
3 Art is part of our culture. What other things do you think are part of popular culture?

Listening

4 **a** ⬤ 2.24 Listen to Jenny and Serge. Match two of the photos with their conversation.

b Listen again and write J (Jenny) or S (Serge). Who …

1 doesn't like going to exhibitions?
2 prefers traditional paintings to modern ones?
3 hates listening to kids singing?
4 loves *Pop Star Search*?
5 prefers watching films?

Pronunciation | *yes/no* questions

5 **a** ⬤ 2.25 Listen to the questions from Jenny and Serge's conversation. Does the voice go up (⤴) or down (⤵) at the end?

1 Is it expensive?   2 Is he famous?

b ⬤ 2.26 Listen and write (⤴) or (⤵), then repeat.

1 Is it nice?   4 It's boring.
2 It's lovely.   5 Are we late?
3 Is it interesting?   6 Does she know?

c Make questions. Practise them in pairs.

it/expensive   *Is it expensive?*
he/know   *Does he know?*

1 it/cheap   3 she/smoke
2 it/new   4 they/work

see Pronunciation bank page 148

Grammar | *like/love/hate/prefer*

6 Look at the answers to exercise 4b. Tick (✓) the correct statements in the Active grammar box. Then choose the correct option to complete the examples.

Active grammar

1 After *like/love/hate/prefer* we can use:
a a noun. ☐
b the infinitive of a verb without *to* (e.g. *buy*). ☐
c the *-ing* form (e.g. *buying*). ☐
We don't like go/going to art galleries.
'Do you prefer pop music to rap music?'
'No, I prefer listening/listen to rap music.'

2 We use *prefer* for something we like:
a more than another thing. ☐
b the same as another thing. ☐
I prefer classical music than/to pop.

see Reference page 97

7 **a** What do you like? In pairs, ask and answer questions.

1 go/museums?
2 listen/rap music?
3 watch/TV talent shows?
4 go/modern art exhibitions?
5 watch/TV documentaries?

A: *Do you like going to museums?*
B: *No, I don't. I hate going to museums.*

b Which do you prefer? Ask and answer questions.

1 go to restaurants/eat at home?
2 watch DVDs/go to the cinema?
3 read books/listen to music?

A: *Do you prefer going to restaurants to eating at home?*
B: *No, I prefer eating at home.*

c Look at audioscript 2.24 on page 156 and complete the How to… box.

How to… talk about preferences

Say what you like or dislike	I (1) _____ his work. ☺ I (2) _____ listening to those stupid kids singing. ☹
Say you like one thing more than another thing	I (3) _____ traditional paintings to modern ones. I (4) _____ watching films or documentaries. I like serious programmes (5) _____ than talent shows.
Ask someone their opinion	*Do you like … ?* *What do you think about … ?*

Speaking

8 **a** Work in pairs or groups and discuss the questions.

1 Do you prefer modern or traditional art?
2 Do you like these things or not?
• watching the news   • going to operas
• reading magazines   • listening to jazz
3 Look at the photos in exercise 1. Which ones do you prefer? Why?

I like … more than … because … .

b Talk to your classmates and find out how many students prefer:

1 visiting museums to going to concerts.
2 watching films to watching documentaries.
3 romantic films to action films.
4 modern art to traditional art.

Do you prefer visiting museums to going to concerts?

Can do | make and respond to suggestions

1 **a** What do you usually do on Saturdays? Make a list with a partner.

b 🔊 2.27 Listen to these friends and tick (✓) the things they talk about in the boxes in column 1. What do they decide to do?

	1	2
go to a football match	☐	☐
go bowling	☐	☐
go to the cinema	☐	☐
see a band	☐	☐
have dinner	☐	☐
go shopping	☐	☐

c What order do they talk about the things in? Number the boxes you ticked in column 2.

2 Listen again and complete the How to... box. Use audioscript 2.27 on page 157 to help you.

How to... make and respond to suggestions

Make suggestions	*What shall we do at the weekend?*
	How about going (1) _____ ?
	What about (2) _____ for dinner?
	Why (3) _____ we _____ and watch that?
Respond to suggestions	*That's a (4) _____ _____ !*
	That sounds (5) _____ !
	I don't (6) _____ so.
	I (7) _____ really like Thai food.
Decide what to do	*Let's (8) _____ at the station.*

3 **a** Look at the list of places to spend an evening with a friend. Match four of them with the adverts.

a the theatre   f the cinema
b a smart restaurant   g a nightclub
c a shopping centre   h a rock concert
d the bowling alley   i a football match
e a classical concert   j an opera

b Work in pairs and make suggestions.

A: *How about going to the nightclub?*
B: *I don't think so. I'm very tired.*

4 **a** Which activities from exercise 3a do you prefer? Rank them in order 1–10 (1 is your favourite).

b In pairs, compare your lists. Ask about your partner's list and explain your preferences.

My number 1 is 'a classical concert' because I prefer classical music to other types of music.

5 Work in groups to organise an evening out.

1 Ask about your classmates' preferences and find something you all like.
2 Talk about the things you can do in your area and make suggestions for tomorrow evening.
3 Agree a plan for your evening and arrange a time and place to meet.

Comparison of adjectives

We use comparative adjectives to compare two or more things.

We use *than* to introduce the second noun in a comparative sentence.

*This book is **more interesting than** his first book.*

*This house is **bigger than** my old house.*

*The blue shoes are **more expensive than** the black ones.*

This is how we form comparative adjectives:

Regular one-syllable adjectives	add *-er*	old → old**er** cheap → cheap**er** new → new**er**
Longer adjectives	put *more* before adjective	interesting → **more** interesting comfortable → **more** comfortable
Two-syllable adjectives that end in *-y*	remove *-y* and add *-ier*	funny → funn**ier** busy → bus**ier**
Irregular adjectives	*good* *bad*	*better* *worse*

Superlative adjectives

We use superlative adjectives to compare one thing with all the others in a group.

*This house is **the biggest** in the street.*

*The blue shoes are **the most expensive**.*

We usually use *the* before a superlative:

*This is **the most interesting** book about mountain climbing in the library.*

This is how we form superlative adjectives:

Regular one-syllable adjectives	add *-est*	old → the old**est** new → the new**est**
Longer adjectives	put *most* before adjective	interesting → the **most** interesting comfortable → the **most** comfortable
Two-syllable adjectives that end in *-y*	remove *-y* and add *-iest*	funny → the funn**iest** busy → the bus**iest**
Irregular adjectives	*good* *bad*	*the best* *the worst*

Spelling rules

Add *-r/-st* to adjectives that end in *-e*:

nice → *nicer/nicest*

large → *larger/largest*

With adjectives that end in consonant + *-y*, remove *-y* and add *-ier/-iest*:

busy → *busier/busiest*

heavy → *heavier/heaviest*

With adjectives that end in a short vowel + consonant, repeat the consonant and add *-er/-est*:

thin → *thinner/thinnest*

big → *bigger/biggest*

like/love/hate/prefer

We use *like/love/hate/prefer* with a noun (e.g. *tea, the cinema*) or the *-ing* form of another verb to discuss likes and preferences.

*I **love the theatre** but my friends **prefer going** to the cinema.*

We use *prefer* to talk about something we like more than another thing or things.

She prefers tea (to coffee). = She likes coffee but she really loves tea.

*I **prefer tea** to coffee. I **prefer drinking** tea.*

We use *to*, not *than*, after *prefer*.

*She **prefers** Mozart to Beethoven.*

> ### Key vocabulary
>
> **The arts**
> modern/traditional art   painting
> Performance arts: ballet, classical music, dance, film, opera, rap music, rock music, theatre
> TV: documentary, talent show
> Literature: novel, play, poetry
> exhibition   graffiti
>
> **Films**
> bad guy   character   film critic   Oscar
> scene   villain
> Genres:
> an action/adventure film   a cartoon
> a comedy   a documentary   a horror film
> a love story   a musical
> a science fiction film   a thriller
>
> Listen to these words.
> ACTIVE BOOK

 see Writing bank page 143

1 Complete the paragraph with the comparative form of the adjectives in brackets.

Russell   Alan

Alan and Russell are brothers, but they look different. Alan is *younger* (young) than Russell. He is also (1) _____ (tall) and (2) _____ (handsome) than his brother. Alan is (3) _____ (fit) than Russell. Russell is (4) _____ (fat) than Alan but he is also (5) _____ (happy) than his brother. Alan has (6) _____ (dark) skin than Russell and Russell has (7) _____ (short) hair than his brother.

2 Complete the table with the comparative and superlative forms of the adjectives.

	Adjective	Comparative	Superlative
1	realistic	*more realistic*	*the most realistic*
2	bad		
3	beautiful		
4	busy		
5	dry		
6	fit		
7	good		
8	informal		
9	noisy		
10	private		

3 **a** Match 1–8 with a–h.

1	deep/freshwater lake	a	Kilimanjaro
2	high/mountain in Africa	b	the Great Wall of China
3	large/museum in the world	c	Edvard Grieg
4	old/national flag	d	the Bugatti Veyron
5	big/structure in the world	e	the Hermitage
6	famous/Norwegian composer	f	Lake Baikal
7	scary/film	g	Denmark's
8	expensive/car	h	Psycho

b Write sentences about exercise 3a using superlative adjectives.

Lake Baikal is the deepest freshwater lake.

4 Find the mistakes in each sentence and write the correction.

Lucinda doesn't like tennis, she prefers ~~play~~ golf. *playing*

1 I like the radio but my children prefer to watching television.

2 We love read adventure books.

3 Isabel likes romantic films than science fiction ones.

4 Some people hate live in the country.

5 The bus is very slow so I prefer drive my car to work.

6 I like more playing the guitar than listening to CDs.

7 Dario likes swimming to sunbathing.

8 My husband really likes cook Indian food.

5 What type of art are these items?

Toy Story   *a cartoon*

1 *Hamlet*

2 *The Mona Lisa*

3 *The Four Seasons*

4 *Carmen*

5 *Scream*

6 *Anna Karenina*

7 Tchaikovsky's *Swan Lake*

8 Queen's *Bohemian Rhapsody*

6 Match the speech bubbles with a film genre.

> action film   comedy   horror film
> love story   musical   science fiction

2 I didn't like the end of the film. It was really scary.

1 That was great! I laughed so much!

4 That was so exciting, especially the part where James Bond skis down the mountain.

3 It wasn't very realistic. I mean, little green men ...

6 I liked the story but I thought the songs were awful.

5 It was very sad when the man left the woman ...

Lead-in

1 Match the words with their meanings.

1	commuting	a	full of people
2	suburbs	b	travelling to work every day
3	park	c	the busiest time of day
4	rush hour	d	leave a car somewhere
5	crowded	e	places around a city where people live

2 Match the photos with the captions.

1 A businessman travelling to a meeting. ☐
2 Rush hour traffic in Jakarta. ☐
3 Cycling to the office. ☐
4 Commuting from the suburbs into Tokyo. ☐

3 Find these forms of transport in the photos.

> bicycle   bus   car   motorbike   plane   underground train

4 Put the words from the box into the correct column(s).

> ~~airport~~   car   drive   flight   garage   journey   park   passenger
> plane   platform   station   ticket   traffic   train

Air	Rail	Road
airport		

5 Do you travel to work/college by car, by bus, by train or on foot?

A

Vocabulary | transport

1 **a** Match the forms of transport (1–6) with the famous places (a–f). Which of the forms of transport can you see in the photos?

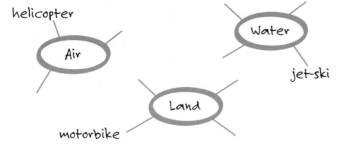

1	bicycles	a	Tokyo
2	yellow taxis	b	London
3	water buses	c	San Francisco
4	high speed trains	d	Amsterdam
5	electric trams	e	Venice
6	red buses	f	New York

b How many transport words can you add to the word maps?

helicopter

Air

Water

jet-ski

Land

motorbike

Reading and listening

2 Look at photos A and D. What's happening? What time of day does this usually happen?

3 **a** Read the text quickly and match two of the photos to it.

b Read the text again and complete the table for Fatima and Jan.

Name	Fatima	Jan	Julia	Billy
Photo				
City				
Form of transport			rollerblading	
Advantages	quick, convenient			
Disadvantages		slow, horrible when it rains		

4 🔘 2.28 Listen to Julia and Billy and complete the table.

City Profiles

This week we look at commuters around the world ...

Fatima da Costa lives in Patriarca, a suburb in the east of São Paulo, Brazil. She works in the centre of the city, near Praça da República. Every day Fatima takes an underground train to work in the morning and back home in the evening. She thinks travelling on the São Paulo underground system – the Metro – is quick and convenient. But the trains are very crowded in the rush hour and she often can't find a seat.

Jan van Looy works in the main train station in Amsterdam. He works for the Dutch Railways but he doesn't catch a train to work. He cycles from his home in the suburb of Sloterdijk. Cycling is very popular in Amsterdam because the city is flat and the distances are not very great. Jan cycles to work because it's very cheap, but it's quite slow and it's horrible when it rains!

D

Speaking

5 Work in groups and discuss the questions. Give your own opinions.

1 Which form of transport is …
- the safest?
- the most convenient?
- the most expensive?
- the most comfortable?
- the cheapest?
- the fastest?

2 How do you get around your town/city?

3 Which form of commuting do you think is best? Why?

Grammar | *-ing* form as noun

6 Look at the examples of the *-ing* form in the Active grammar box. Then find two more examples in the text. Choose the correct words to complete the sentences in the box.

Active grammar

Rollerblading is a bit dangerous when you cross busy roads.

Commuting is really difficult in London.

1 Swimming *is/are* my favourite sport.

2 *Parking/Park* isn't easy in the centre of big cities.

see Reference page 107

7 Choose the correct words in *italics*.

1 *Park/Parking* is impossible in central London.

2 *Bicycles/Cycling* are very popular in Amsterdam.

3 Walking *is/are* good for your health.

4 *Taxis/Taking taxis* are expensive.

5 Waiting for buses *are/is* boring.

Listening

8 a 🔊 2.29 Brendan wants to take his friends for a short break. Listen and answer the questions.

1 Which city does Brendan want to go to?

2 When does he want to leave?

3 How much do the tickets cost?

4 How much does it cost to take a bicycle on the train?

b Match the words (1–7) with their meanings (a–g).

1	destination	a	go and come back
2	one-way	b	more comfortable but expensive seats
3	return	c	the place you want to go to
4	standard class	d	when you leave
5	first class	e	no stops on the journey
6	departure	f	go, but don't come back
7	direct	g	the cheapest seats

c Complete the How to… box. Then check your answers with audioscript 2.29 on page 157.

How to… book a train ticket

Make enquiries	Do you sell (1) _____ for Eurostar trains?
Give details	We (2) _____ to come back three days later.
Ask for more information	What (3) _____ does the train leave London? Is it a (4) _____ train?
Ask about prices	How (5) _____ is that?
Ask for tickets	I'd (6) _____ four tickets, please.

9 Complete the dialogue.

A: Do you sell train (1) _____ for Spain? I'd (2) _____ to go to Barcelona on Wednesday the 12th.

B: One-way or (3) _____ ?

A: One-way. And I'd like to go first (4) _____ .

B: OK. We have a train leaving at 11:30.

A: (5) _____ much is that?

B: It's €200.

A: Is it a (6) _____ train?

B: No, it stops in Lyons.

10 Work in pairs.

Student A: you are a travel agent. Turn to page 131.

Student B: you want to book a train ticket. Look at this information then telephone the travel agent.

You want to travel from New York to Washington DC with a friend. You want to leave next Wednesday and return two weeks later. You can afford a maximum of $500.

Phone the travel agent, get information about trains, dates and prices, then book your tickets.

10.2 Experiences

Grammar	Present Perfect with *been: I/you/we/they*
Can do	describe personal experiences

Reading and listening

1 a Read the text and match the TV programmes with the photos.

19:10 The Countryside Today

Horse-riding and hiking are outdoor activities that many people enjoy. They are healthy and relaxing ways for people to enjoy the countryside – walking is certainly an excellent way to get fit. But for farmers they can have negative results. Today's episode looks at the way horses and hikers can damage fields and farms.

19:30 The Holiday Show

Australia and New Zealand are now popular destinations for travellers from all over the world. This week Jason Morris joins a group of young British students for an action/adventure holiday in Australia. After a long-haul flight of 22 hours they are ready for the experience of a lifetime.

20:25 Extreme Sports Challenge

In today's episode the young presenters Liam and Terri go bungee jumping for the first time. Liam loves extreme challenges but there's a serious problem – Terri is afraid of heights! Can she do the bungee jump or not? Watch tonight's episode and find out.

b Which is the most exciting activity in the photos, do you think?

2 a 🔊 2.30 Listen to an extract from one of the programmes. Which programme is it?

b Read the extract from the TV programme. Is the plane journey Derek's first long-haul flight?

Derek: I haven't been on a long-haul flight before.

c Listen again. Tick (✓) the things the students have done before.

Moira	visit Australia	☐	long-haul flight	☐
Derek	hiking	☐	bungee jumping	☐
Todd	horse-riding	☐	visit Australia	☐
Alicia	bungee jumping	☐	visit America	☐

Grammar | Present Perfect with *been*: I/you/we/they

3 **a** Read the extracts from the TV programme and answer the questions.

a *I haven't been on a long-haul flight before.*

b *Have you been to Australia?*

c *We've all been hiking.*

d *We went horse-riding when we were in Scotland two years ago.*

1 Which extract refers to a particular time in the past? When?

2 Which extracts do not refer to a particular time in the past?

3 Which verb form do we use when we do not refer to a particular time in the past?

b Look at audioscript 2.30 on page 157 and complete the Active grammar box. Then choose the correct words to complete the rules.

Active grammar

+ subject + *'ve* (or *have*) + past participle
We've _____ to America.

− subject + *haven't* (or *have not*) + past participle
We _____ _____ bungee jumping.

? *Have* + subject + past participle
Have _____ _____ to Australia?

Yes, I/we/you/they have.
No, I/we/you/they _____ .

1 We use the Present Perfect to talk about an activity at *any time up to now/a particular time in the past*.

2 *been* is a *past tense/past participle*.

---

see Reference page 107

4 **a** Complete the questions and answers.

1 **A:** Have you _____ to New York?
   B: Yes, I _____ .

2 **A:** _____ your friends been to New Zealand?
   B: No, they _____ .

3 **A:** _____ you been to Canada?
   B: Yes, we _____ last summer, it was great!

b Find the mistakes and correct them using the Present Perfect.

Have you ~~go~~ to England? *been*

1 I wasn't been bungee jumping before.

2 They not have been to Scotland.

3 Have you went to a classical concert?

4 We didn't been on an adventure holiday before.

5 I have been not to Brazil.

6 Did they been hiking before?

Pronunciation | /ɪ/

5 **a** 2.31 Listen to this extract from the TV programme. Are the vowel sounds in the underlined words /ɪ/ (b<u>i</u>g) or /iː/ (gr<u>ee</u>n)?

1 Have you <u>been</u> to Australia?

2 No, we haven't <u>been</u> to Australia before.

b 2.32 There are four /ɪ/ sounds in each of these sentences. Listen and <u>underline</u> the sounds. Practise the sentences.

1 Have you been to the cinema in England?

2 I've been to a disco with him.

3 Have they been to dinner in Finland?

4 We haven't been to Paris in spring.

see Pronunciation bank page 148

6 Write questions about the photos in exercise 1. Then ask and answer them with a partner.

Have you been bungee jumping?

Speaking

7 Work in groups of three.

Student A: look at page 131.
Student B: look at page 134.
Student C: Ask your partners questions with *Have you been to ... ?* If they answer *Yes*, find out when and where they did the activity, and if they liked it. Check any words you don't know in a dictionary before you begin.

Have you been to ...

• an IMAX cinema?
• a bullfight?
• a rock concert?
• a wedding?
• a theme park?
• a circus?

A: *Have you been to an IMAX cinema?*

B: *Yes, I have. I went last week.*

A: *Did you like it?*

103

Vocabulary | activities

1 **a** Which of the activities in the box can you see in the photos?

> climbing Kilimanjaro
> crossing the Sahara
> flying a small aircraft
> flying in a hot-air balloon
> rowing across the Atlantic
> sailing around the world
> walking to the South Pole

b Match the verbs (1–5) with a–e.

1 climb   a a boat, across the lake
2 cross   b a plane, a helicopter, a kite
3 fly   c a hill, a mountain, a tree
4 row   d a boat, a ship, across the ocean
5 sail   e a river, a desert, an ocean

c Have you done any of the things in exercise 1b? What? When did you do it?

Listening

2 2.33 Listen to part of a TV chat show. What is an adventurer?

3 **a** Listen again. Which of these things <u>hasn't</u> Ben Fogle done?

1 cycled across Europe
2 made long solo flights in a small aircraft
3 walked to the South Pole
4 climbed a mountain
5 sailed around the world

b Listen again and complete the chart with details about Ben Fogle's adventures.

Adventure	When?	How long?	How far?
Antarctic	2009	17 days	500+ km
Atlantic			
Sahara			
Monaco			
Kilimanjaro			

Grammar | Present Perfect: *he/she/it*

4 Match the questions (1–4) with the answers (a–d).

1 I've *heard* of Jessica Watson. What's she *done*? ☐
2 What has James Cracknell *done*? ☐
3 What has Ben Fogle *done*? ☐
4 Has he *climbed* a mountain? ☐

a He's *won* two Olympic gold medals but he's also *rowed* across the Atlantic.
b Yes, he has.
c He's *crossed* the Antarctic, he's *cycled* across Europe, he's *walked* and *run* across the Sahara ...
d She's *sailed* around the world.

5 Look at the past participles in *italics* in exercise 4 and complete the chart in the Active grammar box. Then choose the correct words to complete the sentences.

Active grammar

Regular verbs		Irregular verbs	
Infinitive	Past participle	Infinitive	Past participle
climb	*climbed*	*take*	*taken*
row	_____	*do*	_____
cycle	_____	*win*	_____
walk	_____	*run*	_____
sail	_____	*hear*	_____

1 In the Present Perfect, we use *have/has* + past participle with *he*, *she* and *it*.
(We use *have/has* + past participle with *I*, *you*, *we* and *they*.)

2 *Regular/Irregular* past participles have the same form as the regular Past Simple.

see Reference page 107 and Irregular verbs list, page 149

6 Complete the text with the Present Perfect of the verbs in brackets. Find the past participles in the Irregular verbs list on page 149.

Mike Perham is an ordinary young man. He (1) **has been** (be) skiing, he (2) _____ (climb) hills and mountains, and he (3) _____ (leave) school. But in one way Mike is different from most people – he (4) _____ (live) his dream! Mike (5) _____ (cross) the Atlantic in a small boat – solo (but his father followed him) – and he (6) _____ (sail) solo around the world, too. He was 17 when he did that, but Jessica Watson did the same thing at only 16. Also, Mike (7) _____ (write) a book about his experiences at sea.

Now he wants to compete in the next Olympics.

7 a Make Present Perfect sentences.

Jake/run/in a lot of races

Jake has run in a lot of races.

1 Lucinda/not leave/school
2 Kathy/win/a competition
3 Sanjeev/visit/an African country
4 Piotr/not stay/in a five-star hotel

b Ask and answer questions with a partner. Use the prompts in exercise 7a.

A: *Have you run in any races?*

B: *No, I haven't./Yes, I have. I ran in races at school.*

Pronunciation | long and short vowels

8 a ● 2.34 Listen to these long and short vowels, then repeat the words.

Long	Short
/ɑː/ parked	/æ/ had
/ɔː/ walked	/ɒ/ got
/iː/ seen	/ɪ/ written

b ● 2.35 Listen. <u>Underline</u> the word you hear.

1	have	half	4	park	pack
2	feet	fit	5	bald	bad
3	short	shop	6	sleep	slip

see Pronunciation bank page 147

Listening and speaking

9 a ● 2.36 Listen to some people talking about their experiences. Note the past participle they use, and complete their experiences.

1 *met* a famous *person*
2 ____ in a five-____ hotel
3 ____ in a hot-air ____
4 ____ insects
5 ____ an unusual ____

b In pairs, discuss your experiences, and the experiences of your family/friends. Use some of the verbs from the box.

buy   do   drive   eat   fly   go   learn
meet   play   read   see   stay   travel   visit

A: *Have you met a famous person?*

B: *Yes, I've met a famous film star.*

A: *Really? Who did you meet? I haven't met any film stars, but my friend has met Roger Federer – she met him at a tennis match.*

1 Match the directions with the diagrams.

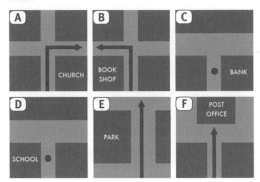

1 Turn left at the bookshop.
2 Go straight on to the post office.
3 The bank is on the right.
4 Turn right at the church.
5 Go along the road next to the park.
6 The school is on the left.

2 **a** Look at the picture. Are the statements true or false? If the statements are false, correct them.

1 The café is on the left.
2 The post office is on the right.
3 The supermarket is on the left.
4 The bus stop is at the end of the road.
5 The motorbike is on the right.
6 The cinema is on the left.

b What else can you see in the picture? Where is it/he/she?

3 **a** ◉ 2.37 Listen to Robin talking to a woman in the street. Answer the questions.
1 What has happened?
2 What does he want to do?
3 Does the woman help him? Why/Why not?

b Listen again and follow the directions on the map. Write the letters of these places.
1 post office ___
2 bookshop ___
3 police station ___

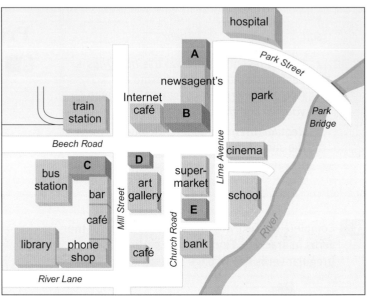

c Listen again and complete the expressions in the How to... box. Check your answers with audioscript 2.37 on page 158.

> ### How to... ask for and give directions
>
> | Ask for directions | : | *Can you tell me the way to the bank?* |
> | | | *(Excuse me,) do you (1) _____ the way to the police station?* |
> | | | *Is there a police station near here?* |
> | Give directions | : | (2) _____ *left at the bookshop.* |
> | | | *Turn right (3) _____ Beech Road.* |
> | | | *Go (4) _____ on for about 200 metres.* |
> | | | *Go (5) _____ the road. It's on the left/right.* |
> | | | *It's at the (6) _____ of the street.* |

4 Work in pairs. Give your partner some directions.
Student A: turn to page 132.
Student B: turn to page 134.

-ing form as noun

We sometimes use the *-ing* form of a verb as the subject of a sentence.

Parking *is really difficult in Madrid.*

We use singular verbs with *-ing* verb subjects.

Flying *is expensive.*

Present Perfect

We form the Present Perfect with *has/have* + the past participle, e.g. *been*.

	I/You/We/They	He/She/It
➕	've (have) + past participle	's (has) + past participle
➖	haven't (have not) + past participle	hasn't (has not) + past participle
❓	Have + I/we/you/they + past participle	Has + he/she/it + past participle
	Yes, I/we/you/they have. No, I/we/you/they haven't.	Yes, he/she/it has. No, he/she/it hasn't.

Have you been *to New Zealand?*

*I've **climbed** a mountain but I **haven't run** a marathon.*

*She's **flown** in a hot-air balloon.*

We usually use the contracted forms, but in formal writing we use the full forms.

The past participle of regular verbs is the same as the regular Past Simple form.

Infinitive	Past Simple	Past participle
play	played	played
arrive	arrived	arrived

But there are a lot of irregular past participles. Some of them are the same as the Past Simple form.

Infinitive	Past Simple	Past participle
buy	bought	bought
have	had	had

But many of them are different from the Past Simple form.

Infinitive	Past Simple	Past participle
see	saw	seen
take	took	taken

Note that the past participle *been* is the past participle of both *be* and *go*.

It's a nice day. → *It's **been** a nice day.*

*I **go** shopping on Saturdays.* → *I **haven't been** shopping this week.*

For more irregular verbs, look at page 149.

We use the Present Perfect to talk about actions and experiences in the past when:

• we are talking about any time up to now.

Have you been to Cuba?

• we don't say a definite time.

We've met the President.

We don't use the Present Perfect with a specific past time. We use the Past Simple.

*I **didn't have** a holiday last year.*

*We **saw** her yesterday.*

We use the Present Perfect to talk about a past experience for the first time.

*We've **been** to Florida ...*

But when we give more information, we use the Past Simple.

*We **went** to Miami two years ago.*

Key vocabulary

Travel and transport

Travel

commuting   crowded   cycling departure   destination   journey one-way/return ticket   passenger rollerblading   rush hour   traffic

Road

bicycle   bus   car   to drive (electric) tram   garage   motorbike to park   taxi

Rail

book a ticket   direct first class/standard class   platform station   ticket   (high speed) train underground train (metro)

Water

boat   jet ski   water bus

Air

aircraft   airport   (long-haul) flight plane

Activities

bullfight   bungee jumping   circus crossing (the desert)   flying go on a camel/cruise   hiking horse-riding   hot-air balloon ice-skating   (rock/mountain) climbing rock concert   rowing   sailing skateboarding   walking

 Listen to these words.

ACTIVE BOOK

 see Writing bank page 144

1 Complete the sentences with the correct form of a verb from the box.

> commute   drive   ~~fly~~   go   pay   swim   take

Flying in first class is very expensive.

1 _____ by credit card is very convenient.
2 _____ is a good way to get fit.
3 _____ to the cinema is my favourite activity.
4 _____ a fast car is very exciting.
5 _____ photos is the best part of a holiday.
6 _____ takes a long time in big cities.

2 Put the words in the correct order to make sentences.

been to China Have you ?
Have you been to China?

1 haven't a long-haul I flight been on
2 adventure holiday you been Have on an ?
3 to We've New York and Boston been
4 horse-riding in been She's Scotland
5 bungee jumping they in New Zealand Have been ?

3 Find four more mistakes in the Past Simple/Present Perfect in this dialogue, and correct them.

Liz: Have you been skiing?
Sue: No, I ~~didn't~~. *haven't*
Liz: It's fantastic.
Sue: When did you go?
Liz: We've been last winter.
Sue: And where did you go?
Liz: Switzerland.
Sue: I haven't went to Switzerland. Was it nice?
Liz: Yes, it was beautiful.
Sue: Was it cold?
Liz: Yes, we've been in January so it was very cold.
Sue: Did you been there in the summer?
Liz: No, I haven't.

4 Some of the past participles in these sentences are wrong. Tick (✓) the correct sentences.
Cross (✗) the incorrect ones and write the correct past participle.

Have you visited the wax museum? ✓ _____
Jonathan has saw a very good film. ✗ *seen*
1 I've runned a marathon. ☐ _____
2 We haven't bought a new car. ☐ _____
3 Has she writed a book? ☐ _____
4 She hasn't play volleyball. ☐ _____
5 They haven't seen an opera. ☐ _____
6 Sue has meet the president. ☐ _____

5 Max and Lorena have made a list of some of the things they have/haven't done in their lives. Study the list then complete the sentences.

	Max	Lorena
see the Taj Mahal	✓	✓
stay in a five-star hotel	✓	✗
go bungee jumping	✗	✓
win the lottery	✗	✗
visit New York	✓	✓
drive a Ferrari	✗	✓
do a university degree	✓	✗
climb a mountain	✓	✓

1 Max and Lorena _____ the Taj Mahal.
2 Max _____ in a five-star hotel but Lorena hasn't.
3 Max _____ bungee jumping.
4 They _____ the lottery.
5 They _____ New York.
6 Lorena _____ a Ferrari sports car.
7 She _____ a university degree.
8 Both Max and Lorena _____ a mountain.

6 Complete each sentence with a travel word.

1 It doesn't stop. It's a _____ flight.
2 Excuse me. Can I have a _____ ticket? I want to come back tomorrow.
3 I prefer travelling in first _____ because the seats are more comfortable.
4 Trains to Edinburgh leave from _____ 10.
5 In London the _____ is between 7:00–9:00 in the morning and 4:00–6:00 in the evening.
6 A Boeing 747 can take more than 300 _____ .

7 Match the activities (1–5) with the places/times (a–e).

1 go to a bullfight
2 go ice-skating
3 go to a rock concert
4 go mountain climbing
5 go hiking

a in the Alps
b in Spain
c in the countryside
d on a lake in winter
e in the evening

11

Lead-in

1 Look at the photos. What are the four learning situations? Which ones have you been in?

2 **a** Which photo (A–D) does each instruction come from?

1	Drive on the left. ☐	5	Put your hands up. ☐
2	Look at the music. ☐	6	Don't go so fast. ☐
3	Follow my movements. ☐	7	Don't shout out the answers. ☐
4	Now start to play. ☐	8	Don't go over the speed limit. ☐

b Work in pairs and discuss the questions.

1 What were the rules when you were at school? Did you usually obey them?

2 What was the punishment when you broke the rules?

3 **a** Match three of the school subjects with the definitions.

> biology chemistry geography history languages literature
> maths physics science

1 the study of the past   3 the study of heat, light, movement, etc.

2 the study of living things

b Do you know all the others? Check their meanings with a partner.

c Can you think of any more subjects?

4 🔊 2.38 Listen and write the number of syllables for each subject in the box in exercise 3a. Which one has the most syllables? Listen again and check your answers.

bi–o–lo–gy = four

Reading

1 Work with a partner and discuss the questions.

1 Do you drive? Do you enjoy driving?
2 Do you always obey the rules of the road?
3 What happens when people break traffic rules in your country?
- fines?
- prison?
- points on their licence?

2 **a** Read the text quickly. Which country is it about?

b Read the text again and find …

1 three traffic offences
2 three punishments
3 two ways to do a driver improvement course
4 what happens at the end of the course

c Do you think Traffic School is a good idea? Do you become a better driver after a course like this? Does this happen in your country?

Grammar | *can/can't, have to/don't have to*

3 **a** Look at the text again and complete the notes.

Points on your driving licence
- In some countries, after you get a certain number of points on your driving licence, you _____ drive.
- But in some countries you have a choice – you _____ get points or you _____ do a driver improvement course.

Driver improvement courses
- At the end of the course you _____ pass an exam, but you _____ take a driving test.

b Complete the Active grammar box by matching 1–4 with a–d.

> ### Active grammar
>
> | 1 *can* | a necessary |
> | 2 *can't* | b not possible |
> | 3 *has/have to* | c not necessary |
> | 4 *doesn't/don't have to* | d possible |

see Reference page 117

Traffic School

Have you ever driven faster than the speed limit, parked in the wrong place or driven through a red traffic light? The answer is probably 'yes'. Every year thousands of motorists become 'offenders' – they break the rules of the road. But what are the punishments for this offence?

In most countries drivers have to pay a fine, usually $100–$300. But in the USA, Australia and some European countries offenders also get points on their driving licence. After they get a certain number of points, they can't drive.

Life is difficult when you can't drive so some states in the USA have introduced a new way to avoid this – Traffic School. Offenders have a choice, they can get points on their licence or they can do a course at Traffic School.

Traffic Schools run 'driver improvement courses'. They cost about $100 and take from four to twelve hours. Most people do the course in a classroom, but in some states drivers can do the course online. Motorists learn the rules of the road and they learn how to be better drivers. They don't have to take a driving test, but at the end of the course they have to pass a written examination.

4 Look at the road signs. Write the rules with *can*, *can't* or *have to*. Use the words and phrases in the box.

> buy petrol   enter   give way   go   go faster than
> overtake   park   ~~stop~~   turn left   ~~turn right~~

1 *You have to stop.*   2 *You can't turn right.*

1   2   3

4   5   6   7

8   9   10

5 **a** 🔊 2.39 Listen to some tourist information. What information is <u>not</u> mentioned?

1 public transport   3 driving   5 hotels
2 immigration   4 flights   6 museums

b 🔊 2.40 Listen to the second part of the tourist information line and complete the leaflet with *can*, *can't*, *have to* or *don't have to*.

DRIVING REGULATIONS IN BRITAIN

Visitors to Britain with a valid driving licence
○ *can* drive in Britain without a British licence for six months.
○ _____ get a British driving licence after six months.

To rent a car, you
○ _____ have a driving licence from your country.
○ _____ have a credit card.
○ _____ be eighteen or over.

When driving in Britain, you
○ _____ keep your documents with you.
○ _____ turn right at a red traffic light.

c Find words with these meanings in the leaflet above.

1 important papers   2 rules   3 officially correct

6 Sami comes from Egypt. He wants to rent a car to drive when he is on holiday in Britain. Write four sentences using *has/have to*, *doesn't/don't have to*, *can* and *can't*.

Sami has to have an Egyptian driving licence.

Pronunciation | /f/ and /v/

7 **a** 🔊 2.41 Listen. Do the <u>underlined</u> words sound the same?

You don't <u>have to</u> be a British citizen to take a British driving test but you <u>have</u> to <u>have</u> a valid British visa.

b 🔊 2.42 Listen. <u>Underline</u> the word you hear. Then repeat.

1 leave   leaf   3 fan   van
2 few   view   4 V   we

c 🔊 2.43 Listen and practise.

1 Philip finds French films very violent.
2 Very few fines feel fair.
3 Fiona Philips never gives fitness advice to fresh fruit fanatics.

see Pronunciation bank page 147

Listening and speaking

8 **a** You are going to hear Steve talking about laws in the USA. Before you listen, look at the prompts in exercise 8b and guess what he says.

b 🔊 2.44 Listen and write sentences from the prompts.

Americans/do/military service
Americans don't have to do military service.

1 Americans/have/identity cards
2 They/drive/when/sixteen
3 They/buy/guns/when/twenty-one
4 Americans/get married/when/eighteen
5 They/have/a bank account/when/eighteen
6 Americans/be twenty-one/go into/bars
7 They/smoke/offices, shops or restaurants
8 Americans/pay/when/go to hospital

9 **a** In pairs, ask and answer questions.

In your country, what do you have to do to …
• get a passport?   • rent a car?
• get a place at university?   • get a credit card?
• open a bank account?   • get a mobile phone?

b Compare the rules in the US with your country. Do you agree with the rules or not?

In my country you have to do military service when you are eighteen.

Listening

1 Did you enjoy your schooldays? (Or are you enjoying them now?) Why/Why not?

2 a 🔵 2.45 Listen to the conversation. Tick (✓) the things the people talk about.

number of years at school ☐
name of secondary school ☐
friends at school ☐
favourite subject ☐
age of leaving school ☐

Sarah

Harumi

Andreas

Ross

b Match the school paths with the people in the photos.

1 high school, teacher training college, sport
2 primary school, secondary school, work
3 gymnasium, university, law
4 elementary school, high school, university

c Listen again and answer the questions.

1 How long was Harumi at school?
2 When can you leave school in New Zealand?
3 What kind of school did Andreas go to?
4 What new technology did Ross use at school?

Vocabulary | schools and subjects

3 a Write the words and phrases from the conversation in these groups.

1 types of school: *primary school, ...*
2 types of higher education: *university, ...*
3 subjects: *sport, ...*

b Can you add any more words to the groups?

Grammar | review of *wh-* questions

4 a Match 1–5 to a–e to complete the questions.

1 Where   a was your favourite subject?
2 What   b did you leave school?
3 How long   c of new technology did you use?
4 When   d did you go to school?
5 Which kinds   e did you spend at school?

b Match the question words with the words and phrases in the box.

How? *the way something works*

How long? Which? Where? Whose? What? Why? When? How much? How many? Who?

> a choice between two (or more) things
> numbers and quantity   people   periods of time
> places   possession   prices or cost   reason
> ~~the way something works~~   things and ideas   times

see Reference page 117

Pronunciation | intonation of *wh-* questions

5 a 🔵 2.46 Listen to the questions from exercise 4a. Does the voice go up (⤴) or down (⤵) at the end?

b 🔵 2.47 What about this question?

Did you leave school at eighteen?

c Now listen again and repeat the questions in exercise 5a.

6 a Make questions for these answers. Choose a suitable *wh-* word.

1 I started studying English six months ago.
2 I live in the centre of the city.
3 I haven't got any pets.
4 My best friend is Sonya – I work with her.

b In pairs, ask and answer the questions.

see Pronunciation bank page 148

Speaking

7 Write five *wh-* questions to ask about a person's education. Ask and answer in groups.

A: *Where did you go to primary school?*

B: *When did you leave secondary school?*

C: *What did you study at university?*

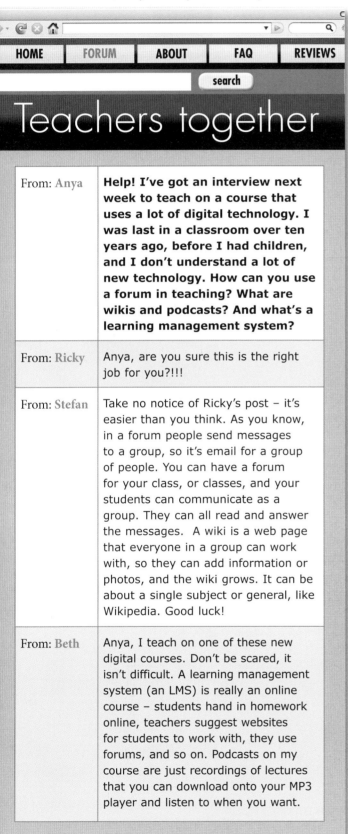

Reading

8 **a** Look at the posts on the teachers' message board. What is their main topic?

1 They're discussing new technology in different jobs.

2 They're exchanging ideas for lessons.

3 They're giving helpful information to a teacher.

b Read the posts again. Are the statements true (T) or false (F)?

1 Anya can use all new technology. ☐

2 She wants to study on a new course. ☐

3 Stefan explains all the new words for Anya. ☐

4 Stefan and Beth give Anya useful information. ☐

c Do the statements describe Anya (A), Ricky (R), Stefan (S) or Beth (B)?

1 He/She works with new technology. ☐

2 He/She isn't very helpful. ☐

3 He/She asks for help. ☐

4 He/She writes about another person's message. ☐

5 He/She gives Anya a well-known example. ☐

Vocabulary | new technology

9 Complete the sentences with words from the box.

> download forum LMS online podcasts ~~posts~~ wiki

There were several *posts* on the forum in answer to my question.

1 I often _____ music from iTunes onto my iPod.

2 Taking a test _____ is great – you get your marks immediately.

3 Our class has a really good _____ on the Internet. We often discuss problems on it.

4 My Spanish class has an online _____ . We use it as a dictionary – we all add words and definitions to it.

5 For this course we use an _____ . The students do most of their work online.

6 The BBC has a really good list of _____ that you can download. You don't have to pay for some of them.

Speaking

10 Work in groups and discuss the questions.

1 Have you ever studied a subject using new technology? Did you enjoy it?

2 Do you use any of the new technology in the text? What do you think of it?

Reading and listening

1 What do you think 'Lifelong learning' is? Where can you go to study after school/university in your country?

2 **a** Match the adverts (A–D) on the right with the types of learning (1–4).

1 distance learning ☐ 3 professional training ☐
2 language school ☐ 4 education for older people ☐

b 🔊 2.48 Listen to four people talking. Write 1–4 next to the adverts in the order the speakers talk about them.

3 Listen again and complete the table.

	Bexley Green College	Open University	MicroMatters Ltd	University of the Third Age
Where do you study?	at the college/at a local university			
How much does it cost?		about £600 a year		
How much time does it take?			two or three days	
Examples of subjects				

Vocabulary | education

4 **a** Find words or phrases in the box to match the definitions (1–5).

> academic   course   distance learning   evening classes   full-time
> lecturer   part-time   professional   student   trainee   trainer
> tutor   well-qualified

1 an adjective to describe work/study that is more than sixteen hours a week
2 a teacher in higher education
3 someone who is learning a particular job
4 a type of teaching and learning which is not classroom-based
5 an adjective to describe work/study of only a few hours a week

b Put some of the words into categories. In pairs, compare your categories.

learners: student ...   teachers: trainer ...

c In pairs, add more words to the categories.

Speaking

5 Work in groups and discuss the questions.

1 Do you have all these types of learning in your country?
2 Have you ever tried/Would you like to try any of them?
3 Do you think that studying part-time is a good idea? Why/Why not?
4 Do you want to study any other subjects in the future? What? When?

(A) ☐

U3A

UNIVERSITY OF THE THIRD AGE
Lifelong learning for retired or older people

(B) ☐

micromatters Ltd

Computer training specialists
Improve your computing skills on
courses from one day to four weeks
All computing skills

(C) ☐

BEXLEYGREEN
Language and Business College

*Do you want to learn another language
or improve your business skills?*

We have classes week days and evenings
in six different languages and a range of
business topics.

(D) ☐

The Open University

• study part-time in your own home
• improve your career prospects
• gain new skills and confidence
• study for pleasure

Listening

6 **a** 🔊 2.49 Listen to a phone call and answer the questions.

1 Which college from exercise 2 is the caller phoning?
2 Where is the caller phoning from?
3 What's her problem?
4 Do they solve her problem at the end? If so, how?

b Listen again and complete the application form.

Online application for courses

Name: _____
Email: n.kop23@freemail.ru
Nationality: _____
Course choice:
_____
_____
_____

Course start date: _____

Payment:
Cash (in person only) ☐
Cheque ☐
Credit card ☐
Bank transfer ☐

I accept the college terms and conditions ☐

Click here to read conditions

Send

Grammar | the imperative

7 **a** Complete the sentences from the phone call. Listen again if necessary.

1 _____ on 'apply now'. 3 No, _____ do that!
2 Now _____ the start date.

b Match the columns in the Active grammar box. Then choose the correct words in *italics*.

Active grammar

With the imperative, we use …

1 the infinitive verb ⎱ for ⎰ a negative instruction
2 *Don't* + infinitive ⎰   ⎱ a positive instruction

We *usually use/don't usually use* the pronoun *you* before an imperative verb.

see Reference page 117

8 **a** Match signs 1–3 with the instructions (a–c).

a Don't bring your dog in here.
b Wear a hard hat.
c Don't smoke.

b Now write instructions for signs 4–6.

9 Work in pairs. Write instructions for a drinks machine. Use the symbols and the notes to help you.

1 put/cup/machine
   Put the cup into the machine.
2 choose
3 pay/correct
4 not/notes
5 press/button/take/drink

Windham Catering College

- Learn to cook delicious Italian food!
- Courses in Italian cookery
- Twelve weeks starting September, January or April.
- Wednesday evenings at
- Windham College, Fairfield Road, Windham
- Enrol from 27 August
- Price: £225.00 per twelve-week course

1 Look at the advert for a cookery course. Work in groups and discuss the questions.

1 Have you ever done a cookery course?

2 Have you done a course at a local college? What did you study?

3 Do you enjoy learning new skills?

2 a 🌐 2.50 Listen to Peter. He's phoning the college about the cookery course. Tick (✓) five things he asks about or checks.

start date ☐	ingredients ☐
tutor ☐	location of college ☐
times of lessons ☐	price ☐
size of class ☐	

b Listen again and make notes about the answers to his questions.

3 a Complete the sentences from the conversation.

1 *Let me* _____ – you send the form to me?

2 _____ *I just check* the date it starts?

3 *Can you* _____ *that, please?* A break in ...

4 It's on a Wednesday evening. *Is that* _____ ?

5 *Can I* _____ what time the lessons start?

6 _____ , *what was* _____ ?

b Check your answers with audioscript 2.50 on page 159.

c Now write the parts of the sentences in *italics* in exercise 3a in the correct places in the How to... box.

How to... check information and ask for repetition

Checking information	: _____
	: _____
	: _____
	: _____
Asking for repetition	: _____
	: _____

4 Work in pairs to enrol for a course.

Student A: look at the information on page 132.

Student B: look at the information below.

Student B

Roleplay 1

You want to enrol for a scuba diving course. You have this information:

Keith's Scuba School

Courses in scuba diving every weekend at Grenville Lake. Twelve hours over two days, lunch included.
Price: **from £400**
Call 07896 112435 for more details.

You want to find out ...

- When does the course start?
- Is it one weekend or more?
- Do they take beginners?

You want to check ...

- the exact price
- the exact times over the weekend

Remember to check information and ask for repetition.

Roleplay 2

You work at a horse-riding school. Answer Student A's questions, using the information below.

- Lessons are usually two hours and they can be weekday mornings or any time on Saturday.
- A beginner has to have at least six lessons before they can go on rides outside the school.
- There are special lessons for beginners every Saturday morning at 10:00.
- Beginners' lessons are £50 for two hours – that includes an hour of one-to-one teaching, then an hour's ride with the tutor.
- It costs £5 to hire a hard hat for two hours.

You start the phone call:

Hello, Grant's Stables and School. Can I help you?

can/can't

We use *can* to say that something is possible or to give permission.

*Hotel guests **can** use the health club.*

We use *can't* to say that something isn't possible or isn't allowed. We often use *can't* to explain rules.

*You **can't** drive through a red traffic light.*

We use *can* to ask about rules or ask for permission.

***Can** we take photographs in the museum?*

*Excuse me. **Can** I use your telephone?*

have to/don't have to

	I/You/We/They	He/She/It
⊕	have to	has to
⊖	don't have to	doesn't have to
❓	Do ... have to?	Does ... have to?

We use *have to* to say that something is necessary. We use it to explain rules.

*In Britain you **have to** drive on the left.*

*My brother **has to** do military service.*

We use *don't have to* to say that something isn't necessary.

*It's informal – you **don't have to** wear smart clothes.*

*She's a member of the club so she **doesn't have to** pay.*

Note the difference between *can't* and *don't have to*.

*You **don't have to** wear a suit.* (It isn't necessary, but you can wear one if you want to.)

*You **can't** wear jeans here.* (It isn't allowed.)

We can use *have to* to ask about rules.

*Do I **have to** get a visa?*

Wh- questions

The common *wh-* question words in English are *what, who, when, where, how, which, whose* and *why*.

We form a lot of questions with *How* + adjective/adverb: *how much, how many, how long, how tall.*

We usually answer these questions with a number, price, quantity, etc.

***How much** was your car? It was 3,000 euros.*

Note the answers to *How long/tall/heavy/wide*, etc.

*How tall are you? I'm 1.8 metres **tall**.*

*How high is Mount Everest? It's about 8,850 metres **high**.*

In *wh-* questions, the verb *to be* and modal verbs (e.g. *can*) come after the question word but before the subject.

*Where **is** your new apartment?*

*Who **can** you see?*

In all tenses the auxiliary verb usually comes before the subject.

*When **is** Tim coming home?*

*Who **did** you see at the party?*

The imperative

We use imperatives to give instructions to people. The positive imperative is the infinitive of the verb, without *to*:

***Stand** up!*

***Come** here, please.*

***Leave** the shopping on the kitchen table.*

The negative imperative is *Don't* + infinitive without *to*:

***Don't do** that!*

***Don't tell** Jake that I'm here.*

***Don't arrive** before nine o'clock.*

We don't often use a subject pronoun with the imperative because it can sound quite rude:

~~*You come here!*~~

It is incorrect to use a subject pronoun with a negative imperative:

~~*You don't do that!*~~

Key vocabulary

Education

School subjects

biology chemistry economics English
geography history languages law literature
mathematics (maths) physics politics science
sport

Institutions

language school primary school/elementary school
secondary school/high school
(teacher training) college university

Types of learning

distance learning evening classes full-time
part-time training

People

lecturer student trainee trainer tutor

Driving

(buy) petrol driving licence driving test give way
overtake park traffic lights

Digital technology

academic course download forum
interactive whiteboard
learning management system (LMS) online
podcast post professional well-qualified wiki

 Listen to these words.

ACTIVE BOOK

 see Writing bank page 145

11 Review and practice

1 Complete the rules using *have to/don't have to*, *can* or *can't* and the phrases in the box.

> be a hotel guest   find a restaurant here
> park here   show your passport

1  You _____ .

2  You _____ .

3 You _____ .

4 **PASSPORT CONTROL** You _____ .

2 Mike has made these notes about the rules in his new office. Complete the sentences with *has to*, *doesn't have to*, *can* or *can't*.

Office rules
Hours are from 9 a.m. to 5:30 p.m.
But OK to go home at 4 p.m. on Wednesdays.
One hour for lunch (but any time between 12 and 3).
No smoking, eating or drinking in the office.
Don't make personal phone calls.
But personal emails from my computer are OK.
Don't use my mobile phone in the office.
Wear a suit and tie, but informal clothes are OK on Fridays.

Mike *has* to start work at nine o'clock.

1 He _____ smoke in the office.
2 He _____ have more than one hour for lunch.
3 He _____ work after 4 p.m. on Wednesdays.
4 If he wants to, he _____ have lunch at two o'clock.
5 Mike _____ wear a suit to work from Monday to Thursday.
6 He _____ make personal phone calls.
7 He _____ use his mobile phone in the office.
8 He _____ wear a suit on Fridays.
9 He _____ send personal emails from his computer.

3 Complete the questions with *wh-* question words. Then match the questions (1–8) with the answers (a–h).

1 *Where* did you go on your last holiday?
2 _____ did you go? Was it in the summer?
3 _____ did you get there? By plane?
4 _____ did you do there?
5 _____ did you stay, one or two weeks?
6 _____ did you go with? Friends from work?
7 _____ did you go there?
8 _____ did it cost?

a We went skiing.
b It was my mother's 60th birthday.
c No, we went in February.
d Three weeks, actually.
e I went to Colorado, in the US.
f It was very expensive!
g Yes, by plane and bus.
h No, I went with a big family group.

4 It is the first day of school for a group of children. Write the instructions the teacher gives them.

not be late   *Don't be late!*

1 be friendly/other children
2 not eat and drink/classroom
3 not run/school buildings
4 not shout
5 stand up/when the teacher comes in

5 Complete the definitions.

1 _____: learning without classes, e.g. on the Internet
2 _____: a person learning a skill, e.g. computing
3 _____: the study of novels, plays, poetry
4 _____: a school for young children
5 _____: working or studying for only a few hours a week
6 _____: the study of numbers

6 Underline the odd one out in each group of words.

professional   distance learning   training

1 languages   mathematics   college
2 tutor   trainee   trainer
3 primary school   high school   elementary school
4 primary school   college   university
5 fine   petrol   points
6 driving licence   park   give way
7 online   forum   sport
8 message board   driving test   wiki

12

Lead-in

1 Write labels for the photos, using one word or phrase from box A and one from box B.

> A   cycling   sailing   trekking   ~~white-water rafting~~

> B   bridge   canyon   ~~river~~   tunnel

Picture A: white-water rafting on a river

2 Work in groups and discuss the questions.

1   Do you know any famous people who do the activities in exercise 1?
2   Do you think any of these activities are dangerous? Why do people do them? Think about these things: excitement, danger, charity, fitness.
3   Make a list of other 'extreme' activities.

3 **a** 🔘 2.51 Listen to Paul and Mia. Which photos do they talk about?

b Listen again and answer the questions.

1   Which activity didn't Mia enjoy?
2   Which activity not in the photos do they talk about?
3   Which was their favourite activity?
4   What is Paul's ambition for next year?

4 Work in pairs. Ask and answer the questions.

1   Have you done any of the activities in exercise 3? Did you enjoy it?
2   Do you want to try any of the activities in the future?
3   Do you have any other ambitions for the future?

No more continents?

For centuries natural barriers such as rivers, mountains and seas have made travel difficult. Now, with modern technology, we are crossing these barriers all over the world.

Britain was an island for 8,000 years. But the Channel Tunnel opened in 1994 and connected Britain to mainland Europe. The Oresund Bridge and Tunnel opened in 2000 and connected Sweden to Denmark and the rest of Europe. Now there are more projects to link different parts of the world. In Europe the Italian government is going to build a 3.3 kilometre-long bridge between Sicily and the Italian mainland. In Asia, Indonesia is going to build the Sunda Strait Bridge between the islands of Java and Sumatra. It's going to have a road and a railway line on it.

But there are bigger projects, to join continents! Spain and Morocco are thinking of building a tunnel connecting Europe to Africa. There is a design for a 38 kilometre railway tunnel between Punta Palomas on the south coast of Spain and Punta Malabata in northern Morocco, near Tangier. And the United States and Russia are discussing a project to connect Alaska to Siberia, joining the continents of North America and Asia.

It's a wide world, but it's certainly getting smaller.

Reading and vocabulary

1 Look at the map and answer the questions.

1 How many continents are there? What are they?

2 How do we travel between continents?

2 **a** Read the text quickly. Is it about …

1 the past and the present?

2 the past, the present and the future?

3 the present and the future?

b Read the text again and match places 1–6 with a–f. Then match the pairs with A–F on the map.

1	Britain	a	the Italian mainland	☐
2	Sicily	b	Denmark	☐
3	Java	c	Sumatra	☐
4	Alaska	d	mainland Europe	*B*
5	Sweden	e	Morocco	☐
6	Spain	f	Siberia	☐

c Work in pairs and discuss the questions.

1 Can you think of any other places that a bridge or tunnel can connect in the future?

2 Do you think connecting continents is a good idea? What are the advantages and disadvantages of this?

3 **a** Look at the words in the box and underline them in the text. In the box, which …

1 three verbs have the same meaning?

2 three words are about geography?

connect   continent   island   join   link   mainland

b Complete the questions about the text with words from the box, then write the answers.

1 When did a tunnel _____ Britain to mainland Europe?

2 What is going to link Java with the _____ of Sumatra?

3 Which _____ is Siberia part of?

c Write three more questions about the text for your partner to answer.

Grammar | *be going to*

4 Look at the sentences and tick (✓) the correct explanation.

They are going to build the Sunda Strait Bridge.
It's going to have a road and railway line on it.

We use *going to* for …

1 intentions (things people plan to do in the future) ☐
2 things happening now ☐

5 Complete the Active grammar box.

Active grammar

	I	*We/You/They*	*He/She/It*
⊕	*'m (am) going to* + infinitive	____ *going to* + infinitive	____ *going to* + infinitive
⊖	*'m (am) not going to* + infinitive	*aren't (are not) going to* + infinitive	*isn't (____) going to* + infinitive
❓	*Am I going to* + infinitive?	____ *we/you/ they going to* + infinitive?	____ *he/she/ it going to* + infinitive

see Reference page 127

6 Write sentences and questions with *be going to*.

Ford/build/a new electric car

Ford is going to build a new electric car.

your company/open/a new office/next year/?

Is your company going to open a new office next year?

1 Britain/not/build/any more airports
2 the Americans/build/a tunnel/?
3 they/open/a new bridge/in 2030
4 I/start/a new course/in September
5 my parents/retire/next year
6 we/not/have/a holiday/next summer

Listening

7 a 🔊 2.52 Listen and answer the questions.

1 What time of year is it?
2 How is Julie going to get to Belgium?

b Listen again and complete the sentences.

1 Julie _____ her grandparents.
2 Julie's grandparents _____ to a small flat.
3 Julie _____ fly there.
4 She _____ the car to the station at Ashford.
5 Omar _____ away this summer.

c What are your plans for your next trip? Where are you going to go and how are you going to get there?

Pronunciation | sentence stress, /ə/

8 a 🔊 2.53 Listen. What do you notice about the pronunciation of *to*?

We're <u>going</u> to take the <u>train</u>.

b 🔊 2.54 Listen and repeat the sentences, then mark the stress.

1 She's going to get fit.
2 They're going to sell their car.
3 We're going to learn French.
4 I'm going to buy a laptop.

see Pronunciation bank page 148

Vocabulary | future time

9 a Listen to the dialogue from exercise 7 again. Tick (✓) the time expressions you hear.

by Saturday ☐
in two years' time ☐
last year ☐
later this year ☐
next summer ☐
next week ☐
next year ☐
the day after tomorrow ☐
the week after next ☐
three years from now ☐
today ☐
tomorrow ☐

b Put the time expressions in the correct order.

1 last year   2 today

c In pairs, ask and answer questions about your intentions using future time expressions.

A: *What are you going to do tomorrow?*

Speaking

10 'Can you find someone who's going to …'

Work in groups of four.

Student A: turn to page 130.
Student B: turn to page 132.
Student C: turn to page 133.
Student D: talk to the students in your group. Ask them questions and find someone who is going to …

1 buy a new mobile phone
2 write a novel before they retire
3 change their job soon
4 have more than three children
5 run a marathon

If you can, find out <u>when</u> they are going to do it.

12.2 Fame and fortune

Grammar	infinitive of purpose; revision of *be going to*
Can do	explain the reasons for your actions/plans

A

Listening

1 **a** How can people become famous? Make a list.

enter a pop star competition

be on a reality TV show

b Work in pairs and discuss the questions.

1 Do you watch talent shows on TV?

2 Do you know any famous winners?

3 Why do people want to become famous, do you think?

4 Would you like to be famous?

2 **a** 🔵 2.55 Listen to the poem and tick (✓) the correct sentence.

The poem says ...

1 fame is great. ☐

2 fame is not really great. ☐

b Read the poem on page 159 (Track 2.55) and check your answer.

c Do you agree with the ideas in the poem?

Pronunciation | rhymes

3 **a** 🔵 2.56 Listen to these lines from the poem again. What happens at the end of each line?

Because when you're a star

Everyone knows who you are,

They know what you do,

But do they really know <u>you</u>?

b 🔵 2.57 Do the words rhyme? Listen and ⟨circle⟩ the odd one out in each line.

1 me being see free tree

2 fly high stay cry my

3 together there never forever clever

4 fame same name game am

5 nice price advice drive rice

4 **a** Work in pairs. Use words from exercise 3b to complete the lines from the song.

Being with you I want to <u>fly</u>,

Don't ever leave me or make me _____ .

Perhaps I'm not very handsome or _____ ,

But we're going to stay together _____ .

When I'm in trouble I call out your _____ ,

Because of you I don't need fortune or _____ .

When you look at me what do you _____ ?

Don't you know your love will set me _____ ?

b Do you have any favourite songs in English? Can you remember any of the lines?

Listening

5 **a** Look at photos A–C. How can these people become famous?

A – He can join a famous club and score lots of goals.

b Match four words or phrases from the box to each photo, A–C. Use a dictionary if necessary.

> acting   ball control skills   drama
> election   football team   perform
> a play   politician   politics
> reserve team   training session   vote

B

C

6 **a** ● 2.58 Listen to three interviews and match them to photos A–C.

b Listen again and choose the correct answer.

1 Victoria is a *university student/TV producer*.

2 Helena is a *politician/student*.

3 Lewis is in the *first team/reserve team*.

c Listen again and write sentences with *be going to*. Then match your sentences with reasons a–c.

1 Victoria ...   2 Helena ...   3 Lewis ...

a to try to get a place in a professional team.

b to try to become a famous performer.

c to learn more about elections.

Grammar | infinitive of purpose

7 Read the sentences in the Active grammar box and tick (✓) the correct answer to the question.

Active grammar

I'm going to practise with them twice a week <u>to improve my physical fitness</u>.

I'm going to work really hard <u>to get into the first team</u>.

What does the <u>underlined</u> phrase do?

1 It explains the purpose or reason for something. ☐

2 It gives more information about the verb. ☐

---

see Reference page 127

8 Put the words in the correct order to make sentences.

parties Julie goes to have to fun

Julie goes to parties to have fun.

1 become Marcie's going lawyer to an exam take to a

2 the Karl to gym goes get to fit

3 magazines My reads to his improve English friend

4 money I play lots lottery to the win of

9 Read the sentences. Are the reasons true for you? If not, change them so they are true for you.

I go on holiday to sunbathe and get tanned.

No, I go on holiday to visit new places.

1 I'm learning English to get a better job.

2 I go to nightclubs to meet new people.

3 I watch television to find out about other countries.

4 I go to work to have fun and relax.

5 I listen to pop music to improve my mind.

Speaking

10 **a** Work in groups. You all want to become rich and famous. What is the best way to do it?

• start an Internet company

• start a pop group

• enter a talent competition

• write a bestselling book

• make a film

• do something really unusual or strange

b Choose one of the ideas. Think about your reasons and plan what you are going to do. Then compare your ideas with other groups.

Reading

1 Read the text quickly and answer the questions.

1 What kind of text is this?
a a news report   c an advert
b a description of a sport
2 Why do people go on this type of expedition?
a to help other people   c to go sightseeing
b to relax

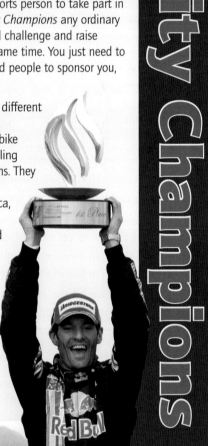

Celebrities like Australian Formula 1 star Mark Webber and pop stars Ronan Keating and Cheryl Cole are well known for taking part in challenging charity events to raise money for people in need.

Stars from the worlds of music, film and sport often go trekking, kayaking and mountain biking to raise money for their favourite charities. But you don't have to be famous or a sports person to take part in a charity event. At *Charity Champions* any ordinary person can take a physical challenge and raise money for charity at the same time. You just need to choose your challenge, find people to sponsor you, and get fit!

There are more than thirty different challenges to choose from, including treks, mountain bike rides, mountain climbs, sailing and horse-riding expeditions. They take place throughout the year in Africa, Latin America, the Caribbean, the Middle East, Asia and Europe, and there are three levels of difficulty, so there really is something for everyone.

Our most popular challenges include trekking on the Inca Trail or along the Great Wall of China, or climbing Mount Kilimanjaro. Visit our website and find your perfect challenge.

Charity Champions

2 **a** Match the words and phrases from the text (1–6) with the correct meanings (a–f).

1 charity   a something difficult for
2 raise money   our bodies
3 physical   b happen
  challenge   c long, often difficult, journey
4 expedition   d give money to someone for
5 take place   completing a charity event
6 sponsor   e organisation that helps people
                  f make money for someone/
                     something

b Read the text again. Are the sentences true (T) or false (F). Correct the false ones.

1 The text describes a beach holiday. ☐
2 The expeditions are all very easy and relaxing. ☐
3 The expeditions take place all over the world. ☐
4 You can find more information on the Internet. ☐
5 People have to climb mountains in a charity challenge. ☐

3 Read some more information about *Charity Champions*. Answer your partner's questions.

Student A: turn to page 132.
Student B: turn to page 134.

Listening

4 **a** 🔊 2.59 David is phoning *Charity Champions*. Listen and number his questions in the order he asks them.

a Do you have to be very fit? ☐
b Where do the challenges take place? ☐
c Who chooses the charity? ☐
d Who pays for the expedition? ☐
e How do I raise money for the expedition? ☐
f What kind of activities are they? ☐

b Work in pairs and answer the questions.

5 Listen again and complete the chart.

David likes/loves ...	He doesn't like ...
hiking	*horses*
David would like/love to ...	He wouldn't like to ...

Grammar | *like* and *would like*

6 Choose the correct forms in the Active grammar box. Then complete the rule with *like* or *would like*. Use exercise 5 to help you.

> **Active grammar**
>
> We use *like* (*love*, etc)/*would like* with nouns and the -ing form of verbs.
>
> We use *like* (*love*, etc)/*would like* with *to* + the infinitive of the verb.
>
> We use _____ to express future desires and ambitions, and we use _____ to express present likes and dislikes.

see Reference page 127

7 Choose the correct form of the verb.

1 Angeles likes *dance/dancing* and she would like *to be/being* a professional dancer.
2 Giorgio doesn't like *learn/learning* English. He'd like *to leave/leaving* his classes.
3 Johann and Bettina would like *to travel/travelling* but Bettina doesn't like *fly/flying*.
4 My father doesn't like *live/living* in the city but he wouldn't like *to leave/leaving* his house.
5 Susanna loves *stay/staying* at home with her children. She wouldn't like *to get/getting* a job.
6 My best friend from Spain would like *to visit/visiting* me in the summer. She'd like *stay/to stay* for two weeks.

8 Look at the table. Work in groups and discuss the questions.

1 Have you been to any of the places?
2 Which of the challenges would you like to do? Which places would you like to visit?

Charity Champions	*summary of expeditions*	
Expedition	**Country**	**Level of difficulty**
Great Wall of China Trek	China	challenging
Sahara Desert Trek	Morocco	challenging
Kilimanjaro Climb	Tanzania	extreme
London to Paris Cycle Ride	UK, France	challenging
Grand Canyon Trekking Expedition	USA	challenging
Mongolian Horse-riding Challenge	Mongolia	challenging
Fastnet Sailing Challenge	UK, Ireland	tough
North Pole Trek and Ski Expedition	North Pole	tough

Pronunciation | /aɪ/ and /eɪ/

9 a 2.60 Listen and repeat this sentence. Do the underlined words have the same vowel sound?

I'd really <u>like</u> to <u>play</u> the classical guitar.

b 2.61 Listen. Underline the word you hear. Then repeat.

1 wait — white
2 Dave — dive
3 late — light
4 main — mine
5 lake — like

see Pronunciation bank page 147

Speaking and writing

10 a Make a list of four or five ambitions.

Visit Machu Picchu.

b In groups, compare your ambitions, then compare as a class. Is there a top ambition in the class?

A: *I'd like to trek to Machu Picchu.*
B: *Oh no. I don't like trekking.*

c Write a paragraph describing your ambitions. Use the verbs in exercise 6.

I'd love to do some trekking in another country in the future. I'd like to trek to Machu Picchu, for example.

12 Communication

Can do | ask about and discuss plans

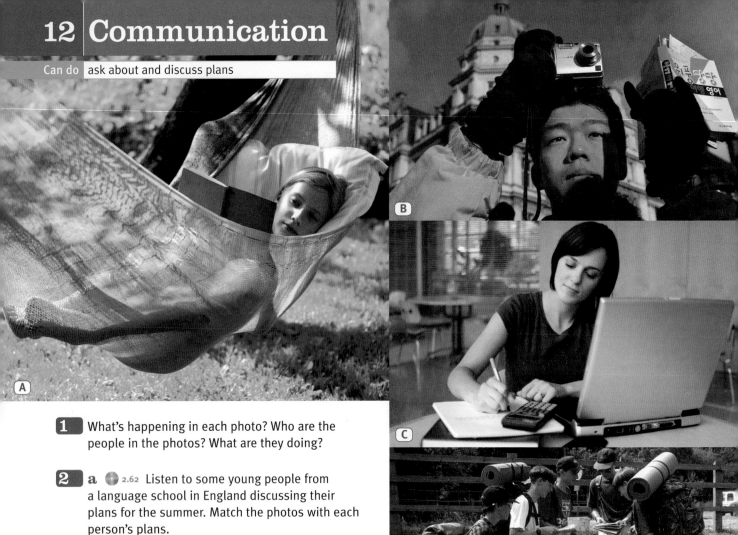

1 What's happening in each photo? Who are the people in the photos? What are they doing?

2 a ⊕ 2.62 Listen to some young people from a language school in England discussing their plans for the summer. Match the photos with each person's plans.

1 Martina = photo ____   3 Hiroshi = photo ____

2 Jacques = photo ____   4 Silvia = photo ____

b Listen again and complete the chart.

	Plans *(is going to)*	Ambitions *(would like to)*
Martina		
Jacques		
Hiroshi		
Silvia		

3 Listen again and complete the How to... box. Check your answers with audioscript 2.62 on page 160.

How to... ask about and talk about plans and ambitions

Asking about plans	*What are you all (1) _____ _____ do?*
Talking about plans	*I'm certainly (2) _____ _____ spend two or three weeks at home.*
	I'm (3) _____ _____ go back in September.
Talking about ambitions	*I'd (4) _____ to work for two months.*
	I really (5) _____ to work with children.
	I (6) _____ to start a course ...

4 a Imagine you are finishing your studies and making plans for the summer. Make a list of three or four things you'd like to do. Use ideas in the list below, exercise 2b, or your own plans.

- learn to drive
- take a summer course, e.g. in acting or singing
- work in another country for a charity
- go to the beach every day
- paint your house/flat
- find some work in your town
- learn a new sport, e.g. scuba diving
- travel to visit some of your family/friends

b Work in pairs. Decide on two or three things you're going to do together, then tell the class.

5 In small groups, discuss your plans for the next few weeks and your ambitions for the future.

I'm going to finish this English course, then I'm going to have a holiday. I hope to get a job when I go home. I'd really like to use English in my work.

126

be going to

We form *be going to* with *to be* and the infinitive of a main verb.

***I'm going to take** my driving test next week.*

	➕	➖	❓
I	*'m (am) going to*	*'m (am) not going to*	*Am I going to … ?*
We/ You/ They	*'re (are) going to*	*aren't (are not) going to*	*Are we/you/ they going to … ?*
He/ She/It	*'s (is) going to*	*isn't (is not) going to*	*Is he/she/it going to … ?*

***Are you going to have** a party for your birthday?*
***She is going to become** the next president.*

We usually use the contracted forms in spoken English.

*It**'s** going to be a cold winter.*
*He **isn't** going to retire next year.*

We use *be going to* to express a personal or impersonal intention (a strong wish to do something in the future).

Impersonal intention

*Spain and Morocco **are going to** build a tunnel.*
*They **are going to** close the factory next year.*

Personal intention

***I'm going to** lose weight next year.*
***We're going to** visit Poland next summer.*

Infinitive of purpose

We use *to* + infinitive to show the purpose or reason for an action.

*I'm learning English **to get** a better job.*

(= I want to get a better job. Learning English can help me do this.)

*I went to the shops **to buy** some milk.*

(= I went to the shops because I wanted to buy some milk.)

like/love vs. would like/love to …

We use *(not) like/love + -ing* form to talk about things we enjoy or don't enjoy doing.

*I love **watching** horror films.*
*We like **eating** Italian food.*
*Cara **doesn't** like **getting up** early in the morning.*

We use *would like/love + to + infinitive* to express a desire for something in the future.

*Kev and Jane **would really like to go** to the opera, but they can't afford the tickets.*

We usually use the contracted forms.

***I'd** love to visit the Caribbean next year.*

We use *wouldn't like + to + infinitive* to express a negative desire for something in the future.

*Laura **wouldn't like to be** a housewife. She enjoys working in an office.*

Note the difference between *like/love + -ing* form and *would like/love + to + infinitive*.

*Jessica **likes playing** the guitar.* (She plays the guitar and she enjoys it.)

*Jessica **would like to play** the guitar in a band.* (She doesn't do this but she wants to.)

We also use *want/hope/plan + to + infinitive* to talk about a desire for the future.

*Emin **wants to work** with children. He **hopes to start** a course on teaching in primary schools.*

Key vocabulary

Activities

bungee jumping   challenge   cycling   expedition
horse-riding   kayaking   mountain biking
mountain climbing   sailing   trekking
white-water rafting

Geography

bridge   canyon   link   mainland   tunnel

Fame

acting   ambition   drama   fame   fortune
politics/politician   professional   talent show

Future time expressions

tomorrow   the day after tomorrow   by Saturday
next week   the week after next   later this year
next year   next summer   in two years' time
three years from now

 Listen to these words.

ACTIVE BOOK

 see Writing bank page 146

1 Here are some notes about your town's plans for next year. Use the notes to write five sentences with *be going to*. Begin sentences 1–2 with *They ...* , and sentences 3–5 with *Our town ...* .

||||||||||||||||||||||||||||||||||||||

- open a new bus station in Morton Road
- build an old people's home in the suburbs
- open a local history museum in the town centre
- close the swimming pool in Rectory Road
- introduce a 35 kmph speed limit in the central area
- start a new 24-hour telephone information line

They are going to open a new bus station in Morton Road.

1 _____
2 _____
3 *Our town ...* _____
4 _____
5 _____

2 Use the prompts to write either a negative statement (✗) or a question (?) using *be going to*.

Carla – bring her car [?]

Is Carla going to bring her car?

my sisters – visit us/next year [✗]

My sisters aren't going to visit us next year.

1 Toyota – build new factories/in Europe [✗]
2 you – have holiday/this summer [?]
3 Tom – buy a new mobile phone [?]
4 my parents – sell their house [✗]
5 your father – retire/next year [?]
6 your friends – stay here/tonight [✗]

3 Find the mistakes and correct them.

Dana's going to ~~buying~~ a new car next month. *buy*

1 I going to visit my grandmother soon.
2 The children is going to stay with their uncle.
3 I think we're going go back to Turkey next summer.
4 Are you going to meeting your new girlfriend tonight?
5 She do not going to do her homework this evening.

4 Complete the sentences with a suitable phrase from the box.

> to commute to work   ~~to get healthy~~
> to meet new people   to see the Acropolis
> to send text messages   to use the Internet

I joined a gym *to get healthy* .

1 We went to Athens _____ .
2 They bought a computer _____ .
3 I'm going to join a club _____ .
4 He uses his car _____ .
5 Maria uses her mobile phone _____ .

5 Complete the sentences with the correct form of the verbs in the box.

> ~~become~~   eat   feel   fly   go   live   marry
> ~~play~~   smoke   study   travel   work

Mandy loves *playing* tennis. She would like to *become* a champion one day.

1 I don't like _____ so I wouldn't like _____ to university.
2 Erica and Pietro love _____ and they would really like _____ around the world.
3 Josh loves _____ in restaurants, but he wouldn't like _____ in one.
4 Tanya doesn't like _____ so she wouldn't like _____ a smoker.
5 Harry doesn't like _____ cold so he wouldn't like _____ in a cold country.

6 Use the clues to complete the word puzzle with activities. What is Activity X?

Activities 1, 5 and 8 take place on water – 1 and 5 on rivers and 8 usually on the sea. Activity 2 uses cars and activities 4 and 6 both use the same type of equipment, but activity 4 uses it on high ground. Activity 3 uses an animal but we do activity 7 on our own feet.

```
                              X
                              ↓
1              R _ F _ _ _ _ _ _
2                   D R I V I N G
3          _ _ R _ _ - _ _ _ I _ G
4  M _ _ _ T _ _ _ _ _ K _ _ _ _
5              K _ Y _ _ _ _ _ _
6              C _ _ _ _ _ N _ _
7      _ _ _ _ T _ _ _ _ _ _ _ _ B _ _ G
8          S _ _ _ _ _ N _
```

Communication activities

Unit 2 Lesson 2 Exercise 10

Student A

Read Doug's diary. Ask questions to complete the diary, and answer Student B's questions.

B: *What does Doug do at half past six?*

A: *He gets up. What does he do at seven o'clock?*

B: *He has a big breakfast.*

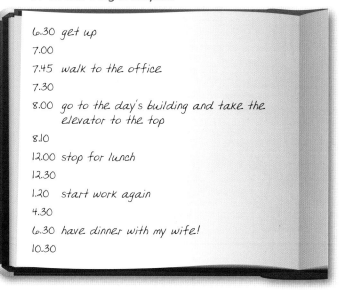

6.30 get up

7.00

7.45 walk to the office

7.30

8.00 go to the day's building and take the elevator to the top

8.10

12.00 stop for lunch

12.30

1.20 start work again

4.30

6.30 have dinner with my wife!

10.30

Unit 3 Lesson 3 Exercise 9

Student A

Read these notes.

Call 1 Your number is 788 032 1349. Answer the phone and start the conversation. (Jason isn't here today. Take a message for him.)

Call 2 Your name is Chris. Phone Student B. You want to speak to Sylvia. Your number is 022 664 337.

Call 3 You work for Henderson Corporation. Answer the phone and start the conversation. (The manager is sick today. Take a message for her.)

Call 4 Your name is Mr/Mrs Osborne. Phone Student B. You want to speak to Mr Preston. Your number is 004 714 932.

Unit 4 Lesson 2 Exercise 9c

Work out your partner's score:

1	X = 2	? = 1	✓ = 0		7	X = 0	? = 1	✓ = 2
2	X = 2	? = 1	✓ = 0		8	X = 0	? = 2	✓ = 1
3	X = 0	? = 1	✓ = 2		9	X = 0	? = 1	✓ = 2
4	X = 0	? = 1	✓ = 2		10	X = 2	? = 1	✓ = 0
5	X = 2	? = 1	✓ = 0		11	X = 2	? = 1	✓ = 0
6	X = 0	? = 2	✓ = 1		12	X = 0	? = 2	✓ = 1

Scores

0–6 = Oh dear. This is an unhealthy diet. You probably feel tired and sleepy a lot of the time.

7–14 = This diet is OK. You probably feel healthy a lot of the time, but eat some fruit and vegetables every day.

15–24 = This is a very healthy diet. Well done! You probably feel fit and happy a lot of the time.

Unit 4 Lesson 3 Exercise 4b

Student A

Answer your partner's questions. Use this information:

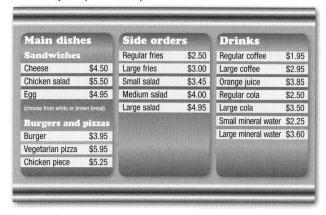

Main dishes		Side orders		Drinks	
Sandwiches		Regular fries	$2.50	Regular coffee	$1.95
Cheese	$4.50	Large fries	$3.00	Large coffee	$2.95
Chicken salad	$5.50	Small salad	$3.45	Orange juice	$3.85
Egg	$4.95	Medium salad	$4.00	Regular cola	$2.50
(choose from white or brown bread)		Large salad	$4.95	Large cola	$3.50
Burgers and pizzas				Small mineral water	$2.25
Burger	$3.95			Large mineral water	$3.60
Vegetarian pizza	$5.95				
Chicken piece	$5.25				

Unit 5 Lesson 1 Exercise 10

Student A

Answer Student B's questions about this villa.

For Sale

Large villa in new development

150 square metres

four bedrooms, three bathrooms

living room, kitchen

patio and two balconies

garage

air conditioning

shared swimming pool

two minutes from shops and restaurants on development

fifteen kilometres from village

€395,000

You want to buy a holiday apartment in New York. Student B has the details. Ask questions to find out these things about the apartment:

1 how big?

2 how many rooms?

3 other features?

4 garden/terrace?

5 where (near shops, etc)?

6 price?

Do you want to buy the apartment?

Unit 5 Communication Exercise 3

Student A

You have this information from the Internet.

www.**furnishyourapartment**.com

Bookshelves	€50
Lamp	€45
Large sofa	€450
Dining table and four chairs	€395
Chair	€125
Large bed	€250
Cupboard	€175
MP3 player	€80
German dishwasher	€395

Today's special bargains:

Flat screen TV	only €100
German washing machine	only €310

Communication activities

Unit 6 Lesson 1 Exercise 9

Student A

Read this text and then give Student B the information (just tell him/her the facts).

Hostal de los Reyes Catolicos

The Hostal de los Reyes Catolicos is a luxury hotel in the city of Santiago de Compostela in the north of Spain, and is very beautiful both inside and outside. It started life in the fifteenth century as a hospital and a hostel for poor travellers, and doctors and nurses worked there. But it changed use many times and finally changed to a luxury hotel in 1953.

Now listen to Student B and complete this chart for another old building. You can use the questions in the chart to get information from Student B.

Name?	
Where is it?	
What was it?	
Who worked there?	
What is it now?	
It closed in …	
… and opened again in …	

Unit 6 Communication Exercise 3

A pairs

You work in a gift shop. Look at the categories below. Choose two categories only, and then make a list of five things you sell in each category. Give each item a price.

- travel guidebooks
- DVDs
- chocolates
- gifts (wallets, diaries, address books)
- stationery (pens, pencils, notebooks)

A1: *Let's sell DVDs and stationery.*

A2: *OK. Which five DVDs?*

A1: *How about a James Bond film for €15?*

When students from B pairs come to your shop, you can answer their questions. But you can only sell them the things on your list!

Unit 7 Lesson 1 Exercise 9

Student A

You have the first half of a story. Use the pictures and notes to tell Student B the story (using the Past Simple). Then listen to the second half of the story.

one morning/set off

notice handbag on the ground

pick up/look in handbag/ some papers

Unit 7 Communication Exercise 4

Student A

a You need to meet Ms Andrews at the airport. Your colleague (Student B) met her last year. Ask questions so you can identify Ms Andrews. Then turn to page 134 and identify her.

b Choose one of these men. This is Mr Gardner. Answer Student B's questions.

Unit 12 Lesson 1 Exercise 10

Student A

Talk to the students in your group. Ask them questions and find someone who is going to …

1 make lots of money
2 get married
3 join a club or team
4 learn how to play a new sport
5 take their driving test

If you can, find out <u>when</u> they are going to do it.

Unit 8 Lesson 1 Exercise 10

Student A

Look at this picture. Student B has the same picture but with six differences. Talk about the pictures and find the differences.

There are some people queuing for food in the centre of the picture.

Unit 8 Communication Exercise 4

Student A

Roleplay 1

You are a shop assistant. You can't exchange the computer because you don't have another one in the shop, but you can give refunds.

Roleplay 2

You bought a wool jacket for €200 last Wednesday. It doesn't fit you. You want a refund or another jacket in a bigger size.

Roleplay 3

You are a hotel receptionist. The hotel has an engineer who can repair central heating, but he isn't working today. The central heating is working in some other rooms. You can move the guest to one of these rooms.

Roleplay 4

Yesterday you bought a ticket on the Anglo Airlines website for a flight to Athens on Saturday. It cost €200. But now you want to fly to Athens on Sunday, not Saturday. Phone the Anglo Airlines office and ask to change your ticket.

Unit 9 Lesson 2 Exercise 7

Student A

Movie madness

The most expensive film ever is *Pirates of the Caribbean: At World's End*. This is the third 'Pirates' film, and stars Johnny Depp. It came to the cinema in 2007 and cost $300 million!

The first films were pictures only; they didn't have sound. The first full-length film with sound was a musical – *The Jazz Singer*, from 1927. This was the first time that people talked in films.

There are lots of ideas about the richest film star. It's difficult – can we compare film stars from fifty years ago with film stars today? Most people agree that the richest male film star today is Tom Cruise, and the richest female film star is Julia Roberts. She has about $212 million, so perhaps she's richer than Tom Cruise ...

Unit 10 Lesson 1 Exercise 10

Student A

You work for Sunshine Travel. Use this information.

- Direct train New York to Washington DC
  Travels on Mondays, Fridays and Saturdays only. First class costs €300 return per person. Standard class costs $180 per person return.
- Slow train New York to Washington DC
  Travels on Mondays, Wednesdays and Sundays. Tickets cost $275 return per person for first class, $125 per person in standard class. There are no tickets available for standard class for next Wednesday.
- New York – Philadelphia, Philadelphia – Washington DC
  Train travels every day. It stops for one hour in Philadelphia station. Standard class only. Tickets cost $150 return per person.

Unit 10 Lesson 2 Exercise 7

Student A

Ask your partners questions with *Have you been on ... ?* If they answer *Yes*, find out when and where they did the activity, and if they liked it. Check any words you don't know in a dictionary before you begin.

Have you been on ...

- an adventure holiday?
- a motorbike?
- a cruise?
- a camel?
- television?
- a jet ski?

A: *Have you been on an adventure holiday?*

B: *Yes, I have. I went last year.*

A: *Did you enjoy it?*

Communication activities

Unit 10 Communication Exercise 4

Student A

Use the map on page 106. Give your partner directions to a place on the map. Tell your partner where you are now, but don't say the name of the place you are giving directions to! Your partner listens and tells you the name of the place.

You are at the hospital. Give your partner directions to ...

1   the art gallery
2   the bank
3   the Internet café
4   the library

Unit 11 Communication Exercise 4

Student A

Roleplay 1

You work at a scuba diving school. Answer Student B's questions, using the information below.

- The next course starts next weekend and it lasts four weekends. It starts at 10:00 on Saturday and goes on until 6:00, with an hour for lunch. On Sunday it starts at 9:00 until 2:00, and then lunch.
- You take all levels, including beginners.
- It's £400 for the course, but you have to hire equipment. That costs from £20 to £50.

You start the phone call:

Hello, Keith's Scuba School. Can I help you?

Roleplay 2

You want to enrol for some horse-riding lessons. You have the information below.

Grants Stables and School

Horse-riding for all levels, classes for beginners and lessons in jumping.

Lessons/rides from £20 per hour

Hard hats necessary

Call Jenna on 01239 48056 for more details.

You want to find out ...
- When are the lessons?
- Is a lesson one hour or more?
- How many lessons do you need before you can ride?

You want to check ...
- the exact price
- the exact times of lessons for beginners

Remember to check information and ask for repetition.

Unit 12 Lesson 3 Exercise 3

Student A

Read the text below and answer your partner's questions.

You have to be very fit to take part in one of our expeditions. Maybe you think you are generally very fit, but even if you are, you have to do a lot of training in whatever activity you choose. It's a good idea to check your fitness with your doctor before you start training, then organise a training timetable. Start by training for half an hour three or four days a week, then every day, then an hour a day. We organise training weekends for people, where we can give you lots of advice and help you with your training.

Ask your partner these questions:
1   Who pays for the expedition?
2   Who chooses the charity?
3   How can you raise more money?

Unit 12 Lesson 1 Exercise 10

Student B

Talk to the students in your group. Ask them questions and find someone who is going to ...

1   visit another country
2   buy a new car
3   start a diet
4   learn another language
5   stop eating meat

If you can, find out <u>when</u> they are going to do it.

Unit 9 Lesson 2 Exercise 7

Student B

Movie madness

The longest film ever is a film called *The Cure for Insomnia* – and it <u>is</u> a cure for insomnia; a good film to watch when you can't go to sleep! It is 87 hours long, and the whole film is the artist LD Groban reading a poem! Sometimes there are scenes of heavy rock bands, but most of it is the poem.

Opinions are different about the most romantic film, but a lot of people think it is *Casablanca*, a film from 1942, and the most romantic scene is where the main character (Humphrey Bogart) says goodbye to the woman he loves (Ingrid Bergman).

Everyone loves a bad guy, and in the opinion of a lot of film critics, the worst villain in a film is Hannibal Lecter, from the films *Silence of the Lambs*, *Hannibal* and *Red Dragon*. Anthony Hopkins played the doctor who killed and ate people in these films. He won the Oscar for Best Actor in the first film, but he was only in the film for sixteen minutes!

Unit 2 Lesson 2 Exercise 10

Student B

Read Doug's diary. Ask questions to complete the diary, and answer Student A's questions.

B: *What does Doug do at half past six?*

A: *He gets up. What does he do at seven o'clock?*

B: *He has a big breakfast.*

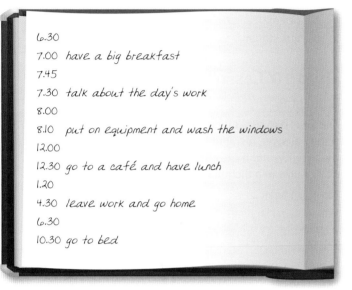

6.30
7.00 *have a big breakfast*
7.45
7.30 *talk about the day's work*
8.00
8.10 *put on equipment and wash the windows*
12.00
12.30 *go to a café and have lunch*
1.20
4.30 *leave work and go home*
6.30
10.30 *go to bed*

Unit 12 Lesson 1 Exercise 10

Student C

Talk to the students in your group. Ask them questions and find someone who is going to ...

1   join a gym
2   learn to play a musical instrument
3   move house or apartment soon
4   go on a skiing holiday
5   get a pet

If you can, find out <u>when</u> they are going to do it.

Unit 5 Communication Exercise 3

Student B

You have this information from the Ardent Catalogue.

Ardent Catalogue Store

Laptop computer	€400
Super vacuum cleaner	€99
American coffee machine	€60
Desk	€99
Large dining table and six chairs	€355
Small sofa with two chairs	€325
Microwave	€60
Luxury bed	€500
Bookshelves	€750
Cupboard	€99
DVD recorder	€150

Unit 6 Lesson 1 Exercise 9

Student B

Listen to Student A and complete this chart for another old building. You can use the questions in the chart to get information from Student A.

Name?	
Where is it?	
What was it?	
Who worked there?	
What is it now?	
It changed in ...	

Now read this text and then give Student A the information (just tell him/her the facts).

Tate Modern

The Tate Modern is a gallery for British and international modern art in the centre of London. It started life in the early part of the twentieth century as a power station. Engineers and power workers produced electricity for London. The power station closed in 1981 and it opened as an art gallery in 2000.

Unit 7 Lesson 1 Exercise 9

Student B

You have the second half of a story. Listen to Student A tell the first half, then use the pictures and notes to tell Student A the end of the story (using the Past Simple).

1 papers boring/ also house key

2 go to the police station/hand bag in

3 woman come to house/ her bag/give £500

Communication activities

Unit 7 Communication Exercise 4

Student B

a Choose one of these women. This is Ms Andrews. Answer Student A's questions.

b You need to meet Mr Gardner at the airport. Your colleague (Student A) met him last year. Ask questions so you can identify Mr Gardner. Then turn to page 130 and identify him.

Unit 8 Lesson 1 Exercise 10

Student B

Look at this picture. Student A has the same picture but with six differences. Talk about the pictures and find the differences.

There are some people queuing for food in the centre of the picture.

Unit 10 Communication Exercise 4

Student B

Use the map on page 106. Give your partner directions to a place on the map. Tell your partner where you are now, but don't say the name of the place you are giving directions to! Your partner listens and tells you the name of the place.

You are at the library. Give your partner directions to ...

1 the cinema
2 the bus station
3 the newsagent's
4 the school

Unit 10 Lesson 2 Exercise 7

Student B

Ask your partners questions with *Have you been ... ?* If they answer *Yes*, find out when and where they did the activity, and if they liked it. Check any words you don't know in a dictionary before you begin.

Have you been ...

- mountain climbing?
- skiing?
- windsurfing?
- ice-skating?
- horse-riding?
- skateboarding?

A: *Have you been mountain climbing?*

B: *Yes, I have. I went last summer.*

A: *Did you like it?*

Unit 12 Lesson 3 Exercise 3

Student B

Read the text below and answer your partner's questions.

When you join one of our expeditions, we ask you to pay for the expedition and to raise money for charity. You can choose the charity and the amount of money you want to raise, but we ask you to raise as much money as you can. Of course, you have to find people to sponsor your trip, i.e. to help you pay for it, but there are other ways of raising money to pay for your trip and to give to the charity. We can help you with ideas; for example, walking dogs for busy people. Or you can sell your old things and give the money to your charity.

Raising money

Ask your partner these questions:

1 Do you have to be fit to do the expeditions?
2 How much training do you have to do at the start?
3 How can *Charity Champions* help people?

1 A form

Can do | complete a form with personal information

1 Why do people fill in forms? Look at the list of reasons and add two more.

- open a bank account
- apply for a job
- get a passport or identity card
- join a school or college
-
-

2 **a** Look at the form and answer the questions.

1 What is the form for?
2 What do you write where it says 'sign here'?
3 Do we use sentences in forms?

Supersaver Supermarkets

Job Application Form

1 SURNAME *Thomson*

2 FIRST NAME *Steve*

3 DATE OF BIRTH *12 March 1992*

4 AGE *19*

5 MARITAL STATUS *single*

6 NATIONALITY *British*

7 PASSPORT OR IDENTITY CARD NUMBER *1997863*

8 ADDRESS *98 Hart Road, Birmingham*

9 EMAIL ADDRESS *steve.tom@emails.com*

10 TELEPHONE NUMBER *0777 187634*

11 OCCUPATION *student*

12 QUALIFICATIONS *---------*

13 LANGUAGES *English, Italian*

14 NEXT OF KIN *Mr Alfred Thomson (father)*

Please sign here: *Steve Thomson*

b Match the questions with the parts of the form.

a How old are you? — ☑ 4
b What's your phone number? ☐
c What's your family name? ☐
d What's your email address? ☐
e Are you married or single? ☐
f What's your job? ☐
g What's your first name? ☐
h What's your address? ☐
i What's your nationality? ☐

3 **a** Look at the How to... box and complete the exercise.

> ### How to... use punctuation (1): capital letters
>
> Circle all the capital letters in Steve's answers on the form in exercise 1 (e.g. Thomson). Then complete the sentence below with two more things.
>
> We use capital letters at the start of a sentence and for the names of people, places, languages, _____ and _____ .

b There are eleven more mistakes with capital letters in this paragraph. Write the correct capital letters.

M
~~m~~y name is carol wilson. i speak english and arabic. i'm british and i live in manchester. my date of birth is 21 february 1993.

4 **a** You want to open a bank account at Saver Bank. Look at the application form and think about all the information you need.

b Now complete the form.

Saver Bank plc

BANK ACCOUNT APPLICATION FORM

Surname _____

First Name _____

Date Of Birth _____

Age _____

Nationality _____

Passport or Identity Card Number _____

Address _____

Email Address _____

Telephone Number _____

Mobile Phone Number _____

Occupation _____

Please Sign Here: _____

Spotlight on... Sophie Ramos

I'm Sophie, and I'm a police officer. On a normal day I get up at 6:30, have a small breakfast and <u>then</u> I have a swim. I go to work at 8:00 and start work at 8:30. In the morning I walk around the town centre, I talk to people <u>and</u> I check the shops. I have a sandwich at 12:30 and then, in the afternoon, I work in the police station.

I write my notes from the morning and go to meetings. I finish work and go home at 5:30, and I meet my friends and play tennis or walk in the park with them. <u>After that,</u> I go home and have dinner, then I watch TV or read a book. I go to bed at 10:30.

1 Read the text about Sophie and answer the questions.

1 What does Sophie do?
2 Does she have a big breakfast?
3 What does she eat for lunch?
4 Does she check shops in the afternoon?
5 What time does she finish work?
6 What does she do in the evening?

2 a Read the text again and complete Sophie's diary.

Morning
6:30 (1) _____ and have breakfast
7:00 have a swim at the swimming pool
8:00 go to (2) _____
8:30 start work — walk around the
      (3) _____ , talk to people,
      (4) _____ the shops
_____

Afternoon
12:30 have lunch (a (5) _____)
1:30   work in the police station — write
       notes from the morning, go to
       (6) _____
5:30   (7) _____ work and go home
_____

Evening
6:30 meet (8) _____ , play tennis, walk
      in (9) _____
7:30 have dinner
8:30 (10) _____ TV or read a book
10:30 go to bed

b Which word do we often leave out in diaries?

3 a Look at the How to... box and answer the questions.

How to... join sentences (1): and, then, after that

Look at the <u>underlined</u> words in the text. Which word/phrase do we use to ...

1 join two actions that happen at about the same time? _____
2 show that one action happens after another? It usually has a comma (,) after it. _____
3 show that one action happens after another? It doesn't usually have a comma (,) after it. _____

b Use your answers to exercise 3a to complete the sentences.

I get to work at 9:00, (1) _____ I have a cup of tea, start my computer (2) _____ read my emails.
(3) _____ I go to a short meeting with my director.
(4) _____ , I start my work for the day.

4 Complete the diary page for your normal day.

Morning
____ get up
____ have breakfast
____ _____
____ _____

Afternoon
____ have lunch
____ _____
____ go home

Evening
____ _____
____ have dinner
____ _____
____ go to bed

5 Now write a paragraph for a local newspaper about your daily routine. Use your notes in exercise 4 and the text about Sophie to help you.

3 | Short messages

Can do | write a short message

1 Read the messages (A–D) and match them with the descriptions (1–4).

1 a message to a flatmate, asking her to do something

2 a phone message to a girlfriend, giving her information

3 a work message to a manager, telling him about an arrangement

4 a text message from a friend, with some interesting information

2 Answer the questions for each message.

1 Who is the message to?

2 Who is the message from?

3 What is the question in the message?

3 Look at the How to... box and complete the exercise.

> ### How to... use punctuation (2): full stops and question marks
>
> We usually end a sentence with these punctuation marks: . ?
>
> Match the punctuation marks with when we use them.
>
> 1 We use this at the end of a question. ___
>
> 2 This is the normal way of ending a sentence. ___

4 Add full stops and question marks in these messages.

1 Jane – I have a message from Andy☐ He has the tickets for the Kasabian concert next week☐ Can you call him later to make arrangements☐ Bob

2 Joe – Maria has a question for you☐ What time is the meeting on Tuesday☐ Please call her on Monday☐

3 Emma – I have a new job in Rome☐ Are you surprised☐ Call me later for more information☐ Gill

5 In pairs, think of three messages that you want/ need to give to someone and make notes. You can choose from the following:

• a message to your teacher about homework

• a message to your flatmate about shopping

• a message to your mother/father about a phone call

• a message to a friend about an arrangement

• a message to a colleague at work about a phone call

• a message to a friend with some exciting news

6 Now write the three messages.

A

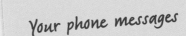

Your phone messages

Louisa – message from Ben – the film tonight is at the Odeon in Hill Street at 8:00. Can you call him before then?

B

Hi Steve. There's a great football match on TV this evening – Arsenal v. Spurs. Can you come and watch it at my house? Dave

C

Sally, we don't have bread for the dinner party tonight. Can you get some when you go to the gym this afternoon? (I'm out all day.)
Thanks.
Suze

D

Mr Owens - message from Michael Thomas. He wants a meeting for all the sales managers on Friday morning. Can you get to the meeting at 8:30? He wants an answer this afternoon.

4 | A personal profile on a website

1 Do you know about *Bebo*, *Facebook* or *Myspace*? Do you use any websites like these? Why/Why not?

2 **a** Read Sandy's profile on a social networking site quickly and choose the best summary.

  1 Sandy tells a story about her life.
  2 Sandy describes her friends and family.
  3 Sandy writes about her hobbies.

PEOPLENET.com

search

Sandy
female
19 years old
Toronto, Canada

| send message | add to friends | add to group | Sandy's photo gallery |

ABOUT ME:

Hi.

I'm Canadian and I live in Toronto. It's a beautiful city. I'm a chef in a French restaurant. I love French food!!

Family and friends are very important to me. My best friend is Cheryl, she's eighteen and she's a student at Toronto University – she's very funny. She doesn't like French food – she likes burgers and hot dogs! My boyfriend is called Felipe. He's from Argentina. He plays the guitar in a rock band. I think he's very handsome!

I live with my mother, my stepfather Harry and my sister, Susy. She's twenty and she's a shop assistant. My aunt and uncle live next to our house – they work with Harry.

SANDY'S INTERESTS:

rock music, swimming, cycling, French food, horror films

SANDY'S FRIENDS

b Read the text again and match the people with the descriptions.

1	Sandy	a	is her stepfather.
2	Felipe	b	is very funny.
3	Susy	c	loves French food.
4	Harry	d	plays in a rock band.
5	Cheryl	e	is twenty.

3 **a** Look at the How to... box and complete the exercise.

> ## How to... use pronouns (1)
>
> Look at these extracts from the text. When we write about a person the first time, we use their name. But when we write about them again, we use a pronoun.
>
> My best friend is Cheryl, she's eighteen and she's a student at Toronto University.
>
> My boyfriend is called Felipe. He's from Argentina.
>
> Look at the text again. Which pronouns do we use for
>
> 1 a man? _____
> 2 a woman? _____
> 3 a place? _____
> 4 two or more people? _____

b Rewrite the sentences using pronouns.

My uncle is thirty-eight. My uncle's an engineer in Mexico City.

My uncle is thirty-eight. He's an engineer in Mexico City.

  1 This is a photograph of my aunt. My aunt is Brazilian.
  2 I'm twenty-one and my brother is twenty-three. My brother's a professional footballer.
  3 My grandparents are retired. My grandparents are Russian.
  4 I live in San Francisco, in California. San Francisco's a very big city.
  5 I'm nineteen and I come from Iceland. Iceland's a cold country but Iceland's very beautiful.

4 **a** Think about your friends and family. Make a list of four or five people and write some notes about them.

Ali – nineteen – my best friend – likes motorbikes

b Now write your personal profile for a social networking site. Use your notes to help you.

My name's _____ . I'm _____ ...

5 An email to a friend

Can do | start and end an informal email

```
To:  Fran
Cc:
Subject: Australia
```

A   Hi Fran

B   Thanks for your email.

I'm so glad that you want to come to Australia. It's a very interesting country, and there's a lot to see.

As you know, I come from Sydney, but I live in Perth now. Perth is in the west and it's a big city. It's got a lot of shops and some lovely squares. We can travel around when you come – the Great Barrier Reef is in the north of the country and there are some very nice beaches there. We can swim and sunbathe, or we can visit the Reef – that's fantastic. There are deserts in the centre of Australia, but they aren't very interesting. In the east there are some long, wide rivers and famous beaches and there are mountains in the south. We can go there, too.

C   Australia is very good for holidays. See you here later this year!

D   Lots of love

E   Monica

---

1 Read the email and answer the questions.

Are there mountains in Australia?

Yes, there are. They're in the south.

1   What is there in the north of Australia?
2   Where are the deserts in Australia?
3   Is there a big city in the west?
4   Where are the famous beaches?

2 **a** Read the email again. Match the descriptions in the box with the features A–E in the email.

> closing sentences ☐   ending ☐
> greeting ☐   name of the sender ☐
> opening sentence ☐

b Complete the explanations using the descriptions in the box above.

1   An informal email begins with a _____ , often *Hi* + name or *Dear* + name.
2   In the _____ we often say thank you for an email, phone call, etc.
3   In the _____ we often talk about a future plan (e.g. *See you later this year*).
4   The _____ is usually *Lots of love* or *See you soon.*
5   The email usually ends with the _____ .

3 Look at the How to... box and complete the exercise.

> **How to... join sentences (2): *and*, *but*, *or***
>
> We use *and*, *but* and *or* to join sentences. Find these three words in the email and match them with their meanings (a–c).
>
> 1 *and*   a gives different information
> 2 *but*   b gives another choice
> 3 *or*   c adds and combines information

4 Complete the sentences with *and*, *but* or *or*.

1   We come from Texas _____ we live in New York.
2   There's a concert hall in the town _____ there's a theatre, too.
3   We can eat at home _____ we can go to the café.
4   There's a good film on at the cinema this week, _____ John doesn't want to see it.
5   Would you like to go to the beach _____ visit a national park today?

5 **a** A friend wants to visit you in the summer. Make a few notes about your country to tell him/her.

b Think about the beginning and ending of the email, and write these parts of the email.

c Now write the email to your friend. Use *and*, *but* and *or* to join sentences.

Tell us about a place you visited recently.
Remember to answer these questions:
• Exactly when and where did you go?
• Where did you stay? (i.e. hotel, campsite)
• How much did your trip cost (approximately)?
• What did you like about the place?
• What didn't you like about the place?

Reykjavik, Iceland

Reviewer: *Neil Strachan, Glasgow*

My wife and I went to Reykjavik for a weekend last month. We chose Reykjavik because it only takes two hours from Glasgow. We arrived early on Friday morning so we had a full weekend there.

We stayed three nights in the city centre – and what a city! It's lively and fun, and it has a pretty lake in the centre. It's a small city so it's easy to walk around, but it is expensive. We took a trip in the countryside around Reykjavik and we loved that because everything is different from Scotland. The only problem is the weather – it's very cold, and it's dark most of the time because it's very far north. We'd like to go again in summer, when it's light.

1 Read the text. Does it answer all the *TravelBuddy* questions?

2 Read the text again and complete the chart.

Reykjavik	
Positive things	Negative things
lively and fun	

3 Look at the How to... box and complete the exercise.

> ### How to... join sentences (3): *because, so*
>
> We often join sentences with *because* or *so*. Underline *because* and *so* in the text and choose the correct option in the sentences below.
> 1 We use *because/so* to introduce a reason (why we do something).
> 2 We use *because/so* to introduce a result (what happens after we do something).

4 **a** Complete the sentences with *because* or *so*.
1 I had some bad fish at dinner _____ I was ill all last night.
2 I was ill all last night _____ I had some bad fish at dinner.

b Complete the sentences with *because* or *so* and your own ideas.
1 I left the English class ...
2 The coat was very expensive ...
3 Sam was late for work ...
4 Jan doesn't like Harry ...
5 The weather was awful ...

5 **a** Choose a city you know. Make notes to answer the questions.
• Where is it?
• When did you go there?
• Who did you go with?
• How did you get there?
• How long did you stay?
• What did you do there?
• Did you like it? (Why/Why not?)

b Check that your notes also include the points from the *TravelBuddy* advice.

c Now write a short text for *TravelBuddy* about a visit to the city.

7 | Short messages on cards and notes

Can do | respond to an event in writing

1 **a** Do you ever send cards to people? Why? What sort of messages do you write inside the cards?

b Match the situations (1–8) with one of the messages (A–E).

(A) *Get well soon*

(B) **Congratulations!**

(C) Thank you

(D) Good luck!

(E) **Happy Birthday!**

1 Your cousin starts a new job next week.
2 Your friend's wedding is on Saturday.
3 A colleague retires at the end of this week.
4 Your uncle gave you a present.
5 Your best friend is twenty-one tomorrow.
6 Your aunt is in hospital.
7 Your sister had a baby.
8 You stayed for a weekend at somebody's house.

2 Read the messages (a–h) and match them with the situations in exercise 1b.

a It's wonderful news about your new baby – I'm really pleased for you and wish you all the best for the future.

b Have a great birthday! I hope you get lots of lovely presents.

c Thank you very much for the present – I love it!

d I'm sorry to hear that you aren't well. I hope you get better soon.

e I hope everything goes well in your new job.

f Congratulations on your happy day and all the best for many happy years together.

g Thank you for a lovely weekend – I had a really good time and I look forward to seeing you again soon.

h We hope that you enjoy your retirement.

3 **a** Look at the How to... box and complete the exercise.

> ### How to... use punctuation (3): dashes and exclamation marks
>
> We often use dashes (–) and exclamation marks (!) in informal writing (cards, emails, notes, etc.). Match the punctuation marks with when we use them.
>
> 1 We use this at the end of a sentence when something is surprising, exciting or interesting. ___
>
> 2 We use this to join two pieces of information in the same sentence. ___

b Choose the correct underlined punctuation marks.

1 Thank you for the present you sent me . / – It's fantastic ! / .
2 Clare had a baby . / – he's got blue eyes and blond hair.
3 That's a fantastic result. Congratulations . / !
4 It's my birthday and I'm having a party . / ! Can you come?

c Decide where to put the dash in the sentences.

1 Thanks for the present it's just what I wanted.
2 I'm really pleased you got the job good luck!
3 Enjoy your trip send me a postcard!
4 I'm sorry I missed your birthday I was on holiday.

4 Find the phrases in the box in the messages in exercise 2 and use them to complete the sentences.

> I hope   I'm really pleased   I'm sorry

1 Good luck! _____ you pass the exam next week.
2 _____ to hear that you are ill.
3 _____ to hear about your new baby. Does she look like you?
4 Happy Birthday! _____ you have a fantastic party!
5 _____ you can't come to the party.

5 **a** Look at the four situations.

- Your cousin is taking an important exam.
- It is your aunt's fiftieth birthday next week.
- Your teacher is ill in hospital.
- Your best friend's wedding is next month.

1 You want to send cards to these people. Choose a suitable message for each person from exercise 1 (A–E).
2 Think about what you want to write inside each card and underline phrases on this page.

b Now write the cards.

1 This is a postcard of Punta del Este in Uruguay. What kind of things do people do here? Make a list.

sunbathe

2 Lara is having a holiday in Punta del Este. Read the postcard to her sister in England and answer the questions.

1 What is the name of Lara's sister?
2 Where are Lara and her family staying?
3 What is the weather like?
4 How many children does Lara have?

Dear Polly

1 Well, we are at Punta del Este and it's (beautiful) We're staying in a lovely apartment near the beach.

2 The weather is fantastic so I spend most of my time relaxing by the wonderful swimming pool. It's lunchtime now so I'm eating some salad here.

3 John and the children are down at the amazing beach now. Patrick is on a jet ski and Melanie is having some windsurfing lessons! We're all having a great time!

4 Well, it's time for another swim.

See you soon.

Love Lara

Polly Graham
65 Dorset Str.
Birmingham
B22 78T
England

3 **a** Look at the How to... box and complete the exercise.

> **How to... make your writing more interesting**
>
> When we write we use different adjectives to make our writing more interesting. Often the adjectives we use have similar meanings, e.g. *great, wonderful*. (Circle) the positive adjectives with similar meanings in Lara's postcard (the first one has been done for you).

b Work in pairs. Make a list of ten positive adjectives.

4 Improve the text by using positive adjectives to replace *nice*.

fantastic
We're having a ~~nice~~ day today! The weather is nice and we're having a nice meal in a nice restaurant. The restaurant is in a nice old building in the village. The village is really nice.

5 Answer the questions about Lara's postcard.

1 How does she begin and end the postcard?
2 Which paragraph ...
a describes Lara's activities?
b describes her family's activities?
c gives a reason for ending the postcard?
d describes the apartment?

6 **a** Imagine you are on a weekend away with your family. Read the questions and make a note of the answers.

1 Where are you?
2 Where are you staying?
3 What is the weather like?
4 What are you doing?
5 What is your family doing?

b Now write a postcard to a friend.

9 | A biography

1 a Read the biography and answer the questions.

1 When did Russell Crowe move to Australia?

2 What was unusual about his early life?

3 What jobs did he do before he became a film star?

4 What was his first famous film?

5 Where does Crowe live now?

MY FAVOURITE FILM STAR

1 **R**ussell Crowe was born in New Zealand in 1964 but his family moved to Australia when he was only four. His parents were chefs in the film business, and they travelled around a lot, so Crowe lived in a lot of different places and homes until he was fourteen, when the family moved back to New Zealand.

2 Crowe began acting when he was six – in an Australian TV series. He also worked in *Neighbours*, the famous Australian soap opera. When he was sixteen, he started singing and after that, he worked as a waiter, a salesman and in many other jobs. In 1986 he went back to New Zealand and worked in the theatre for two years.

3 He started making films in the 1990s. His first famous film was *LA Confidential*, in 1997. After that, he starred in many other famous films, such as *Gladiator* and *A Beautiful Mind*.

4 Now Russell Crowe is married to Danielle Spencer, a singer and actress who worked with him in Australia. They have two sons and live near Sydney, in Australia.

b What kind of information does a biography usually give about a person? Tick (✓) one sentence.

a It gives their opinions and ideas about life. ☐

b It gives details of the different stages of their life. ☐

c It lists all their films (or plays, or books). ☐

2 Look at the How to... box and complete the exercises.

How to... use paragraphs

Look at the text and choose the correct answer.

We use paragraphs in our writing to group *different*/*similar* ideas together.

Look at the biography of Russell Crowe and match each paragraph with these parts of his life.

a his first acting jobs ☐

b his famous films ☐

c his early life ☐

d his personal life ☐

3 In this short biography there is one incorrect sentence in each paragraph. <u>Underline</u> the sentence. Which paragraph does each sentence come from?

1 ■ Angelina Jolie was born in California in 1975. She went to movies with her mother when she was a child and became interested in acting. She also appeared in music videos when she was a teenager.

2 ■ Angelina became a fashion model when she was fourteen. She made her first film when she was sixteen. Other famous films include *A Mighty Heart* and *Changeling*.

3 ■ Her first major film was *The Bone Collector* in 1999. Jolie also has adopted children from different countries. Then she became an international superstar when she made *Lara Croft: Tomb Raider* in 2001.

4 ■ She met Brad Pitt in 2005 and they now have three children together. Her parents were actors. She does a lot of charity work.

4 a Think of someone you know a lot about, e.g. a pop star, a sports star or a public figure. Make some notes about them. Try to use the verbs in the box.

acted	is married to	lived	lives	moved
starred	started	was born	went	worked

b Put your notes into four groups (a–d in exercise 2). Now write a short biography. Follow these steps.

1 Write your notes into sentences.

2 Link the sentences using time expressions if you can.

3 Organise your sentences into four short paragraphs.

1 Read the blog and answer the questions.

1 Who wrote the blog?
2 Why didn't he get on the bus?
3 How much did the taxi cost?
4 Why did Karl go into the bank?
5 Why was his boss angry?

Karl's Blog
Saturday 12th April

Well, today was another disaster! I was really, really late for work – again!!

First, I slept late (as usual!) so I didn't have time for breakfast. Why is it difficult to get up in the morning during the week? I put on my suit and ran for the bus. There was a lot of rain last night and the road was wet. Well, I ran very fast and I fell over – it's OK, I wasn't hurt – but my suit got wet! So then I ran home to change. Later, I went back to the bus stop and the bus came – but it was full of people and there was no space for me. Then I had a fantastic idea – get a taxi!

I saw a taxi and got in it. It took me all the way to my office – FANTASTIC! Then the driver asked me for £10, but I didn't have any money. Why didn't I take any money with me? I haven't done that before! No problem, I said to the driver, I've got a cash card. So the taxi driver took me to the cash machine at the bank near my office. Well, I put the card in the machine but it didn't come out. It was terrible! In the end, I went into the bank and they opened the machine and gave me my card (and some money!).

Of course, when I got to the office my boss was there. I was TWO HOURS late for work – she was really angry with me!

2 a Read the blog again. Are the statements T (true) or F (false)?

1 A blog is like a diary. ☐
2 We use formal language in blogs. ☐
3 We can include photos in blogs. ☐
4 We don't talk about our problems in a blog. ☐
5 Anybody can write a blog. ☐
6 You can't find blogs on the Internet. ☐

b Complete the 'blog rules' with the words in the box.

> adjectives exclamation forms friend
> interesting life opinions

How to write a personal blog
• Write about your own _____ .
• Imagine you are talking to a _____ .
• Give your own _____ about things.
• Use lots of _____ such as *fantastic* and *terrible*.
• Use _____ marks (!).
• Don't use full _____ , e.g. *I have got*, *did not*; use contractions, e.g. *I've got*, *didn't*.
• Try to tell an _____ story about your life.

3 a Look at the How to... box and complete the exercise.

> ### How to... join sentences (4): *first, later, in the end*
>
> We often use *first*, *later* and *in the end* when we tell a story or describe things that happen one after another.
>
> <u>Underline</u> *first*, *later* and *in the end* in the text and decide if the statements below are true or false.
>
> | | True | False |
> |---|---|---|
> | We use *first*, *later* and *in the end* ... | | |
> | a at the beginning of a sentence. | ☐ | ☐ |
> | b to give reasons. | ☐ | ☐ |
> | c to explain when different things happened. | ☐ | ☐ |

b Choose the correct words in *italics*.

I had a terrible experience this morning. (1) *Then/First*, I went to the newsagent's at the end of my street. I bought some chocolate and put it in my pocket. Then I went to the library and did some homework. (2) *Later/In the end*, I remembered that I needed a new notebook so I went to the big supermarket. I spent a long time in the shop but I didn't see any notebooks. I was hungry (3) *first/so* I started to eat the chocolate. Suddenly, the security guard ran towards me (4) *and/later* stopped me. He said I was a thief – I was eating the supermarket's chocolate but I didn't pay for it! I was really angry. (5) *In the end/First*, we went to the manager's office and I explained the situation – so everything was OK.

4 a Make short notes about something interesting that happened to you recently. Just write the key points.

b Now write a blog about what happened to you. Look at the list of rules in exercise 2b and make sentences from your notes.

11 | An Internet message board

Can do | write a message for an online message board

1 Have you ever read an Internet message board, or posted a message on one?

2 Look at the message board and answer the questions.

1 What kind of people use this message board?
2 Who posted the first message?
3 What does Craig want to know?
4 Does Colin think media studies is useful?
5 What does Ken do on the message board?

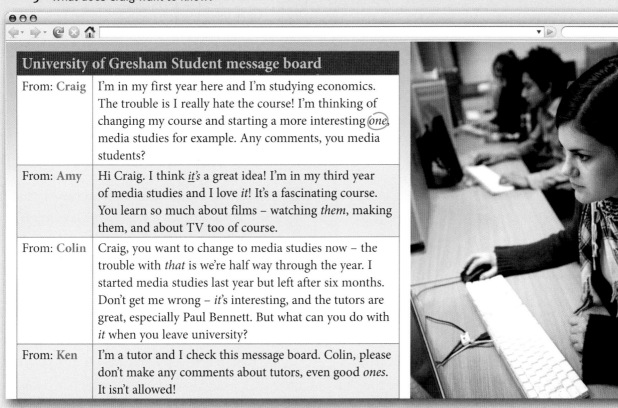

University of Gresham Student message board	
From: **Craig**	I'm in my first year here and I'm studying economics. The trouble is I really hate the course! I'm thinking of changing my course and starting a more interesting *one*, media studies for example. Any comments, you media students?
From: **Amy**	Hi Craig. I think *it's* a great idea! I'm in my third year of media studies and I love *it*! It's a fascinating course. You learn so much about films – watching *them*, making them, and about TV too of course.
From: **Colin**	Craig, you want to change to media studies now – the trouble with *that* is we're half way through the year. I started media studies last year but left after six months. Don't get me wrong – *it's* interesting, and the tutors are great, especially Paul Bennett. But what can you do with *it* when you leave university?
From: **Ken**	I'm a tutor and I check this message board. Colin, please don't make any comments about tutors, even good *ones*. It isn't allowed!

3 Look at the How to... box and complete the exercise.

> ### How to... use pronouns (2)
>
> Look at the pronouns in *italics* in the text.
> Circle the pronouns which refer back to nouns.
> Underline the pronouns which refer back to an idea.

4 **a** Look at this question on a message board. What does the writer want to know?

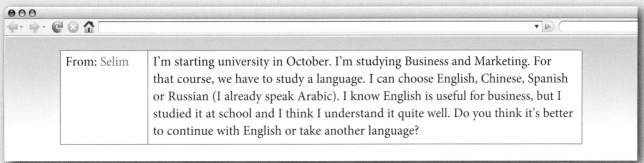

From: Selim	I'm starting university in October. I'm studying Business and Marketing. For that course, we have to study a language. I can choose English, Chinese, Spanish or Russian (I already speak Arabic). I know English is useful for business, but I studied it at school and I think I understand it quite well. Do you think it's better to continue with English or take another language?

b In pairs or small groups, discuss Selim's question. What do you think?

5 Now write a message back to Selim.

12 A short informal letter

1 What are the situations in your country when people say *thank you*? How do they do it? Do they usually phone, write letters, send cards, text messages or emails?

2 **a** Read the text quickly. What kind of text is it?

A   81 Wormsley Road
Stockport
Manchester

B   18th July, 2010

C   Dear Uncle Harold

D   Thank you for the lovely present. It arrived in the post this morning.

E   It was very generous of you. It's perfect and I'm going to wear it every day.

F   I'm looking forward to seeing you at Mum's birthday party next month.

  Thanks again,

G   love

  Carrie

b Read the text again and answer the questions.

1 Who wrote the letter?
2 What did Uncle Harold do?
3 What did Carrie receive, do you think?
4 What does she say about the future?
5 Do we use full forms, e.g. *I am happy* or contractions, e.g. *I'm happy* in letters like this?

c Do you ever write notes or letters like this? Why? Who to?

3 **a** Match the descriptions (1–7) with the parts of the letter (A–G) in exercise 2.

1 date
2 closing sentence
3 greeting
4 ending
5 address
6 opening sentence
7 main paragraph

b Which of the sections do we use ...

1 to talk about the future?
2 to give more information?
3 to say what has happened or to explain the reason for the letter?

4 Look at the How to... box and complete the exercise.

How to... use punctuation (4): apostrophes

Circle three examples of apostrophes (') in the letter and decide if they ...
a show possession.
b show contractions.
Now write the apostrophes in the correct places in the sentences.
1 Theyre very excited about Janes wedding.
2 I dont like Michaels new girlfriend.

5 Rewrite the note using all the apostrophes you need.

Dear Auntie Alice,
I'm
~~I am~~ really sorry to hear that you are not feeling well.

I hope that you are not going to stay in hospital very long and that you will soon get better.

I am going to send you some roses because I know you are very fond of flowers. They are from Dads garden. I hope you like them.

Joanne and the children send you their love,

Saul

6 **a** Your grandmother has sent you an expensive birthday present. You want to send her a thank you letter.
Plan your letter. Look back at Carrie's letter, and think about the questions below. Make notes.

• What was the present?
• When/How did you get it?
• How do you feel about it?
• Why is the present useful for you? How do you plan to use it?
• When are you going to see or speak to your grandmother again?

b Now write your letter.

Pronunciation bank

English phonemes

Consonants

p	b	t	d	k	g	tʃ	dʒ
park	bath	tie	die	cat	give	church	judge
f	v	θ	ð	s	z	ʃ	ʒ
few	visit	throw	they	sell	zoo	fresh	measure
h	m	n	ŋ	l	r	j	w
hot	mine	not	sing	lot	road	yellow	warm

Vowels and diphthongs

iː	ɪ	e	æ	ɑː	ɒ	ɔː	ʊ	uː	ʌ
feet	fit	bed	bad	bath	bottle	bought	book	boot	but
ɜː	ə	eɪ	əʊ	aɪ	aʊ	ɔɪ	ɪə	eə	ʊə
bird	brother	grey	gold	by	brown	boy	here	hair	tour

Sound–spelling correspondences

Sound	Spelling	Examples			
/ɪ/	i	this	listen		
	y	gym	typical		
	ui	build	guitar		
	e	pretty			
/iː/	ee	green	sleep		
	ie	niece	believe		
	ea	read	teacher		
	e	these	complete		
	ey	key	money		
	ei	receipt	receive		
	i	police			
/æ/	a	can	man	pasta	land
/ɑː/	a	can't	dance*		
	ar	scarf	bargain		
	al	half			
	au	aunt	laugh		
	ea	heart			
/ʌ/	u	fun	sunny	husband	
	o	some	mother	month	
	ou	cousin	double	young	
/ɒ/	o	hot	pocket	top	
	a	watch	what	want	

Sound	Spelling	Examples			
/ɔː/	or	short	sport	store	
	ou	your	course	bought	
	au	daughter	taught		
	al	bald	small	always	
	aw	draw	jigsaw		
	ar	warm			
	oo	floor	indoor		
/aɪ/	i	like	time	island	
	y	dry	shy	cycle	
	ie	fries	die	tie	
	igh	light	high	right	
	ei	height			
	ey	eyes			
	uy	buy			
/eɪ/	a	lake	hate		
	ai	wait	train	straight	
	ay	play	say	stay	
	ey	they	grey	obey	
	ei	eight	weight		
	ea	break			
/əʊ/	o	home	phone	open	
	ow	show	throw	own	
	oa	coat	road	coast	
	ol	cold	told		

* In American English the sound in words like *can't* and *dance* is the shorter /æ/ sound, like *can* and *man*.

Weak forms

Word	Strong form	Weak form	Examples of weak forms in sentences
a, an	/æ/, /æn/	/ə/, /ən/	I've got **a** new car. Did you bring **an** umbrella?
at	/æt/	/ət/	Let's meet **at** six o'clock.
and	/ænd/	/ən/	I'd like a burger **and** fries.
are	/ɑː/	/ə/ (or /ər/ before vowels)	What **are** your phone numbers?
been	/biːn/	/bɪn/	I've **been** to San Francisco.
can	/kæn/	/kən/	She **can** sing very well.
do	/duː/	/də/	**Do** you like skiing?
does	/dʌz/	/dəz/	**Does** she work hard?
has	/hæz/	/həz/, /əz/	**Has** he left? Where **has** she been?
have	/hæv/	/həv/, /əv/	**Have** you seen the film? What **have** you got?
than	/ðæn/	/ðən/	She's taller **than** Juan.
them	/ðem/	/ðəm/	Let's take **them** to the cinema.
to	/tuː/	/tə/ (before consonants)	I want **to** go home now.
was	/wɒz/	/wəz/	He **was** an architect.

Pronunciation bank

Word endings

-s endings: Present Simple/noun plurals (Lessons 2.2, 2.3)

• after /p/, /t/, /k/, /f/ and /θ/, add /s/

help → helps, wait → waits, talk → talks, laugh → laughs, book → books, laptop → laptops, bath → baths

• after vowel sounds and /b/, /d/, /g/, /v/, /l/, /m/, /n/, /ŋ/ and /ð/, add /z/

dry → dries, go → goes, enjoy → enjoys, rob → robs, read → reads, bag → bags, love → loves, feel → feels, swim → swims, clean → cleans, sing → sings, breathe → breathes

• after /s/, /z/, /ʃ/, /tʃ/ and /dʒ/, add /ɪz/

miss → misses, organise → organises, wash → washes, watch → watches, judge → judges

Past Simple endings (Lesson 6.1)

• after /p/, /k/, /f/, /s/, /tʃ/, /ʃ/ and /θ/, say /t/

help → helped, talk → talked, laugh → laughed, miss → missed, watch → watched, wash → washed

• after vowel sounds and /b/, /g/, /v/, /z/, /dʒ/, /l/, /m/, /n/, /ŋ/ and /ð/, say /d/

dry → dried, enjoy → enjoyed, play → played, rob → robbed, jog → jogged, organise → organised, judge → judged, love → loved, kill → killed, dream → dreamed*, clean → cleaned, bang → banged, breathe → breathed

* Some verbs which end in /m/, /n/ or /l/ can form the past with -ed or -t: *dreamed/dreamt, learned/learnt, spelled/spelt*

• after /t/ and /d/, say /ɪd/

wait → waited, add → added

Weak forms

a/an (Lesson 1.3)

We usually use the weak vowel /ə/ in *a* and *an*:
He's a doctor. It's an answering machine.

can/can't (Lesson 3.2)

We can say *can* in two ways. We usually use the weak form /kən/ in statements and questions:
I can swim. Can you swim?

We use the strong form /kæn/ in short answers:
Yes, I can.

We always use the strong form of *can't* /kɑːnt/ in statements, questions and short answers:
I can't swim. Can't you swim? No, I can't.

Comparatives (Lesson 9.1)

In comparative sentences the -er ending is always weak:
It's colder here.

We usually say *than* with the weak vowel /ə/ too:
She's slimmer than me.

been (Lesson 10.2)

In Present Perfect sentences we pronounce *been* as /bɪn/:
Have you been to Australia?

going to (Lesson 12.1)

With *going to* we always use the weak vowel /ə/ in *to*:
We're going to take the train.

Stress

Main stress (Lessons 1.1, 3.3, 5.3)

When we say a word with more than one syllable, we stress one syllable more than the others. This syllable has the main stress:

<u>moun</u>tain, <u>beau</u>tiful, a<u>part</u>ment, infor<u>ma</u>tion.

You can check the main stress of a word in a dictionary. They often show it like this: ˈmaʊntɪn

Contrastive stress (Lesson 6.3)

Sometimes, we want to answer a question with information that is different from the information in the question, e.g.

Were you born in London?
No, I was born in Mumbai.

We always stress the different information.
No, I was born in <u>Mumbai</u>.

Sentence stress (Lessons 8.1, 12.1)

We stress one or two words more than other words in a sentence. We usually stress the words which have 'meaning', e.g. the nouns and verbs, and not the 'grammar' words, e.g. pronouns and articles:
She's <u>dancing</u>. They're <u>talking</u>. Are you <u>listening</u>? She's <u>going</u> to get <u>fit</u>. We're <u>going</u> to learn <u>French</u>.

Intonation

Intonation of yes/no questions (Lesson 9.3)

Use a rising intonation (⌐◢) in most questions we answer with *yes* or *no*.

Are you ready?

Is it expensive?

Do you like going to museums?

Intonation of wh- questions (Lesson 11.2)

Our voice often falls when we ask a *wh-* question. It falls on the main verb.

What are you doing here?   When did you arrive?

Irregular verbs

Verb	Past Simple	Past Participle
be	was/were	been
become	became	become
begin	began	begun
break	broke	broken
bring	brought	brought
build	built	built
buy	bought	bought
can	could	been able
catch	caught	caught
choose	chose	chosen
come	came	come
cost	cost	cost
dig	dug	dug
do	did	done
draw	drew	drawn
drink	drank	drunk
drive	drove	driven
eat	ate	eaten
fall	fell	fallen
feed	fed	fed
feel	felt	felt
find	found	found
fly	flew	flown
forget	forgot	forgotten
get	got	got
give	gave	given
go	went	gone/been
grow	grew	grown
have	had	had
hear	heard	heard
hold	held	held
hurt	hurt	hurt
keep	kept	kept
know	knew	known
learn	learned/learnt	learned/learnt

Verb	Past Simple	Past Participle
leave	left	left
let	let	let
lose	lost	lost
make	made	made
mean	meant	meant
meet	met	met
pay	paid	paid
put	put	put
read/ri:d/	read/red/	read/red/
ride	rode	ridden
ring	rang	rung
run	ran	run
say	said	said
see	saw	seen
sell	sold	sold
send	sent	sent
shine	shone	shone
show	showed	shown
sing	sang	sung
sit	sat	sat
sleep	slept	slept
speak	spoke	spoken
spend	spent	spent
stand	stood	stood
steal	stole	stolen
swim	swam	swum
take	took	taken
teach	taught	taught
tell	told	told
think	thought	thought
throw	threw	thrown
understand	understood	understood
wear	wore	worn
win	won	won
write	wrote	written

Audioscripts

Do you know...?

Track 1.01

a b c d e f g h i j k l m n o p q r s t u v w x y z

Track 1.02

a h j k b c d e g p t v f l m n s x z i y o q u w r

Track 1.03

oh/zero, one, two, three, four, five, six, seven, eight, nine, ten

Track 1.04

eleven, twelve, thirteen, fourteen, fifteen, sixteen, seventeen, eighteen, nineteen, twenty, twenty-one, twenty-two, thirty, forty, fifty, sixty, seventy, eighty, ninety, a hundred

Track 1.05

1 Listen.
2 Look at page ...
3 Ask and answer.
4 Read.
5 Write.
6 Complete.
7 Match.
8 Repeat.
9 Correct.
10 Check your answers.
11 Read the tip.

Track 1.06

M = Man, W = Woman
M: How do you say *coche* in English?
W: Car.
M: How do you spell that?
W: C–A–R.
M: And what does *grandmother* mean?
W: She's your mother or father's mother.
M: I don't understand. Can you repeat that?
W: Yes. She's your mother or father's mother.
M: Oh. OK. Thanks.

Unit 1

Track 1.07

M = Man, W = Woman
1
W: Hi, I'm Silvia. What's your name?
M: Hi, Silvia. My name's Pedro.
2
M: What's your name, please?
W: It's Caroline Stacey.
M: How do you spell that?
W: It's C–A–R–O–L–I–N–E S–T–A–C–E–Y.
3
M: Hello. My name's John Logan.
W: Hello. I'm Maria Burton. Nice to meet you.

Track 1.08

020 651 3472

Track 1.09

M = Man, W = Woman
1
M: What's your number?
W: It's 01452 946 713.
2
W: What's your phone number, please?
M: 02096 659 248.
3
M: Is your mobile phone number 951 327 946?
W: Yes, that's right.
4
W: Excuse me. Can you tell me your phone number?
M: Of course. It's 02096 639 247.
W: Thanks.

5
M: Can you give me your mobile number, please?
W: It's 01542 984 731.
M: 01542 984 731?
W: Yes. That's right.

Track 1.10

1 Australian 2 Argentinian
3 Brazilian 4 Italian 5 Germany
6 Iranian 7 Spain 8 Polish
9 English 10 Chinese 11 France
12 Greece

Track 1.11

Australia	Australian
Argentina	Argentinian
United States of America	American
Brazil	Brazilian
Italy	Italian
Germany	German
Iran	Iranian
Russia	Russian
Spain	Spanish
Poland	Polish
England	English
Turkey	Turkish
China	Chinese
Japan	Japanese
France	French
Czech Republic	Czech
Greece	Greek

Track 1.12

I'm Brazilian. I'm from São Paulo.
1 Jennifer López is American. She's from New York.
2 We're Polish. We're from Warsaw.
3 A: Excuse me, where are you from?
   B: I'm from Colombia.
4 A: What is it?
   B: I think it's a Japanese car.
5 A: Who are they?
   B: They're students in my class. They're from Brazil.

Track 1.13

This is a picture of my wedding. This is me and this is my husband Rafael. Rafael's sisters' names are Nathalia and Alessandra. They're from Brazil. Rafael's mother is Nilza and his father is Almir. This is my brother, he's called Connor. Our parents are called Kim and Steve. My grandparents, my mother's mother and father, are called Eileen and Seamus.

Track 1.14

This is a picture of my family from Canada. This is my mom and this is my dad and this is my brother, Ben. His wife is Sheri and these are their two daughters, Julia and Erica. This is my grandmother, Margaret and my grandpa, Jack. They live in southern Ontario. This is my sister, Emily. Her husband's name is Tom and their son's name is James. This is my uncle, Jay. His wife's name is Shelley. And this is their dog. His name is Shadow.

Track 1.15

Mike

Let's see, interesting jobs in my family. Well, erm, my parents are retired, so that isn't very interesting. My sister, my sister's in marketing – she's a marketing director, and, oh yes, her husband, my brother-in-law, is a television producer. Um, my sister-in-law is a lawyer, and, who else? Oh, my uncle. My uncle's a farmer.

Helen

My family's jobs? Well, yes, there are some interesting jobs in my family ... my parents are landlords in a restaurant, and my brother is a chef there, so that's a real family business. My other brother's an engineer and my sister's in computing – she's a computer programmer. Um, let's see, who else? Well, my cousin's a teacher – not very interesting, erm, oh, I know, her father – my uncle – is a sea captain – a captain of a very big ship. Now, that's different!

Track 1.16

a an

Track 1.17

an actor an architect a chef
a computer programmer a dentist
a doctor an engineer a farmer
a lawyer a sea captain
a shop assistant a TV producer

Track 1.18

1
A: Open your mouth, please. Say Aah.
B: Unnngh.
A: That's good. Thank you.
2
Stop ... Stop now. Good boy! OK, now come here, here boy. Good dog!
3
A: Look at these plans. They aren't correct, are they?
B: No, I think you're right.
A: OK. Let's think. What ...
4
Number 3 is ready. Jane, where are you? Number 3 to table, please. Quick!

Track 1.19

M = Man, W = Woman
1
W: Good morning.
M: Hi.
W: Are you a new student?
M: Yes, I'm in the elementary class.
2
W: No, she's his girlfriend.
M: Oh, OK. Well, see you later.
W: Bye.
3
W: Excuse me.
M: Yes?
W: Are you the teacher?
M: No, I'm a student in the ...
4
W: Great. Thanks for your help ...
M: OK. Bye.
W: Goodbye.
5
W: Good evening.
M: Hello. We've got a reservation for dinner at 8 o'clock.
W: Yes, come this way ...
6
M: Great party!
W: Yes. See you at the next one!
M: Yes. See you soon.

Track 1.20

1
M = Maria, C = Clara
M: Hello, I'm Maria.
C: Hello Maria, I'm Clara.
M: Pleased to meet you. Where are you from?
C: I'm from Alicante.
M: Oh! Do you work there?
C: No, I'm a student.

150

2

J = Jordi, K = Krystof

J: Excuse me, are you Krystof?
K: Yes, I am. What's your name?
J: My name's Jordi. Are you Polish?
K: Yes, I am. I'm from Warsaw.
J: What do you do?
K: I'm a teacher.

Unit 2

Track 1.21

What time is it?

1 It's six o'clock.
2 It's ten past two.
3 It's quarter past eight.
4 It's twenty past three.
5 It's half past seven.
6 It's twenty-five to two.
7 It's quarter to four.
8 It's five to five.

Track 1.22

1 I get home late at night, at about quarter to twelve.
2 We leave work at ten past five in the afternoon.
3 I get up at quarter past seven in the morning.
4 We have dinner at half past six in the evening.

Track 1.23

M = Man, W = Woman

W: When do you get up?
M: At ten in the evening.
W: Do you work at night?
M: Yes, I do.
W: What do you do in the afternoon?
M: I sleep.
W: When do you have dinner?
M: I have dinner at about eleven in the morning.
W: Do you work in an office?
M: No, I don't.
W: Where do you work?
M: I work in a hospital.
W: So, what do you do?
M: I'm a doctor.

Track 1.24

walks, listens, organises

Track 1.25

cleans, talks, washes, likes, goes, watches

Track 1.26

1 The teacher talks in English in class.
2 Jake washes his hair every morning.
3 Matt likes his new job – it's very interesting.
4 Tracy goes to work at 9:00 in the morning.
5 My brother watches football on TV every evening.
6 Patrick plays games on the computer at work.

Track 1.27

M = Man, W = Woman

W: Does Jeanette like her work?
M: Yes, she does. She loves it.
W: Does she clean the shark tank?
M: Yes, she does. And she feeds the sharks.
W: Do the sharks eat every day?
M: No, they don't. They eat three times a week.
W: So… does Jeanette work every day?
M: No, she doesn't. She works five days a week.

Track 1.28

Hi, I'm Jodie and this is Hell's Kitchen, New York City. It's the home of a famous flea market, you know, where people sell old things, things they don't want any more. It's right in the centre of the city, so it's very busy. The market is open Saturday and Sunday from 9:00 in the morning to 6:00 in the evening, and people come here every weekend to buy and sell all kinds of things.

My brother Karl and I come here every weekend, too. We have a stall and I sell old clothes, shoes, bags, scarves and things like that. Karl doesn't sell clothes – he sells things like mobile phones, laptop computers and digital cameras. Our things are all useful, or beautiful, and they're quite cheap, but some people sell really expensive, useless things! We love it here – it's really good fun!

Track 1.29

K = Karl, J = Jodie

K: Hey, Jodie. You're here already.
J: Hey, Karl. Yeah, I'm early today.
K: So, everything's ready.
J: That's right. Here are all my clothes – my bags, shoes and scarves, oh, and I have some watches today, too – they're nice, don't you think?
K: Yeah, they're great! What are those books?
J: Oh, a friend has a book store. He wants to sell some of these old books.
K: OK. What's the time?
J: Quarter to nine. Do you have your things?
K: Yeah, here they are – some fantastic mobile phones today, and these two laptops.
J: Oh, they're good. Listen, do you want a coffee before we start?

Track 1.30

K = Karl, J = Jodie, Ja = Jane

J: It isn't very busy today, is it? I know, let's go and have a look at Jane's clothes stall.
K: OK. … Hi, Jane! Only us! Oh, look – this is horrible! What is it?
J: I'm not sure … is it a belt?
K: I really don't know, and look over there. Now that's really ugly!
J: Oh, it is. What is it?
K: I think it's a coat. But she has some nice scarves. Look.
J: Oh, yeah, these are pretty. … Jane, hi, I want one of these scarves. OK?
Ja: Sure. Put it over there and come back later.
J: OK, thanks. Karl, just look at those shoes, they're so old-fashioned!
K: Yeah, but that bag is really useful – I like that.
J: Come on Karl, there are some people at our stall.

Track 1.31

this   these

Track 1.32

big, clean, green, listen, niece, read, sister, swim, teacher, think

Track 1.33

Matt

On holidays I like to go on city breaks, erm, I go with my girlfriend and we like to walk around the city and look at the sights. We get up at about nine o'clock and don't go to bed until quite late. We take with us our camera because I like taking photographs of the buildings, erm, and we also take a guidebook so we can find our way around.

Wendy

When I go on holiday, I love to go to Thailand, because my brother lives there and I can visit him and spend some time with my nephews and nieces. I love to go to the beach, er, I always get up early and get a book and take it down to the beach with me, and I take my brother's children with me, um, I always take some presents with me when I go, to give to the children, er, they love presents from England, particularly from London. In the evening I usually spend some time with my brother, in his house, talking, and maybe eat another meal and get some good sleep, and then the next day back to the beach!

Gareth

I go on holiday with my family, er, we usually go skiing in Italy or Austria. We like that, er, all of us, the kids, too. So we get up quite early, er, at about eight o'clock, so that we can start skiing in the morning, then we ski all day. Boring, isn't it? But we love it! We come back to the apartment at about four o'clock and have a big meal, then we play games with the children. Um, when they go to bed we just read books or play more games, but we go to bed early, too because we're always tired. Oh, we always take sunscreen with us, um, because it's often hot and sunny, and of course we take games and books for the evenings.

Unit 3

Track 1.34

Stig

In my lunch break, I usually have lunch at my desk and at the same time I check my email and read the news. Er, when I finish my lunch I usually go for a walk. Sometimes I go to the park, sometimes I go to the shops, er, but I always leave my desk at least for fifteen to twenty minutes at lunchtime.

Amber

Um, at lunchtime, I, um, sometimes go into town, um, and go shopping, um, but I don't always take a lunch break and I quite often sit at my desk, um, and carry on working. Um, occasionally I surf the Internet, um, but usually I work through my lunch break.

Matt

In my lunch break I usually surf the Internet but sometimes I go to the gym or walk through the park. Occasionally I visit a café and I sit and have lunch and read my book.

Ailsa

Um, I usually go up to the canteen to have lunch with some colleagues and sometimes when I'm busy, I stay at my desk and have a sandwich. There's a bus into the town centre, so I often take the bus into town to do some shopping or go to the bank. I never go to the gym at lunchtime.

Track 1.35

W1 = Woman 1, W2 = Woman 2

W1: Hello, Mrs Smith. How's your Susie?
W2: She's fine, thank you, Mrs Jones. And how's Jonny?
W1: He's OK, thanks. He can play the guitar now, you know.
W2: Oh, Susie can play the guitar, and she can play the piano, too.
W1: Well, Jonny can't play the piano but he can sing.
W2: Oh, can he? Susie can sing …
W1: Can Susie dance?
W2: Yes, she can. Can Jonny dance?

Audioscripts

W1: No, he can't. He doesn't have time to dance. He can play football – he's in the school team, and he can play tennis, and …

W2: Susie can't play football – she doesn't like it. It's not a nice game for a girl. But she can play tennis, and she can ski, of course. Tell me, can Jonny ski?

W1: No, but he can speak French, you know …

W2: Oh, of course Susie can speak French, and she can speak Spanish, too, and she can …

W1: Jonny can ride a bike and he …

W2: Susie can't ride a bike but she can drive a car. Can Jonny drive?

W1: Of course he can't drive. He's only ten!

Track 1.36

Can you dance? Yes, I can. No, I can't.

Track 1.37

six
sixteen
sixty
six hundred
six hundred and one
six hundred and sixty
six thousand
six thousand, six hundred and sixteen
sixty thousand
six hundred thousand
six million
six billion

Track 1.38

sixteen sixty fourteen forty

Track 1.39

1 forty 2 eighty 3 seventeen
4 thirteen 5 ninety 6 sixteen

Track 1.40

1

T = Tony, J = Jane

T: This is 054 898 4567. Please leave a message after the tone.

J: Hi, Tony, it's Jane. Let's meet outside the cinema at ten to eight. See you there, OK? Bye.

2

M = Mandy, S = Steve

M: Hello, this is Mandy and John's phone. We're not here right now so please leave a message with your name and number and the time of your call. Thank you.

S: Mandy, it's Steve Henshaw here. It's twenty past three on Wednesday. Can you call me? My number's 068 919 0752. Thanks.

3

M = Michael, C = Carol

M: This is Michael Brown's voicemail. Please leave a message now.

C: Good morning, Mr Brown. This is Carol at Benson Cameras. Your new camera is here. Can you come to the shop and get it this week? We are open from nine o'clock until half past six every day.

4

J = Judy, D = Damian

J: Hi, I'm not here right now so please leave a message after the beep. Thanks.

D: Judy, it's Damian. Why don't we meet for dinner this evening? How about the Italian restaurant in Green Street at twenty-five past eight? Give me a call. I'm in the office all afternoon.

5

R = Reception, M = Mary

R: Good morning. Brandon Travel Agency.

M: Hello. Can I speak to David Renton?

R: I'm afraid he isn't in this morning. Can I take a message?

M: Yes, can you ask him to call Mary Wilde?

R: Of course. What's your telephone number?

M: It's 713 391 8834.

R: Sorry? Can you repeat that?

M: 713 391 8834.

R: Fine.

M: Thanks. Bye.

Track 1.41

M = Man, W = Woman

W: Hello.

M: Hello, can I speak to Laura, please?

W: She isn't here right now. Can I take a message?

M: Yes, please ask her to phone Jeffrey.

W: OK. What's your number?

M: It's 011 908 5561.

W: OK. Bye.

Track 1.42

I = Interviewer, D = Dario, L = Lizzie

I: Dario, what's your phone number?

D: It's 887 715 992.

I: Do you have any special abilities?

D: Well, I can play the piano and the guitar, and I can drive. I love driving.

I: Can you speak any foreign languages?

D: No, I can't. Only English!

I: Can you use computers at all?

D: Yes, but I only use them to play games!

I: And what do you need?

D: Well, it's my sister's wedding next month. We need a photographer; we want good photos.

I: OK.

I: Lizzie, what about you? Do you have any special abilities?

L: I can play a lot of different sports.

I: Really? Which ones?

L: Football, basketball and tennis.

I: What about practical skills?

L: Well, I'm a good cook. And I like cleaning and housework.

I: What about computers?

L: Oh, I really don't understand computers! Actually, that's what I need. Can someone repair my new laptop?

I: I see. And what's your phone number, Lizzie?

L: My mobile number is 0777 334 898.

I: Right.

Unit 4

Track 1.43

1

Well, my husband's from Brazil so we eat a lot of Brazilian food. My favourite is a dish called *feijoada*, made from black beans, and rice and meat. We eat that quite a lot because it's very cheap to make. We don't eat much fast food, except sometimes on the weekends and we also eat lots of seafood.

2

Oh, in Canada we eat a lot of seafood, especially lobster and scallops, anything that comes from the sea. But we don't eat much lamb or duck and we don't eat many takeaways. But my favourite food is maple syrup and I usually have it twice a week on pancakes.

3

My family's from Iran. We eat a lot of rice and stews. The stews are made with meats and lots of dried fruits and lots of delicious spices. I think my favourite food is a dish called *fesenjan*, made with nuts and fruits and spices, and my children love it and, best of all, it's really easy to cook. We don't eat any pork or ham, and Iranians don't eat much seafood.

Track 1.44

Hello and welcome to *In The Rubbish Bin*, the show where we look at people's lives by looking at their rubbish. I'm Laurence Redburn.

Today we look at the diets of two very different families. I have their rubbish bins in the studio, with a typical day's rubbish, so, let's start with rubbish bin 1. What does this family eat and drink? We have some cans … cola cans – not very healthy. Mmm, instant coffee. Some boxes … cheese and tomato pizza, burgers. Some biscuits, and … crisp packets – all fast food, and not very healthy. Do they eat any vegetables or fruit? I don't think so. Oh dear, not a healthy diet. A lot of this food is bad for you, so this family is probably not very healthy.

Now let's look at rubbish bin 2. This is very different – it's good. This family eats a lot of fruit and vegetables … some potatoes, carrots … bananas and apples. What do they drink? We have a juice carton, a milk carton and we have a water bottle – very good, all very healthy so far. Tea bags … well, OK. They eat some pasta, and fish – that's good. I can't see any fast food here. I think this is a very healthy family.

Track 1.45

W = Woman, L = Laurence

W: But Laurence, that's really not fair!

L: What do you mean?

W: Well, this bin doesn't really show our diet.

L: Go on.

W: OK, we eat a pizza once a week – I don't think that's bad – and the children eat some burgers. And, yes, we sometimes drink some coffee, and the children drink a can of cola once or twice a week, but we don't drink any tea, and we drink a lot of water – about ten litres a week. We also eat a lot of vegetables every day, and we eat some meat and chicken. We don't eat any sweets or chocolate – that's good, isn't it?

L: Well, yes, but where are the water bottles and vegetables in your bin?

W: We recycle them, of course!

Track 1.46

pasta, some

Track 1.47

salad, butter, lamb, apple, lunch, carrot

Track 1.48

W = Waitress, S = Sam, J = Jenny

W: Hi. What can I get you today?

S: Hi. I'd like a cheese sandwich, please.

W: On white or brown bread?

S: On brown, please.

W: Would you like fries?

S: Yes.

W: Regular or large size?

S: Large.

W: And your friend?

S: Jenny, what would you like?

J: Do you have salads?
W: Yes. Small, medium or large?
J: Can I have a medium salad?
W: Sure. Anything to drink?
J: Sam, do you want some juice?
S: No, thanks. I'll have a coffee.
J: OK, a small cup of coffee for …
S: No, no, a large one.
J: OK. A large cup of coffee for him and a small glass of mineral water for me.
W: Fine. Coming right up!

Track 1.49

W = Waitress, S = Sam, J = Jenny

W: OK, here we are. Two vegetarian pizzas.
S: No, they're not for us. Our order is a sandwich with fries and a salad.
W: Oh, sorry, that's the wrong order. Just a moment.
J: Two vegetarian pizzas? I really like them! Can we change our order?
S: Of course not.
W: OK. I think this is your order. A medium salad for you, sir.
S: Oh no, the salad's for her.
W: OK. Right. A medium salad and a small glass of mineral water for you, madam; and a cheese sandwich on brown bread with large fries and a large cup of coffee for you, sir.
S: Yes. Thanks. Can we pay now?
W: Sure.
S: How much is that?
W: That's sixteen dollars and seventy cents, please.
S: Can I pay by credit card?
W: Of course.

Track 1.50

W1 = Woman 1, M1 = Man 1, W2 = Woman 2, M2 = Man 2

W1: Hello.
M1: Good morning to you! Can I help you?
W1: Yes, I need some fruit. I'd like three bananas, a kilo of apples and a melon, please.
M1: We don't have any melons today. Sorry.
W1: OK, just the bananas and apples then, please.
M1: A kilo of apples – they're two euros a kilo, and three bananas. Here you are.
W1: Thank you. How much is that?
M1: That's three euros and fifty cents, please.
W1: Three euros, fifty. Here you are. Thank you. Bye.
M1: Bye.

W2: Can I help you?
W1: Yes, I'd like 500 grammes of beef, 400 grammes of this fish, and a chicken, please.
W2: Um, I don't have any chickens left, I'm afraid.
W1: Oh dear. OK.
W2: That's 500 grammes of beef and 400 grammes of fish. That's eighteen euros altogether. Thank you.

W1: Hello.
M2: Hello there. What can I do for you?
W1: I'd like some cheese, please.
M2: Certainly. Which cheese?
W1: Umm, can I have 200 grammes of that one, please?
M2: Of course. Is that it?
W1: No, do you sell milk?
M2: Yes, it's in the fridge.
W1: Ah, can I have two litres, please?
M2: Yes. Right, that's two euros eighty.

Unit 5

Track 1.51

A = Estate agent, J = Jon

A: Unusual Homes. Good afternoon. Can I help you?
J: Yes. I'm interested in the house in Italy with the unusual roof.
A: Oh, yes, I know it.
J: Can I ask you a few questions about it?
A: Of course.
J: Well, first, how many bedrooms does it have?
A: Umm, let me see. It has five bedrooms.
J: Oh, good. And is there only one bathroom?
A: No, there are two bathrooms.
J: Excellent. Is there air conditioning?
A: No, you don't need air conditioning in a house of that type. But there is central heating.
J: Mmm, OK. Is there a garden?
A: Yes, there's a large, sunny garden; it has a lot of outside space.
J: OK, good. Is the house near a village?
A: Yes, it is. The village is one kilometre away.
J: Oh, good. So are there many shops in the village?
A: I'm afraid I don't know. There's a cash machine in the village, so there are probably shops.
J: Are there any schools in the area?
A: Well, yes, there's a school in the village.
J: Oh, that's good. OK. Now, can I check, how much is the house?
A: It's 300,000 euros.
J: Oh, that's not bad. Can I see it?
A: Yes, of course. Tell me when you can get to Italy, and then I can call the owners and …

Track 1.52

A = Insurance agent, P = Pete

A: Allied Insurance. Can I help you?
P: Yes. I need some home insurance.
A: OK. Can you answer a few questions?
P: Sure.
A: What's your full name?
P: It's Peter Morgan.
A: Are you married?
P: Yes. But we haven't got any children.
A: OK, Mr Morgan. Have you got your own house?
P: No, I haven't. I've got a modern studio apartment in the centre of town, but it's rented.
A: Has it got a garden?
P: No, it hasn't got a garden, but it's got a small terrace.
A: Is there a kitchen in the apartment?
P: Not a big one, but there's a kitchen area with a fridge, a microwave and a sink. But I haven't got a cooker.
A: What about furniture?
P: We've got a coffee table. It's valuable because it's very old. And there are two chairs, they're made of wood. And we've got a sofa.
A: No dining table?
P: No, we always eat on the sofa!
A: OK. Now, electrical equipment. Is there a TV?
P: Yes, of course. And we've got a music system.
A: Any computers?
P: Yes, I've got a laptop computer – I use the Internet a lot.
A: And have you got a mobile phone?
P: Yes, I have.

Track 1.53

A: OK, Mr Morgan. Have you got your own house?
P: No, I haven't. I've got a modern studio apartment in the centre of town, but it's rented.
A: Has it got a garden?
P: No, it hasn't got a garden, but it's got a small terrace.

Track 1.54

He's got a laptop, a cat and a watch.

Track 1.55

1 hat 2 on 3 top 4 packet

Track 1.56

Ana

I'm Ana. I'm from Spain and I love this country – in Spain there are so many places and things to see. There's even a famous desert in Spain – it's true – the Almeria Desert. It's in the south of Spain. They make a lot of films in this desert because it's really hot and dry. There are also a lot of beautiful beaches in Spain.

Marcin

My name's Marcin and my home is in Poland, in the east of the country. There are some beautiful lakes in the east of Poland – it's a lovely area. A lot of Polish people take their holidays here. In fact, it's quite popular now with people from other countries, too.

Costas

I'm Costas. I live in Greece, on the island of Kefalonia. People don't think that Greece is a green country, with a lot of trees, but Kefalonia is a very green island. There's a lovely forest in the north of the island. Of course, there are also beaches on Kefalonia – it's a very popular holiday island.

Yumiko

My name's Yumiko. I come from Japan, from a city called Osaka. It's a huge city in the west of Japan, and it's very busy and noisy, and it's not very friendly. There are a lot of shops and offices in the city, and people are always in a hurry. I don't like it here – I like the mountains.

Track 1.57

river desert

Track 1.58

river desert detached famous luxurious noisy popular

Track 1.59

1 It's really hot and dry.
2 It's quite popular now with people from other countries, too.
3 Kefalonia is a very green island.
4 It's very busy and noisy, and it's not very friendly.

Track 1.60

Hello. My name's Megan, and I come from Wales. I don't live there now; I live in England, but Wales is still my home. I come from the south of Wales, a village near Cardiff, the main city in Wales. My parents still live there.

Wales is a lovely country. It has mountains in the north and hills in the south, and there are a lot of beautiful beaches in the west. There are also a lot of rivers in Wales – our word for them is 'aber' – yes, we have our own language!

I like Wales because it's very beautiful and because the people are really friendly.

Unit 6

Track 1.61

art gallery, bank, bar, bus station, café, cinema, factory, hospital, library, museum, post office, restaurant, school, train station

Track 1.62

A = Angeles, J = Jason
A: Oh, that's an interesting building. What is it?
J: The Hoover Building? Oh, that's a supermarket.
A: A supermarket? You have lovely supermarkets here, Jason!
J: Well, they planned it as a factory in the 1930s. So it was a factory for years before it was a supermarket.
A: Oh, I see.
J: Yes, in fact, my grandfather worked there in the 1960s, after he married my grandmother. But he stopped working there a long time ago. He produced electrical equipment.
A: Really?
J: Yes, it only opened as a supermarket about 30 years ago.
A: That's interesting. You know, there's a building in Madrid like that, I mean, it changed from one thing to another – the Reina Sofia. It's an art gallery now.
J: Oh, yes. I know it. I visited it when I was in Madrid last year. It's fantastic! It's all 20th century art, isn't it?
A: That's right. It's my favourite gallery – you know I studied modern art – I often go there. I love *Guernica*, you know, the famous painting by Picasso.
J: Of course. What was it before, then?
A: It was a hospital – doctors and nurses lived and worked there, and looked after sick people. They started changing it into a gallery in 1980, then the gallery opened in 1992.

Track 1.63

worked, opened, started

Track 1.64

changed, lived, looked, planned, produced, studied, visited

Track 1.65

I = Interviewer, S = Sean, M = Meera
1
I: Sean, can I ask you some questions for our series on immigrants?
S: Sure.
I: Are you Irish or American?
S: Well, I'm a New Yorker! No, that's a joke. I'm American, of course. Well, that's what my passport says! But my family were Irish, so I'm Irish-American.
I: Did you grow up in the USA?
S: Yes, I did. I was born in New York and I went to school in Brooklyn – that's a suburb of New York. And I still live there.
I: Where did your family come from?
S: My great-great grandparents came from Waterford. That's a city on the south coast of Ireland.
I: Why did so many Irish people go to the USA?
S: Well, life was very difficult in Ireland. There wasn't enough food or work for all the people in the 1840s and 50s, so poor people came to America to look for jobs and a better life.

2
I: Why are there so many Indian people in England, Meera?
M: Well, for hundreds of years India and Pakistan were part of the British empire. So there were a lot of connections between the countries. Rich Indians sent their children to school in England and poor people came here as servants.
I: Were you born in London?
M: No, I was born in Mumbai, in India. But my family came to the UK in the 1980s. My father worked as a teacher and my mother worked in a restaurant. There were lots of jobs for Indians in Britain in those days.
I: Did you go to school in India?
M: No, I didn't. I didn't go to school there because my parents moved here when I was five, so I went to school in England.
I: Do you ever go to India?
M: Yes, I went there last year – for my cousin's wedding. It was fantastic. The people were so friendly! But it was very hot. I was happy to come home to London!

Track 1.66

Heather
I was born in Canada and my family lives in Canada. I grew up in New Brunswick and I went to French school in New Brunswick. I left home in 2005 and went travelling overseas. I went to all sorts of different countries and I met my partner overseas in 2006. I came to England in September 2007.

Stig
I was born in Norway but I didn't grow up there. We moved to England when I was five. So I didn't go to school in Norway, I went to school in England. I went to university in London. I studied economics but I didn't get a job in economics, I became an English teacher instead.

Track 1.67

1
Were you born in London?
No, I was born in Mumbai.
2
Did you visit Venice?
No, we visited Rome.
3
Was it nice?
No, it was horrible.

Track 1.68

C1 = Customer 1, S = Shop assistant,
C2 = Customer 2, C3 = Customer 3
C1: Excuse me. Where can I find men's shoes?
S: Men's shoes. That's on the top floor.
C1: Where are the stairs?
S: There are escalators on your right.
C1: Right. And have you got any maps of London?
S: No, we haven't. Sorry.
C1: OK. Thanks.
S: Can I help you?
C2: Yes. I'd like a laptop computer.
S: You need the computer department.
C2: Where's that?
S: In the basement. There are stairs on your right.
C2: Thanks very much. Oh, and I need a present for my son. Do you sell CDs?
S: Yes, we've got a music department on the ground floor.
C2: Great.
C3: Hello, is this the information point?
S: Yes. How can I help you?
C3: Where can I find dining tables and chairs?
S: That's in the furniture department on the top floor.
C3: Is there a lift?
S: Yes. Go to the end of the beauty hall and turn left.
C3: I need some other things. Have you got a store guide?
S: Yes. They're just here.
C3: Can I have a copy, please?
S: Of course.
C3: How much is that?
S: It's free.

Unit 7

Track 2.01

1 G has got blue eyes.
2 B has got long fair hair.
3 F has got dark skin.
4 G has got short grey hair.
5 F has got a beard.
6 B is slim.
7 C is young.
8 F is bald.
9 A is tall.
10 C is short.
11 E wears glasses.
12 F has got a moustache.

Track 2.02

C = Carol, M = Marianne
C: So, Marianne. What's your news?
M: Something exciting happened yesterday.
C: What?
M: Do you remember that man on the beach – the one I told you about in my email?
C: Er, yes.
M: He spoke to me! He's really friendly. He's Brazilian. He works in one of the big hotels on the beach, so he speaks good English.
C: What does he look like?
M: Well, he's very handsome, and tanned of course. About 22 or 23 I think. He's slim and he's got dark hair.
C: Long or short?
M: Short. And he's got a little beard.
C: What's his name?
M: Luis.
C: And has he got a wife or girlfriend?
M: No, he's single at the moment …
C: So, do you think he likes you?

Track 2.03

In Canada we celebrate Canada Day on July the first. This is basically Canada's birthday and the day that united Canada as a single country. The first Canada Day was in July 1867. On July the first we celebrate, everyone has the day off work and we have festivals, parties, there's usually a parade – just general celebration for everyone.

We celebrate Halloween on October the thirty-first and this is a day when people of all ages celebrate, dress up in costumes, children go around in their neighbourhood from door to door collecting candy and yelling 'trick or treat!'. If you're at home you have candy and treats by the door to give to everyone that comes by. They also usually carry a charity box and collect donations from people as well as the candy.

Track 2.04

first second third fourth fifth sixth seventh eighth ninth tenth eleventh twelfth thirteenth fourteenth fifteenth twentieth twenty-second thirtieth thirty-first

Audioscripts

Track 2.05

M = Mike, J = Jane
M: Hi, Jane, it's me.
J: Oh, hello, Mike. What's the problem?
M: You didn't write the names or addresses on those presents. I want to wrap them and take them to the post office. Who are they for?
J: Sorry.
M: The DVDs. Are they for Gordon?
J: Yes, they're his.
M: What about the trainers ... are they Davy's?
J: Yes, the trainers are his.
M: What about the clock? Who is that for?
J: That's for my mum and dad.
M: OK, so the clock's theirs. And the handbag? Is that for Tara?
J: The handbag? Of course not. That's mine!
M: It's yours? Oh. So what did you get for Tara? I know it's her birthday next week.
J: The diary, that's hers.
M: Right. OK. Well, what about the umbrella?
J: The umbrella?
M: Yes, there's an umbrella on the table.
J: A black one?
M: Yes.
J: That belongs to us. It's ours!
M: Is it? Oh yes. Of course ...

Track 2.06

birthday, brother, bathroom

Track 2.07

1 free 2 think 3 thick 4 thirst
5 three

Track 2.08

1 sixth 2 eighth 3 eat 4 hate
5 thin 6 three 7 lift 8 fifth

Track 2.09

G = Geoff, I = Isabel
G: What's wrong, Isabel?
I: I don't believe it. It's my computer. Look – nothing!
G: Phone the computer department then. They can repair it.
I: That's not the problem. I need to finish writing up the sales information for the meeting this afternoon.
G: So? You've got time.
I: No, I haven't. I also need to meet Mr Schäfer at the airport before the meeting. He arrives in half an hour.
G: Oh, I see ... . Look, I can meet him. I've got time.
I: Oh, can you, Geoff? That's really nice of you. He's on flight ...
G: Wait a minute! I don't know Mr Schäfer – do you?
I: Well, I met him about three years ago.
G: So what does he look like?
I: He's quite tall, about two metres, I think.
G: How old is he?
I: He's middle-aged. I think he's in his forties, his late forties now.
G: OK. What colour is his hair?
I: Well, he had brown hair when I met him, dark brown hair, but maybe he's grey now.
G: Oh, this isn't easy. Does he have long or short hair?
I: Short, I think, yes, quite short.
G: Right. Let's think, what's his body type?
I: Pardon?
G: Is he fat, thin ... ?
I: Oh, slim, quite slim, I think.
G: What colour is his skin? Dark, fair ... ?
I: He was very pale when I met him – yes, I remember that. Very pale.
G: And what colour are his eyes?
I: Oh, come on, Geoff! I can't remember that! I didn't look into his eyes, you know!
G: OK, OK. Is there anything else you can remember? Any other features I can look out for?
I: Um, yes. He had a beard, quite a short beard, and he had glasses. Does that help?
G: Yes, it does. What's he like?
I: Oh, he's nice. He's very friendly.
G: OK, that's fine. Well, see you later with Mr Schäfer. Good luck with your computer.
I: Oh, Geoff, wait a minute.
G: Yes?
I: Why don't you just hold up a card with his name on?

Unit 8

Track 2.10

M = Man, W = Woman
M: I want to go shopping at lunch time, I really need some new clothes. Are there any good clothes shops around here?
W: Well, there's a shop that sells nice jeans on the main road.
M: Oh, I think jeans are uncomfortable. I never wear them.
W: Really? I wear jeans all the time, even to work.
M: But jeans are very casual. You can't wear jeans to a formal business meeting!
W: That's true, but I never go to formal meetings. Now, what about shirts and pullovers? Tight shirts and pullovers look good.
M: Actually, I prefer loose shirts. And I don't wear pullovers very often. I prefer smart jackets.
W: Even in the winter?
M: Yes. But I usually wear a coat. Winter coats are usually warm and comfortable.
W: Really? I think winter coats are too heavy. I hate them!

Track 2.11

J = Jools, A = Anna, W = Whitney
Ju = Justin, P = Pam, M = Mika
J: Hello there, everyone! It's festival time here in the UK and today we're bringing you some pictures and information about late summer festivals around the world. Let's start in the US. Our reporter Anna Lindstrom is at the Boston Carnival right now. How's it going, Anna?
A: Hi, Jools. It's great. It's a really hot, late August day. I'm having a good time – everyone is having a good time.
J: What's happening right now?
A: Well, I'm standing in the street and I'm watching some fantastic dancers. They're moving slowly towards me. They're wearing really colourful costumes and they're dancing really well.
J: Sounds good.
A: Yes, and I'm with Whitney, who makes food for all the partygoers here. Whitney, what are you doing?
W: Well, I'm cooking some lovely Caribbean chicken curry.
A: Mmm, it smells wonderful.
J: Thank you, Anna. Now, Boston isn't the only place having a party at this time of year. Our reporter Justin Leonard is at the Mariachi festival in Guadalajara, Mexico. Justin, how's it going over there?
Ju: Hi, Jools. It's great here. I'm sitting in the town square and I'm listening to some fantastic mariachi music. In this band the guitarists are all playing together; it's lovely.
J: It sounds noisy there.
Ju: It is! The spectators aren't just listening, they're clapping and shouting and singing with the music.
J: Thank you, Justin. And in Helsinki, Finland, Pam Sykes is reporting on the Helsinki Festival.
P: Hello, Jools. Well, it's quiet here – it's not like Mexico. This is an arts festival, so it's all in cinemas, theatres and concert halls. Some people are queuing behind me to go into a theatre. I have Mika here with me. Mika, what are you queuing for today?
M: I'm not queuing for the theatre – I'm with my children – they're over there; they're waiting to see some funny films, some old films with Charlie Chaplin.
P: That sounds like fun! Thank you, Mika. Back to you, Jools.
J: Thanks, Pam. Now, in the studio this afternoon ...

Track 2.12

1 She's dancing.
2 They're talking.
3 Are you listening?
4 We aren't leaving.

Track 2.13

OK, I'm looking at a picture of a street scene. It's a festival, I think. At the front of the picture two women are dancing. They're enjoying it! They're wearing really colourful costumes. On the left there are some people watching the dancers, and at the back of the picture there are some buildings, shops, and maybe houses, I think. There are musicians playing on the right of the picture – they're all wearing black so they're all together; they're part of the festival. I think everyone's having a good time!

Track 2.14

1
Woman: Ailsa, what's the weather like in Scotland right now?
Ailsa: In the south of Scotland it's quite warm and sunny but in the north, in the highlands, there's still snow on the mountains.
2
Woman: What's the weather like in Canada at the moment?
Heather: Well its summertime in Canada right now, but it's actually not that warm. It's 15 degrees and really foggy today.
3
Woman: Hi, Stig. What's the weather like over there?
Stig: At the moment in Norway it's late summer and today it's warm and sunny.
4
Woman: Amber, what's the weather like in Brazil now?
Amber: Well, this morning it was really hot and sunny but now it's raining.

Track 2.15

cold, hot, foggy, snowing

Track 2.16

1 cold   gold
2 top   told
3 snow   hot
4 not   lot

Track 2.17

old, clock, cost, note, hotel, not, on, wrote, own, bottle

155

Audioscripts

Track 2.18

J = Jan, L = Luke

J: Hello.

L: Jan? It's Luke.

J: Luke? You don't usually call at this time. You always phone in the evenings.

L: I know. But I'm not at work. I'm at home.

J: Oh. Are you sick?

L: No, but I can't get into the office. The underground isn't working today.

J: Really? Why?

L: It's snowing here.

J: Snowing! So what?

L: Well, it's really snowing a lot. So the trains and buses aren't running. People can't get to work and lots of people are staying at home.

J: But it snows all through the winter in New York. Nothing stops because of that!

L: I know. But it hardly ever snows in London. It's a shock for us.

J: That's crazy!

L: Well, at least it isn't raining!

J: Yes, I hate rainy weather. I always feel sad and depressed when the sky is grey and there's no sun.

L: I know what you mean. London's always dark in December and January.

J: Yeah, I prefer snow really. Everything looks so beautiful ...

L: Mm. I suppose so ...

Track 2.19

1

R = Receptionist, W = Woman

R: Can I help you, madam?

W: Yes, I'm calling from room 342.

R: Yes, madam.

W: Well, it's very hot in here. I think there's a problem with the air conditioning.

R: Oh, I am sorry, madam. Is the air conditioner turned on?

W: Yes, it is. But it isn't working. Can you send somebody to repair it?

R: Of course. I'll ask the engineer to go to your room.

2

S = Shop assistant, M = Man

S: Can I help you?

M: Yes. I bought this DVD player from you, but it isn't working.

S: I see. Have you got your receipt?

M: Yes, I have. Can I exchange it for another one?

S: Of course. Just a moment. Here you are.

M: Thanks very much.

3

S = Shop assistant, W = Woman

W: Excuse me. Can you help me?

S: Yes, madam?

W: I bought this pullover yesterday and it doesn't fit.

S: Do you want to try a different size?

W: No, I'd like a refund.

S: Have you got your receipt?

W: Yes. Here it is.

S: OK. So that's 150 euros. Here you are.

Unit 9

Track 2.20

Ai = Ailsa, Am = Amber

Ai: Um, what have you got under painting?

Am: Um, I put cartoon under painting.

Ai: Yes.

Am: What about you?

Ai: Yes, I've, I've got cartoon as well, and I also put modern art under painting.

Am: Oh, yes, of course. And literature?

Ai: Um, I've got three things under literature: horror, novels and poetry.

Am: Oh, I put horror under film.

Ai: Yes, I think it can go there, too.

Am: Um, what about music?

Ai: Under music I've got classical music ...

Am: Yep, me too.

Ai: Um, opera ...

Am: Yeah ...

Ai: And rock music.

Am: And opera can also perhaps be classed under theatre?

Ai: Yeah, I agree.

Am: With dance and ballet.

Ai: Yeah. Under, so what have you got under theatre?

Am: Um, dance, ballet, and I think that's all I had.

Ai: OK, I also put comedy and plays.

Am: Oh, comedy can also go under literature, can't it?

Ai: Yeah, and film.

Am: Yeah.

Track 2.21

1 easier than

2 faster than

3 colder than

4 healthier than

Track 2.22

P = Petra, N = Nick

P: It says here that 70 percent of Americans got news about the election on the Internet. I think that's amazing.

N: Amazing? I don't find it surprising at all. I mean, with an election, people want to find out news very quickly, and it's faster on the Internet than on TV. How many Americans use the Internet for news every day?

P: Erm, well, it says 37 percent here.

N: Well, there you are, about half of the first number.

P: Mmm, do you think the number is the same here?

N: I think that it's probably the same. I think a lot of younger people use the Internet for news stories, but older people are more traditional – they read newspapers or watch the news on TV.

P: I don't think that it's just older people. I believe that newspapers are still better than other news sources because you can read them anywhere – on the train, in a restaurant, even in front of the TV!

N: Yes, I suppose so. What do you think of getting news on your mobile phone, then?

P: Well, it's OK, but in my opinion, it's better to read a newspaper or watch TV for news, to get more information and other people's opinions.

Track 2.23

P = Presenter, M = Mariela

P: Good evening. Tonight we've got Mariela Dolcino with us to talk about her favourite films from the last ten years. As you know, Mariela is the film critic for *The Sunday Reporter*. Welcome to the show, Mariela.

M: It's good to be here, Neil.

P: OK. Let's start with the best. Mariela, what do you think is the best film of the last ten years?

M: Well, there's no competition for me. I know a lot of people think it was the films in the *Lord of the Rings* series, and they were good, but for me the best film in the last ten years was *Slumdog Millionaire* – it was so different, very clever, and it had the best photography, I think.

P: I think a lot of people agree with you. What's the most exciting film of the last ten years, do you think?

M: That's easy – *Casino Royale*. I think it's the best James Bond film – Daniel Craig was fantastic in the character of James Bond – he's by far the best Bond in my opinion.

P: OK. Were there any surprises for you in the last ten years?

M: Surprises? Let me see ... well, yes. I think the biggest surprise was *An Inconvenient Truth* – you know, the Al Gore documentary about the environment. It was really interesting, and I think a lot of people understood the problem better when they watched it.

P: What about foreign language films? Any good ones there?

M: Well, lots, of course, but the one that I think was best was *The Lives of Others*, the German film. It was a lovely film, very sad, but the most interesting foreign language film of the last ten years, and for me the most successful winner of the Oscar for the best foreign language film.

P: Mmm, I liked that one, too. You don't like violent films, do you?

M: No, I don't, but there's one violent film that I want to talk about – *No Country for Old Men*. That was very violent, possibly the most violent film of the ten years, but it was very good – and the actor Javier Bardem was really fantastic as the bad guy – it's not usually the kind of part he plays, but you can believe that he's a real villain in this film!

P: And any good comedies?

M: Oh, yes, my favourite was *Little Miss Sunshine* – it really was the funniest film of the last ten years for me, especially the scene when the little girl is at the Little Miss Sunshine competition, but it's also quite sad in places.

P: Well, I think that's all we have time for ...

M: No, wait a moment. There's one more film I really want to mention, and that's *Chicago*. I don't usually like musicals at the cinema, but it really was the freshest musical for a long time – it was really good.

P: OK. Thank you very much, Mariela, and now we turn to ...

Track 2.24

J = Jenny, S = Serge

J: I'm going to the Banksy exhibition. Do you want to come?

S: Is it expensive?

J: No, it's free.

S: Er, no thanks. I don't like going to exhibitions really. They're boring.

J: But Banksy's really good. I love his work.

S: Who's Banksy? Is he famous?

J: Yes. He's a really famous modern artist. He paints graffiti on the sides of buildings.

S: That sounds stupid. I prefer traditional paintings to modern ones. Anyway, I want to stay at home. It's the final of *Pop Star Search* on TV this evening.

J: Oh no. I hate listening to those stupid kids singing.

S: Well, I love it. It's so exciting.

J: It's rubbish.

S: Oh, you hate everything on TV.

J: No, I don't! But I like serious programmes more than talent shows. I prefer watching films or documentaries. Programmes that make you think.

S: But I don't want to think when I watch TV. I just want to relax.

Track 2.25

1 Is it expensive? 2 Is he famous?

Track 2.26

1 Is it nice?
2 It's lovely.
3 Is it interesting?
4 It's boring.
5 Are we late?
6 Does she know?

Track 2.27

M = Matt, W = Wendy, G = Gavin
M: What shall we do this weekend?
W: Oh, I don't know.
G: How about going to the cinema?
M: Ooh, what's on?
W: Ahh, I think there's a new *Harry Potter* …
M: Oh no, I don't like that.
W: Oh, don't you? I love that!
M: I, I saw the last one and it was really boring.
W: Oh, it was great! I read the book. I loved it.
G: I don't think so.
W: Oh, it's two against *Harry Potter*. OK, OK, not *Harry Potter*.
M: What about going out for dinner?
W: Mmm … yeah … Thai food – anybody like Thai food?
G: It's OK.
M: I don't really like Thai food.
W: How can you not like Thai food? I love Thai food.
M: And restaurants are quite expensive. Um, there's a football match on Saturday, why don't we go and watch that?
G: I think that's a great idea.
W: Ahhh … mmm … OK, I do quite like football. Yeah, ah, hang on though, because football could be a bit expensive.
M: My brother's band, they're on at the local club this weekend. Why don't we go and see them?
W: Ah, yeah, that'd be great.
G: That sounds good.
W: I'd love it.
M: Let's meet at the station.
W: Good idea. What time?
M: About seven?
W: Seven's good.
G: Seven's fine.
W: Fantastic, seven o'clock at the station.
M: See you there.
W: Yeah.

Unit 10

Track 2.28

Julia

The way I commute to work is probably quite unusual! I rollerblade! I live in Surfside, a suburb in the north of Miami and I work at a hotel on Miami beach. It takes about twenty-five minutes to get to work. And of course it costs nothing. It's usually warm and sunny in Miami and rollerblading is very healthy – I really enjoy it. But rollerblading is a bit dangerous when you cross busy roads. And it's tiring!

Billy

Commuting is really difficult in London. It's a huge city and there's a lot of traffic. You can't really commute by car because it's impossible to park in the centre of London. There's a good underground system but there aren't any stations near my house so I get the bus to work. It isn't expensive but it's sometimes quite slow because of all the traffic. And I hate waiting at the bus stop in the winter, it's very boring!

Track 2.29

B = Brendan, T = Travel agent
B: Good morning. Do you sell tickets for Eurostar trains?
T: Yes. What's your destination?
B: Paris.
T: And when do you want to go?
B: I'd like to go on Friday the fifth of June.
T: Return or one-way?
B: I'd like return tickets, please. We want to come back three days later. And I'd like four tickets.
T: OK. I'll just check. OK, do you want first or standard class?
B: Oh, first class is expensive. I'd like standard class. How much is that?
T: Let me see. Four return tickets in standard class, and your departure date is the fifth. That's £280.
B: Right. What time does the train leave London?
T: At ten thirty in the morning.
B: Is it a direct train?
T: Yes. There are no stops.
B: And can we take our bikes on the train?
T: Yes, but it costs an extra £20 for each bike.
B: Fine. I'd like four tickets then, please. Can I pay by credit card?
T: Sure. Put your card in the slot …

Track 2.30

**J = Jason, D = Derek, A = Alicia,
M = Moira, T = Todd**
J: I'm here at Heathrow Airport with a group of friends from Lancaster University: Derek, Moira, Todd and Alicia. Today's the start of an amazing adventure for them. In half an hour they get on a plane to begin the holiday of a lifetime. Derek, how are you feeling right now?
D: To be honest, Jason, I'm feeling quite nervous … nervous but excited.
J: Why are you nervous?
D: Well, this is my first long plane journey. I haven't been on a long-haul flight before so it's my first time … and Australia is a long way away.
J: Are the rest of you experienced travellers?
A: We've been to America!
M: Yes, the three of us have been on a long-haul flight before. I went to Florida last year with Todd and Alicia.
J: Have you been to Australia?
M: No, we haven't.
D, A, T: No, we haven't been to Australia.
J: So I guess you're all very excited about those activities in Australia? Have you been horse-riding, hiking or bungee jumping before?
T: Alicia and I have been horse-riding. We went when we were in Scotland two years ago. But Derek and Moira stayed in the hotel! So they haven't been horse-riding before.
M: It was cold!
D: But we've all been hiking. We went last year.
J: And have you ever been bungee jumping?
D: Oh no. We haven't been bungee jumping. It's the first time for all of us.
M: I'm very nervous about it!

Track 2.31

1 Have you been to Australia?
2 No, we haven't been to Australia before.

Track 2.32

1 Have you been to the cinema in England?
2 I've been to a disco with him.
3 Have they been to dinner in Finland?
4 We haven't been to Paris in spring.

Track 2.33

P = Presenter, A = Author
P: Let's talk about your new book now. It's called *Modern-day Adventurers*. What exactly do you mean by 'adventurer'?
A: Mmm, that isn't an easy question. It's probably best to give you some examples of adventurers.
P: OK …
A: Take Jessica Watson.
P: I've heard the name. What's she done exactly?
A: She's sailed solo around the world, you know, on her own, and she's only sixteen. And then there's Ramona Cox.
P: I haven't heard of her.
A: She's done lots of solo flying – long flights in small aircraft. But perhaps the most remarkable adventurer is Ben Fogle, the TV presenter. He's cycled across Europe, he's walked, and run across the desert, he's …
P: Hold on … what hasn't he done?
A: I don't know! His most famous adventure was crossing the Antarctic; it was a race actually – a race of over 500 kilometres to the South Pole. He and James Cracknell did it in January 2009, and it took seventeen days.
P: James Cracknell … now what has he done?
A: He's won two Olympic gold medals in rowing – that's how you know him, but he's also rowed across the Atlantic, with Ben Fogle – that's over 2,500 kilometres; they did that in 2006, again in a race. It took them fifty days and they came fourth.
P: Very impressive! And you mentioned the desert.
A: Oh, yes. Ben Fogle has done the Sand Marathon – that was in 2004; it's a race across 200 kilometres of the Sahara Desert. That took him seven days. And he's also cycled across Europe – that was when he was much younger. He cycled to Monaco with a group of friends in 1993, and they did it in nine days.
P: What about mountains? Has he ever climbed a mountain?
A: Yes, he has. He's climbed several! He climbed Kilimanjaro in 2006 – that was his fourth peak of over 6,000 metres …
P: This is amazing …
A: Yes, well, now you know what I mean by adventurer!

Track 2.34

parked, had, walked, got, seen, written

Track 2.35

1 have 2 fit 3 short 4 park
5 bald 6 sleep

Track 2.36

1
Matt: Have you ever met anyone famous?
Amber: No, I haven't, but my brother has. He works in the film industry so he meets famous people all the time.

2
G = Gavin, W = Wendy
G: Have you ever stayed in a five-star hotel?
W: Yes I have, ah …
G: You have?
W: Yeah in, um, Venezuela, in, ah, the capital city of Caracas, I stayed in the Hilton there and I think that's a five-star.

3
A = Amber, M = Matt
A: Have you ever flown in a hot-air balloon?
M: I haven't. Have you?
A: Yes, I have. It was a birthday present from my husband. It was amazing.

157

4
W = Wendy, G = Gavin
W: Have you ever eaten insects?
G: No, I haven't. I have a friend who has ...
W: Really?
G: ... but I don't think it's a good idea.
W: Why not?
G: I don't like the idea of eating insects.
W: Ah. I've, I've eaten insects in Thailand on holiday.
G: You have?
W: Mmm, it wasn't very nice.

5
A = Amber, M = Matt
A: Have you ever played any unusual sports?
M: Well, I don't really play it, but I like to go rock climbing.
A: Oh, wow, that is quite unusual.

Track 2.37

R = Robin, W = Woman, M = Man
R: Excuse me. I've lost my wallet. I think somebody has stolen it. Is there a police station near here?
W: I'm afraid I don't know. I haven't been to this part of town before. Why don't you ask in the library over there?
R: OK. Thanks. ... Excuse me. Do you know the way to the police station?
M: The police station. Yes, it's easy. You turn left at the next road, Mill Street ...
R: Turn left, OK ...
M: Then go straight on for about 200 metres. Then you get to the post office.
R: The post office.
M: Yes, it's on the right.
R: On the right, OK.
M: Next to the post office, turn right into Beech Road.
R: Beech Road. OK.
M: Go along the road, then turn left at the bookshop, into Lime Avenue.
R: Yes, OK.
M: The police station is in Lime Avenue. It's at the end of the street, on the left.
R: OK, thanks very much.

Unit 11

Track 2.38

biology, chemistry, geography, history, languages, literature, maths, physics, science

Track 2.39

Welcome to the free Tourist Information Line for visitors to Great Britain. For information on visas and immigration, please press one. For information on driving in Britain, please press two. For information on hotels, please press three. For information on public transport in Britain, please press four. To return to this menu at any time press the star key.
You have chosen option two: driving in Britain.

Track 2.40

If you have a valid driving licence from your own country, you can drive in Britain without a British licence for six months. After six months, you have to get a British driving licence. To get a British licence you have to take a driving test. You can find information about the British driving test on our website.
To rent a car in Britain you have to have a valid driving licence from your country and a credit card. Drivers under the age of eighteen can't rent cars in Britain.
When you are driving in Britain, you don't have to keep your documents with you. The

British drive on the left side of the road and, unlike the United States, you can't turn right at a red traffic light.
For more information on British driving regulations, please look at our website.
That is the end of the driving section. To return to the main menu press the star key.

Track 2.41

You don't have to be a British citizen to take a British driving test but you have to have a valid British visa.

Track 2.42

1 leaf 2 few 3 fan 4 V

Track 2.43

1 Philip finds French films very violent.
2 Very few fines feel fair.
3 Fiona Philips never gives fitness advice to fresh fruit fanatics.

Track 2.44

We don't have a lot of rules in the United States really. I mean we don't have to do military service and we don't have to have identity cards. You can drive when you're sixteen and you can even buy a gun when you're twenty-one! And in most states you can get married and have your own bank account or credit card when you're eighteen. Actually, you can usually get married when you're sixteen, but you have to have permission from your parents.
But some things aren't so easy. You have to be twenty-one to go into a bar or a nightclub, and smoking is difficult – you can't smoke in offices, shops or restaurants. And of course we have to pay when we see a doctor or go to hospital, which is pretty expensive.

Track 2.45

P = Presenter, S = Sarah, H = Harumi,
R = Ross, A = Andreas
P: Now, as you know, the government is thinking of making the school-leaving age eighteen, up from sixteen, and of course there was a report recently which suggested that children should start serious learning at six, not four or five. In the studio we've got four people from different educational backgrounds: Sarah, from England; Harumi, from Japan; Andreas from Germany, and Ross, from New Zealand. Good morning all.
All: Hi/Hello.
P: Sarah, let's start with you. Where did you go to school?
S: Mmm, my primary school was in a little village in the west of England ... then I went to the secondary school in the local town when I was eleven. I left when I was sixteen to start work. I trained to be an electrician.
P: So you had, what, eleven, twelve years at school. Harumi, you went to school in Japan. How long did you spend at school?
H: Well, I went to elementary school then high school in Kyoto – for about thirteen years, yes, six to eighteen. Then I went to university and studied English.
P: That's why your English is so good. Ross, when did you leave school?
R: I left at eighteen too – though you can leave at sixteen, or even fifteen in New Zealand if your parents agree. I went from high school to a teacher training college and studied sport – that's what I teach now.
P: What about you, Andreas? Did you leave school at eighteen?
A: At nineteen actually. Then I went on to university and studied law – that was

another seven years after about fourteen years at school!
P: What a punishment! What was your favourite subject at school? Law?
A: No, come on! I went to a gymnasium, which is an academic school, but they don't do law, even there. No, I really liked politics and economics, and maths, surprisingly.
P: OK, one other thing. Another current topic is the use of new technology in schools – how much to have in schools and so on. Which kinds of new technology did you use? Sarah?
S: Hah! New technology – you're joking, aren't you? When I was at school a CD player was new technology!
P: Ross, I think you're the youngest here. Did you use much new technology at school?
R: Yeah, we used email at school and we also had forums, you know, where you can send messages to whole groups, like the history forum, the sports forum. And in my last year, we had interactive whiteboards, you know, so the teacher had the whole book up on the board. That was cool!

Track 2.46

1 Where did you go to school?
2 What was your favourite subject?
3 How long did you spend at school?
4 When did you leave school?
5 Which kinds of new technology did you use?

Track 2.47

Did you leave school at eighteen?

Track 2.48

H = Host, C = College, OU = Open University, MM = MicroMatters, U3A = University of the Third Age
H: Good afternoon. Welcome to *Live to Learn*. People today often want to continue learning throughout their lives, but what are their choices? First, let's talk to Aileen Murphy, head of Bexley Green Language and Business College.
C: Good afternoon. Well, at Bexley Green College, we offer a range of languages and business topics, so it's a good place to get more skills.
H: Which languages do you teach at the college?
C: Well, English, of course – we have a lot of students from overseas, all over the world really, who take English and perhaps a business course, too – we have very well-qualified business tutors. But we also offer French, Spanish, German, Russian and Chinese for English speakers. A lot of our students are business people who want to learn another language.
H: How much do the courses cost?
C: It depends. Our most popular course is a ten-week part-time language course of about ten hours a week, and that costs about £800.
H: And your classes are all at your college?
C: No, most of our classes are at the college, but we have evening classes at the local university buildings, too.
H: Thank you, Aileen. Now we have Graham Knight, from the Open University.
OU: Well, the Open University is a distance learning university – that is, you study at home, using books, CD-ROMs, the

Internet. There are a few classes during the year, and there are often summer schools. Our students have to study for about twelve hours a week.

H: And what subjects do you offer?

OU: Almost everything! You can study academic subjects like art history or maths, or subjects like computing or nursing.

H: Thank you, Graham. Oh, what about cost?

OU: Most of our courses are about £600 a year, at the moment.

H: Thanks. Now, Beth Anderson works for a professional training company, MicroMatters Ltd.

MM: Right. We offer training courses in computer skills for people who are actually working with computers.

H: Do you offer courses to people who aren't working?

MM: Oh, yes. Most of our courses last two or three days, for people in work, but we also have full-time courses for a week or two weeks, and evening courses.

H: And the cost?

MM: A week's course costs about £900. Of course, we provide everything – the trainers, the training room at our centre, the computers – the trainees don't have to pay for any extras, so we aren't cheap.

H: Thank you. Now, finally, James Beecham, to tell us about the University of the Third Age.

U3A: Good afternoon. The University of the Third Age is for retired people, so it's mostly older people. We have groups across the country, and each group organises its own courses. Usually, the group uses a hall in its town, or a local school, and lecturers come to speak to the group on weekday afternoons. We try to make our type of learning very cheap. The membership cost is different in different groups, but most are around £20 a year – so it's very cheap.

H: Yes, I see. And what kind of courses or subjects do you offer?

U3A: Well, the speakers talk about their special subjects or their interests, so we have a lot of different topics, but it's not usually very academic.

H: Right. Thank you, everyone, for coming. Now, let's move on to ...

Track 2.49

S = Secretary, N = Nadia

S: Good morning. Bexley Green College. Can I help you?

N: Hello, yes. I'm calling from Moscow, Russia. I want to enrol for one of your courses online, but I'm having problems. I tried to send the application through, but I don't think it went.

S: OK. What's your name?

N: Koparova, Nadia Koparova.

S: Could you spell your last name for me?

N: Yes, it's K–O–P–A–R–O–V–A.

S: Thank you. Ummm, no, I don't have a form from you.

N: Oh, what did I do wrong?

S: OK, let's see. Is your computer on?

N: Yes.

S: Do you have the application form on the screen?

N: No, I've got your home page, with phone numbers.

S: Right, click on 'apply now' at the top of the page.

N: OK. Now I've got the application form.

S: OK. Let's go through it together.

N: I don't have a problem with the personal information, but I'm not sure if I filled in the rest correctly.

S: OK, so you've got your personal details. What about the course?

N: I want to do two courses at the same time.

S: That's fine. There are three lines under 'course choice', you just put your two choices on the first two lines. What are they?

N: I want to do 'Advanced Improvers' English' ...

S: That's code 30755 – put that in now.

N: OK, and 'Business for Beginners'.

S: That's code 72592 – put that on the second line.

N: Right.

S: Now enter the start date for the courses.

N: That's 22nd June. OK.

S: And choose how you want to pay.

N: Um, credit card. My number is ...

S: Don't give me the details now; it isn't necessary.

N: OK. Now I click 'send' ...

S: No, don't do that! You have to read and accept the conditions first.

N: Oh, I didn't do that before. So, I read those ... and I click here ... OK.

S: When you click 'accept the conditions', a 'send' box appears.

N: I see. Yes, it's there.

S: Now you click on that and the form comes to us. OK, do that now.

N: Right. Oh, that's OK now.

S: Yes, I can see your form on my screen now. That's all fine, Ms Koparova, you can expect to hear from us in two or three days ...

Track 2.50

R = Receptionist, P = Peter

R: Hello, Windham Catering College.

P: Oh, hello. I'm phoning about the Italian cookery course. I'd like to enrol for it. Can I do that on the phone?

R: No, I'm afraid not. You can enrol by post or online.

P: Oh, I don't have a computer here. How do I enrol by post?

R: Let me take a few details and I can get a form to you. Then you just fill it in and send it back to us with your payment.

P: Oh, let me check – you send the form to me?

R: That's right.

P: Can I ask some questions first?

R: Of course. What would you like to know?

P: Can I just check the date it starts?

R: Yes. All our courses start in the week of 13th September, with a break of one week in the week of 23rd October and ...

P: Can you repeat that, please? A break in ...

R: A break in the week starting 23rd October.

P: OK, and it's on a Wednesday evening, is that right?

R: Yes.

P: Can I ask what time the lessons start?

R: They start at 7:00 and finish at 9:30.

P: That's OK, good. And the price is about £220, I think.

R: Yes, £225 exactly.

P: Does that include the ingredients?

R: No, it doesn't. You have to bring the ingredients – you get a list each week for the next week.

P: Oh, I see. I think that's everything.

R: You know that you have to come to the other building in the evening, don't you?

P: Sorry, what was that?

R: Evening classes aren't in the main building; they're in the annexe. Come to the main building and then take the first road on the left – York Street.

P: Oh, OK. Thanks.

R: Right, your name is ...

Unit 12

Track 2.51

P = Paul, M = Mia

P: Look, here's the photo of us rafting on the Colorado River last summer.

M: Oh, yes. That was so frightening. I didn't really enjoy that – the raft went so fast! It was really dangerous.

P: Well, I thought it was fantastic.

M: I preferred trekking in the Grand Canyon really.

P: Yes, that was fun. But a bit slow. And do you remember when we went on those bikes in the hills behind San Francisco?

M: Yes. I remember cycling up the hills and through all those tunnels!

P: Yes, that was great.

M: Mm, I really enjoyed that. Do you think that was the best part of our trip?

P: No, horse-riding was the best. That was really exciting.

M: Yeah, you're right. I think horse-riding was my favourite, too. It was a lot of fun.

P: Next year I want to try something different.

M: What?

P: Bungee jumping in New Zealand.

M: Wow. That sounds great!

Track 2.52

O = Omar, J = Julie

O: So, Julie. It's the start of the summer holiday next week. What are your plans?

J: Oh, we're going to visit my grandparents in Belgium.

O: Are you going to take the children?

J: Yes. My grandparents are going to move to a small flat later this year, so this is our last chance to stay with them.

O: Are you going to fly there?

J: No, we're going to take the train the week after next.

O: So you're going to go through the Channel Tunnel?

J: Yes. I'm going to drive the car to the station at Ashford and put it on the train. It's really exciting. What about you, Omar?

O: Well, I haven't got much money at the moment, so I'm not going to go away. I'm going to stay at home ...

J: But that's what you did last year!

O: I know. My life's really boring!

Track 2.53

We're going to take the train.

Track 2.54

1 She's going to get fit.
2 They're going to sell their car.
3 We're going to learn French.
4 I'm going to buy a laptop.

Track 2.55

Everyone Wants To Be Famous

Everyone wants to be famous,
To be someone everyone knows.
To live in a mansion with servants,
And star in the best TV shows.

A sports star, an actor, a winner,
Whatever it takes to get fame.
A model, a dancer, a singer,
So people remember your name.

Audioscripts

But when you're alone
In a hotel or home
The night is so cold
And there's no one to hold.
When life seems so blue
Just who do you talk to?

Because when you're a star
Everyone knows who you are.
They know what you do,
But do they really know you?

Track 2.56

Because when you're a star
Everyone knows who you are.
They know what you do,
But do they really know you?

Track 2.57

1 me being see free tree
2 fly high stay cry my
3 together there never forever clever
4 fame same name game am
5 nice price advice drive rice

Track 2.58

Victoria

I've joined the drama group at university because I really love performing. I'm going to learn how to sing and dance. I want to act in plays and musicals and of course I'd like to be famous one day. Sometimes TV producers watch our student shows so anything is possible!

Helena

My ambition is to become a famous politician, perhaps a minister in the government. At the moment I'm just a student – I'm studying politics at college. But I'm going to work for a politician next summer. I want to learn more about elections and voting. I'm really excited about it.

Lewis

That was my first training session with the team, so I'm a bit tired. It's only the reserve team but I'm going to practise with them twice a week to improve my physical fitness and ball control skills. I'm going to work really hard to get into the first team. I know I'm a good footballer and I'm sure I'm good enough to get a place in a professional team. These days footballers are the biggest stars in the world, and I'd really like to be rich and famous.

Track 2.59

A = Andi, D = David

A: Good morning. *Charity Champions*, Andi speaking. How can I help you?
D: Oh, hello. My name's David MacMahon. I'm thinking of doing one of your challenges, but I want to ask a few questions first.
A: That's fine, David. Please go ahead.
D: Well, first question, where exactly do the challenges take place?
A: All over the world; in Africa, Latin America, and the Caribbean, Asia, the Middle East and Europe.
D: Oh, I see. And what kind of challenges are they? I mean, what kind of activities are they?
A: Well, we have hiking, cycling, sailing, rafting, mountain climbing and horse-riding.
D: Oh good. I like hiking and I love cycling – I use my bike every day – but I don't like horses. And I don't like sailing much.

A: Well, there are quite a few there that you like. What about rafting and mountain climbing?
D: I'm not sure. I mean, I'd like to climb a mountain one day. I haven't done any rafting, but I'd love to try it. Do you have to be very fit?
A: Well, yes, you have to be quite fit. Our expeditions are difficult and you have to have a good level of fitness. Erm, really, you need to choose an activity you know you can do and start training early. We have training weekends, too. People find them very useful.
D: Oh, that sounds good. Er, ... who pays for the expedition?
A: Um, you do. Well, you pay for the expedition, or you raise money to pay for it.
D: And how do I raise money for the expedition?
A: Well, there are several things you can do, for example, you can do a charity dog walk to get money.
D: Oh, I'm not sure about that. I mean, I like dogs but I wouldn't like to walk them.
A: Well, there are other ways. How about working for people, you know, doing their gardens? Anyway, we also ask you to raise money for your charity.
D: Oh, yes, of course. Erm, who chooses the charity?
A: You do. Do you have any other questions, David?
D: Yes, how do I raise money for the charity?
A: The same as for the expedition, or you ask people to sponsor you, you know, a pound for each kilometre on a trek. So do you want to join one of our expeditions, David?
D: I'm not really sure. Can you send me some information?
A: Certainly. I can send you a brochure. Let me take your details and ...

Track 2.60

I'd really like to play the classical guitar.

Track 2.61

1 white 2 Dave 3 late 4 mine
5 lake

Track 2.62

M = Martina, S = Silvia, J = Jacques, H = Hiroshi

M: Oh, I'm so glad the exam's over. Now we can relax a bit.
S: What are you all going to do for the summer, then? What about you, Martina?
M: I'm going home to Krakow next week, and I'm certainly going to spend two or three weeks at home, just relaxing, perhaps sitting in the garden if the weather's good enough.
S: Isn't that going to get boring?
M: Yes, probably. I'd like to work for two months, but it's difficult to get summer jobs at home at the moment.
J: I've got a job.
H: Really, Jacques. What are you going to do?
J: I'm going to take part in a summer camp for young children in Canada, so I can work and make some money, and continue to speak English.
S: Aren't you going to go back to France for the summer?
J: No, I'm planning to go back in September. You know I really want to work with children – I hope to start a course on teaching in primary schools in September.

S: Oh, that sounds lovely. What are you going to do, Hiroshi?
H: Me? I'm going to travel.
M: Travel? Why?
H: Well, I'm a long way from home, so it makes sense to travel in Europe while I'm here. I'm going to go to Paris next week – by Eurostar – and then I'm just going to go where I want. I'm not going to make any arrangements.
J: It sounds fantastic! I'd like to come with you!
H: But you've got a job! No, I want to practise my English. I hope to get a place in a university here next year.
S: You're all so lucky – doing interesting things. I'm going to study all summer.
M: Study – why?
S: I really want to go to medical school and it's very difficult to get a place.
J: Well, good luck!